INTERNATIONAL
Relations

INTERNATIONAL
Relations

JYOTI MALHOTRA

ADROIT

Adroit Publishers
New Delhi

ISBN : 978-81-87393-14-6 (HB)

First Published in 2016

Cover page by Priyadarshani Verma

Requests for permission to make copies of any part of the work should be mailed to:

Copyrights & Permissions Department
ADROIT PUBLISHERS

Published by

ADROIT PUBLISHERS

4675/21, Ganpati Bhawan, Ansari Road,
Daryaganj, New Delhi-110 002

Phone : 011-23266030

Distributors

AKHIL BOOK DISTRIBUTORS

email: akhilbooks@yahoo.com
akhilbks@gmail.com

Typesetting—***Kumud Printographics***, *Delhi-110053*

E-mail: vedkumud123@gmail.com

Printed at: Roshan Offset Delhi-110053

PREFACE

The purpose of this book is to provide you with a basic understanding of foreign affairs and introduce you to the fundamental principles of international relations within the political science framework. We will examine the theories of realism and liberalism as they are understood in world politics. These theories will serve as the foundation for more advanced study in the International Relations field of the Political Science major, and will help you develop the critical thinking skills you need in order to analyze conflicts between states. We will also explore issues that relate to the politics of global welfare, such as war, world poverty, disease, trade policy, environmental concerns, human rights, and terrorism. You will learn about the ethics of war, the global distribution of wealth, the concept of the balance of power and its relationship to the causes of war, and what happens in the international system when the balance of power collapses. At the end of this course, you will have a comprehensive understanding of the basic principles and concepts of International Relations, as well as the analytical ability to examine the global political system.

Upon successful reading of this book, you will be able to:

- discuss and explain the various analytical and theoretical positions used in the subfield of international relations to explain world politics;
- delineate the historical development of interstate relations and the place of the nation state in that development;
- describe specific issues that have relevance to the study of interstate relations, national security, war, economic integration, trade, and so forth;
- describe the differences between national and transnational actors in the international arena, both public and private;
- distinguish between the three levels of analysis of the international system: individual, domestic, and global;
- discuss the role of national power and diplomacy in international relations;
- discuss the nature and development of international organizations;
- identify and discuss major issues associated with international law and morality;
- identify and discuss major issues of the international economy;
- identify and discuss major issues related to human rights;
- identify and discuss global environmental issues; and
- discuss the economic relationship between the North and South.

JYOTI MALHOTRA

CONTENTS

CHAPTER 1

INTERNATIONAL RELATIONS AND POLITICS

INTRODUCTION

There has been a great confusion in defining international phenomenon which came to be described variously by various scholars as international relations, international affairs, world affairs, world politics and international politics.This was due to the fact that there was no systematic study on the subject. The real interest in the subject emerged only after the First World War in 1919 when the first Chair of International Relations was founded at the University of Wales.

Governments not only interact with the people they rule but also with other governments—to trade, to share ideas, to work together to solve global problems, and to resolve disputes. Political scientists have been analysing international relations— relations between states—for centuries, but never more so than during the twentieth century, as scholars tried to explain the reasons for and explore the aftermath of World Wars I and II and the Cold War that followed.

Although numerous international agreements and institutions exist to facilitate smooth relations among the nearly 200 countries in the world, international politics can still be extremely violent. Even though people have fought one another for millennia, political scientists still do not know exactly what causes people and states to go to war, start revolutions, or commit acts of terrorism. Identifying both immediate and long-term causes and consequences of political violence, as well as thinking about the impact of this violence on the international system, has become an important part of political science.

HISTORICAL BACKGROUND OF INTERNATIONAL RELATIONS

The history of international relations is often traced back to the Peace of Westphalia of 1648, where the modern state system was developed. Prior to this, the European medieval organisation of political authority was based on a vaguely hierarchical religious order. Westphalia instituted the legal concept of sovereignty, which essentially meant that rulers, or the legitimate sovereigns, would recognise no internal equals within a defined territory and no external superiors as the ultimate authority within the territory's sovereign borders. Classical Greek and Roman authority at times resembled the Westphalian systems, but both lacked the notion of sovereignty.

Westphalia encouraged the rise of independent nation-state, the institutionalisation of diplomacy and armies. This particular European system was exported to America, Asia and Africa via colonialism and the so called, "standards of civilisation". The contemporary international system was finally established through decolonisation during the cold war. While the nation-state system is considered "modern", many states have not incorporated the system and are termed "pre-modern". Further a handful of states have moved beyond nation-state system and can be considered "post-modern". The ability of contemporary IR discourse to explain the relations of these different types of states is disputed. "Levels of analysis" are a way of looking at the international system, which includes the individual level of transnational and intergovernmental affairs, and global level.

BROADER MEANING OF INTERNATIONAL RELATIONS

Relations at the international level is termed international relations. In the case of international relations, nations work as groups, their needs and wants are called interests or national interests, and disagreement among groups or between interests is called conflict.But the element of power remains the same. International relations, then, becomes a process of adjustment of relationships among nations in favour of a nation or group of nations by means of power. Thus, three important things relevant to international relations are: national interests, conflict and power.

The first is the objective, the second is the condition and the third is the means of international relations. But the second is of greater significance than the first or the third, because if conflict is not there, national interests and power will have little function to perform.

In this sense, international relations can be described as a set of those aspects of relations among independent political communities in which some element of conflict of interest is always present. However, it does not mean that power struggle in a continuing state of conflict against each other. Not every -nation is hostile to every other nation. Nations whose interests are identical or harmonious, are likely to have some sort of co-operation as a basis of their relationships and use this basis in their struggle against their enemies.

Thus, international relations involves conflict as well as co-operation. Joseph Frankel argues that war and peace represent the extremes of the two recurrent modes of social interaction, namely conflict and harmony, and therefore our study of international relations should include both.

a) Conflict occupies a prominent place in International Relations:

But conflict occupies a more prominent place in international relations. This is so due to the fact that co-operation itself is the result of conflict.This is so in two ways. Firstly, nations with identical or harmonious interests co-operate with each other in order to win the conflict with other nations. Secondly, co-operation is sought to be achieved only because international relationships are basically conflict.The study of international relations is primarily a study of the process in which a nation tries to have an advantageous position in a conflict with other nations or groups of nations' by means of power. Conflict cannot be eliminated from international society and the process of adjustment by means of power always goes on.

(b) Conflict is a continuing phenomenon:

Therefore, international relations like all relations, is by nature a continuing phenomenon. This nature of continuity also imparts the central place to conflict in international relations. Even the most co-operative and friendly relationship may at times become conflict. Sino-Indian relations may be cited as an appropriate example in this connection. The relation between India and China were most cordial and friendly for more than a decade. But since 1959 and especially after October, 1962, the two countries have been involved, in a conflict of a serious nature. From the point of view of a student of international relations, the present phase of Sino-Indian relations is a more important subject of study than all the earlier phases. It is because the interest of international relations is to know how conflict is or can be resolved, although the study of cordial relationships is not outside the scope of international relations.

For a student, again, international relations is the study of the control of conflict and establishment of co-operation. But as co-operation is possible only through the control of conflict, he has to pay greater attention to conflict.

(c) International Relations is an interaction of Foreign Policies:

Conflict arises from incompatibility of interests of nations. And nations try to safeguard their interests by trying to influence and control the behaviour of other nations. National interest, however is, served through foreign policy. Thus, nations come into contact with each other through their foreign policies. In this sense, international relations can also be described as an interaction of foreign policies. Feliks Gross maintains that the study of international relations is identical to the study of foreign policy. Russell Field also holds more or less the same view. The argument of the supporters of this view is that it is not possible to understand international relations without understanding the foreign policies of States.This argument has some validity. But it has been challenged by writers like Fred Sondermann and others.

(d) Foreign Policy closely linked but not identical to international relations:

The study of international relations is closely linked to the study of foreign policy but is not identical to it. The study of foreign policies of States is an important aspect of the study of international relations. But the latter is a broader field of inquiry. As a matter of fact, the question of relationship between international relations and foreign policy is made difficult by the fact that neither foreign policy nor international relations has a clearly defined starting point. However, the study of foreign policy provides the most important single helpful factor to the study of international relations. We have said earlier that international relations is a process in which nations try to safeguard their interests, which are not compatible with these of others, by means of power. Since this process apparently works through foreign policies of States, the study of foreign policies may fulfill in some measures the requirements of the study of international relations.

It is only in this sense that the study of international relations centers on the process and effects of interactions between foreign policy decisions. But the study of foreign policies of States does not exhaust the scope of the study of international relations and the former remains subordinated to the latter. Harold Sprout and Margaret Sprout would call foreign policy as sub-category of international relations.

DEFINITION, NATURE AND SCOPE OF INTERNATIONAL RELATIONS

International Relations is an important branch of Social Science. The Scope of International relations is the complex relations existing among the sovereign states of the world. It is mainly concerned, among other things, with the study in depth of all events and situations affecting more than one state.

The great Greek Philosopher Aristotle, said that man by nature is a social animal.

Being a social animal, man can't live in isolation. His basic nature and his basic needs make him to satisfy his numerous needs in association with others. Moreover no man is self sufficient even in his daily needs and therefore, he has to depend upon his fellow man for its existences. Just as no individual can live in isolation, no state can afford to live in isolation. Like the individual no state is self sufficient. Naturally, it has to cultivate relations between states. These relations are the subject matter of International Politics.

DEFINITION

According to Hartman "International Relations as a field of study is focused upon the process by which states adjust their national interest to those of other states".

Padelford and Lincoln define it as the "Interactions of state policies within the changing patterns of power relationships".

According to Quincy Wright "International Relations is the relations between groups of major importance in the life of the world at any period of history and particularly relations among territorially organised nation states which today are of such importance. We will also use the term to designate the studies of discipline, describing, explaining or assisting in the context of these relations. With the assistance of these definitions it can be understood that nations try to protect their incompatiable interest by means of power.

According to Morgenthau. "It is the struggle for and use of power among nations."

Palmer and Perkins opine that International politics is essentially concerned with state system. Sprout and Sprout also defined international politics as those aspects of the interactions and relations of independent political communities in which some element of opposition, resistance and conflict.

NATURE OF INR

International Politics (INP) constitute relations and interactions among nations. As in politics, so in international politics, there are sovereign states whose interests are not identical. Those interests of the sovereign states are called national interest. The sovereign states in order to achieve their interest come into conflict with one another and as a means to achieve the ends, power is generally used. Thus INP is that aspect of interactions and relations of sovereign states in which the element of conflict or interest is present. It is a process in which nations try to protect their incompatible interest by means of power. But international relations are not merely state to state political relations but it is something more than this. As Hartmann says "INRS include all inter-course among states and all movements of peoples, goods and ideas across national frontiers. Thus it is clear that international Relations covers a wider meaning than mere political relations. No doubt political factors dominate over other factors in international Relations namely economic, cultural and religious factors. Therefore it studies the totality of all relations of all those factors between, and among the states of the world.

SCOPE OF INTERNTIONAL RELATIONS

International Politics is an important branch, of social science and it is an inter-disciplinary in nature. Scope means areas of study. The scope of International Relations is not yet well settled. In 1954 the UNESCO published a booklet edited by C.A W Manning. In this book IR has been recognised as an independent discipline. During the last 40 years this discipline has evolved all the traits of an independent study and it can be understood from its progress that it is well on its way to becoming and Independent academic discipline. Most of the scholars of International Relations describe the following aspects in the study of this discipline.

1. State system
2. National Interest

3. National Power
4. Foreign Policy
5. Instruments of international politics – Diplomacy. Foreign policy, international trade, Economic and Military assistance etc.
6. Nationalism, Colonialism and imperialism.
7. Control of inter-state Relations – Balance of power-International law and international organisations.
8. Dynamic elements and new dimensions-Rivalry between super powers and different blocs of nations.
9. World government.
10. War and peace ideologies.
11. Ethnic groups – Races of mankind and Terrorist groups.
12. International Regionalism.
13. Nuclear weapons and its use.
14. International organisation and its role in maintaining world order.

International Relations is a developing subject it has to keep in pace with the highly dynamic, and developing nature of relations among nations. Hence its scope is bound to be ever expanding in content.

DIFFERENCE BETWEEN INTERNATIONAL RELATIONS AND INTERNATIONAL POLITICS

Many writers have shown their inability in drawing a line of demarcation between international Relations and International Politics. Kenneth Thompson and Morgenthau consider IP as an inalienable part of IR. This superfluous resemblance does not make IP the core of IR/-Both are different from each other as shown below:

1. International Relations includes all sorts of relations ie. political, economic, cultural, geographical, legal and non official. So it embraces the totality of relations among people. But International Politics includes only the political aspects of the overall relations. In other words only those relations which arouse actions and reactions are the subjects of IP. Thus it can be said that international politics is the political aspects of international Relations.
2. International Relations is a wider concept whereas international politics is a narrower concept.
3. The methodology of the study of international relations is descriptive while that of international politics is purely analaytical. In international relations the factors are studied chronologically while in international politics the basis of study is what, when and how of the present with a relationship between the past and future.

It is established beyond doubt that international politics derives its strength from international relations. The former uses the latter as the basis and subject matter of study and hence both are one and the same thing. Modern international politics aims at the establishment of peace through the international organisation and international relations too are based on this very principle. Thus, concern for peace is the common denominator between international politics and international relations.

DIFFERENCE BETWEEN INTERNATIONAL POLITICS AND NATIONAL POLITICS

In international politics, there are sovereign states whose interest are not identical.

These interests of the sovereign states are called the national interest. The sovereign states in order to achieve their interests come into conflict with one another and as a means to achieve the ends power is generally used. Thus, international politics is that aspect of interactions and relations of sovereign states in which the element of conflict or interest is present. National Politics, like international politics, also involves a sort of adjustment of relationship within and among individuals or groups.

Politics denotes the struggle for power. Whether it is national politics or International politics, politics is a common word. According to Morgenthau "Power man's control over the minds and actions of other men and political power means the mutual relations of control among the holders of public authority and between the latter and people at large".

There are groups of divergent interest in national politics too and each aims to further its own interest. This incompatibility of interests generates a conflict. Keeping in mind their own interests the groups tend to strengthen their position by making temporary alliances. However, the conflict always remains restricted to a certain level as the government checks the struggle with the help of laws. The governmental intervention may frustrate a group or a section of people from taking the process of politics beyond limits. In national politics the individual is the actor. The individual is generally under the impact of a particular culture, ideology and ethical values. This analysis states that there is an area in which the national and international politics are similar and in some respects they are different from one another.

SIMILARITIES BETWEEN NATIONAL POLITICS AND INTERNATIONAL POLITICS

1. International politics as well as national politics cluster around the interests. Conflict is the result of incompatible interests.
2. In both seeking of power is important as it is the means through which the desires and wants can be fulfilled.
3. Both adopt psychological methods to seek power.
4. In both alliances generally appear from the desire of men states to strengthen themselves against the adversary.

DISSIMILARITIES

1. In international politics only interests are permanent and so the states may use direct means to achieve their goals. The use of cunningness, treachery, and sabotage is the part and parcel of international politics. In national politics some ethical norms have to be observed. The state regulates the conduct of it citizens and punishes them if they jump over the limits.
2. In national politics the individuals are under the coercive authority of the state. The laws are universally binding upon them and the municipal courts have a complete jurisdiction over them. On the other hand, the sovereign states are governed by a weak law called international law and the International Court of Justice too cannot exercise its jurisdiction as freely as the municipal courts do in regard to individuals.

3. In international politics the sovereign states generally resort to wars if their interests are jeopardised and there is apparently no other alternative. National politics is a field which does not interest the ordinary man. The issues involved in international politics to an ordinary man are in comprehensible.

OBJECTIVES RELATED TO THE STUDY OF INTERNATIONAL POLITICS (SIGNIFICANCE)

In this increasingly inter dependent world its study is essential for human survival and human progress. It reveals how men and nations tend to act in given circumstances and so tells us what conditions should be encouraged and what conditions should be discouraged if we are to promote international harmony and well being.

In international relations we deal with nations and human beings. The states are sovereign in nature and sovereign nation states have not yet learned to live in peace. War is the most important problem facing the world community. Today a war cannot be fought with the nuclear weapons, since it would destroy the whole civilisation that mankind has built up. The students of international relations should bear in mind this cold reality. Attempts may be made to put an end to this ugly phenomenon of war.

Again,. no community can live in isolation. What is being witnessed is increasing global inter dependence, both political and economic. A war anywhere or fluctuations in prices of commodities like oil will affect all countries. Under such conditions the study of international relations will help people to know each other and understand the problems which confront them.

Our aim is to create a world state. Every people should have consciousness about the brotherhood of man. A basic knowledge of the cultural or linguistic or racial peculiarities of the people of the world would help us to create more understanding and tolerance.

The objectives can be summed up as follows.

1. To find out ways and means leading to the establishment of peace.
2. To avoid conflict among nations and to seek the areas of co-operation.
3. To give less and less importance to the external sovereignty and to perpetuate the idea of world brotherhood.
4. To help the underdeveloped cities and countries by pooling the resources of economically advanced countries.
5. Liquidation of imperialism and colonialism.
6. To balance the power among nations.
7. To establish collective security for maintaining peace and avoid aggression.
8. To give respect and obey the internation law.
9. To respect and strengthen the working of international organisation
10. To maintain a high standard of International morality.
11. To assure the proper enjoyment of Human rights and fundamental freedoms.

CONCLUSION:

All said, the general definitions should broadly apply to international relations in any period either at the beginning of this century, or during the inter-war years, or after the Second World War.What is significant about the nature of the post-1945 international relations is that various developments in international life have brought about a change in the nature of the concept of sovereign states, the conflicts among States, the national interest, and the means of achievement of national interest, that is, power It is as a result of a change in the nature of all these things that international relations has also undergone a significant change. But change does not mean a complete break with the past.

Even today, therefore, international relations retains some of its old and essential elements. With the change in the nature of international relations, the methods of its study have also changed. The change in both the spheres, however, has come mainly from one fundamental source, namely developments in various aspects of international life. But it is the change only in the concept of conflict, national interest, and power that is primarily concerned with the nature of international relations. The change in the methods of study of international relations is a matter of approach.

QUESTIONS

1. Discuss the nature and scope of international relations?
2. How International Relations is different from International Politics?
3. Analyse the historical background of International Relations?
4. What is the importance and significance of studying International Relations?
5. Draw the line of demarcation between the International Politics and National Politics? Discuss its similarities and dissimilarities
6. **According to Morgenthau.** "It is the struggle for and use of power among nations." Discuss the nature of international relations in the light of above given statement

CHAPTER 2

APPROACHES TO THE STUDY OF INTERNATIONAL POLITICS

INTRODUCTION

Most theories of international relations are based on the idea that states always act in accordance with their **national interest,** or the interests of that particular state. State interests often include self-preservation, military security, economic prosperity, and influence over other states. Sometimes two or more states have the same national interest. For example, two states might both want to foster peace and economic trade. And states with diametrically opposing national interests might try to resolve their differences through negotiation or even war. A **theory of international relations** is a set of ideas that explains how the international system works. Unlike an ideology, a theory of international relations is (at least in principle) backed up with concrete evidence. The two major theories of international relations are realism and liberalism.

APPROACHES TO IR

Historically, international activities were the results of actions taken by central governments, but this is changing in the world of today. Increasingly, these activities involve different actors. **International relations** is the study of the interactions among the various actors that participate in international politics, including states, international organisations, nongovernmental organisations, sub national entities, and individuals. Political scientists develop theories or frameworks, both to understand the causes of events that occur in international relations and to answer the foundational questions in the field.

Realism poses that states exist in an anarchic international system.

- Each state bases its policies on an interpretation of national interest defined in terms of power.
- The structure of the international system is determined by the distribution of power.

Liberalism argues that humans form states that generally cooperate and follow international norms and procedures.

There are several distinct approaches to the study of IR, these include: the traditional approach, the scientific approach, the behavioural and post-behaviouralist approaches, the systems approach and contemporary approaches.

A) Traditional Approach

In view of the complex variables influencing behaviour of states, the traditionalists focus on the observed behaviour of governments. They explain observable government behaviour on the basis of concepts like balance of power, national interest, diplomacy etc. Traditional realists try to understand and resolve the clashing of interests that inevitability leads to war.

This is an approach to international relations that emphasises the studying of such disciplines as diplomatic history, international law, and philosophy in an attempt to develop better insights. Traditionalists tend to be sceptical of behaviouralist approaches that are confined to strict scientific standards that include formal hypothesis testing and, usually, the use of statistical analysis.

B) Scientific Approach

Scientific scholars challenged the traditionalist, arguing that IR is too broad and complex a field to be a sub- discipline of political science. They began constructing conceptual frameworks and partial models of international systems, and tried to collect and analyse data to refute of validate a formulated hypothesis.

Such theorists focus on statistical correlations between variables like incidence of war and alliance policies for e.g. While this approach has brought a methodological rigor to IR, it relies more heavily on process analysis than on experimentation. Even obtaining data is difficult in IR and the units of analysis vary (terrorism for e.g. is a relative term).

C) Behavioural Approach

In the 1960s and 70s, scholars began arguing that politics cannot be studied factually without reference to values. Behavioural approach is informed by socio-anthropological and psychological perspectives. It focuses on understanding the reasons behind the action behaviour of states and other international actors.

This approach has contributed to understanding how people and organisations of different cultures interact, the effects of propaganda and stereo-typical views on conflict situations and international relations. It is difficult to determine the behaviour of states, which is the aggregate behaviour of a large number of individuals and of super-imposing authorities.

An approach to the study of politics or other social phenomena that focuses on the actions and interactions among units by using scientific methods of observation to include quantification of variables whenever possible. A practitioner of behaviourism is often referred to as a behaviouralist.Behaviorism refers to the ideas held by those behavioural scientists who consider only observed behaviour as relevant to the scientific enterprise and who reject what they consider to be metaphysical notions of "mind" or "consciousness".

D) Post-Behaviouralist Approach

In the 1980s, an attempt was made to combine normative and empirical approaches to study IR. This approach can be used to test the validity of the idealists' hypothesis to see if democratic or authoritarian states are more likely to be engaged in internal conflicts

MODERN APPROACHES

The history of modern political thought is the story of a contest between two schools that differ fundamentally in their conception of the nature of man, society and politics. Realism and idealism are the two main competitors for recognitions as the sound approach to the study of international politics. One believes that a rational and moral political order derived from universally valid abstract principles achieved. It assumes the essential goodness and changeability of human nature. It trusts in education, reform and the periodic use of force to remedy these defects. This is the idealistic school. The basic

Assumption underlying realist approach is rivalry and strife among nations in some form or other. It is contest for power or influence always goes on in international society, and this contest cannot be controlled by International law or Government. Therefore, the prime function of Diplomacy and Statesmanship is to check the contest for power and the means to be adopted, for its new balance of power.

A) REALISM

LEADING REALISTS

The philosophy as realism which flourished almost throughout the 18th and 19th centuries has been revived after the second World War. E.H .Carr, George Kennan, Thompson, Schuman and Morgenthau are the leading realists.

Morgenthau is the chief advocate of the realist school Morgenthau's is generally recognised as the main exponent of this theory. It was he who gave theoretical orientation to realism. He is the first to develop a realistic model. According to him, the central focus of realism is power. Other realists who follow Morgenthau have only carried forward the tradition established by him. Since Morgenthau is the chief advocate of the realist school it is proper to discuss in detail his realist theory of International politics. In his famous book 'Politics Among Nations, published in the late forties Morgenthau propounded the theory.

BASIC ASSUMPTION

The basic assumption underlying realist approach is rivalry and strife among nations in some form or other. It is contest for power or influence always goes on in international society, and this contest cannot be controlled by International law or Government. Therefore, the prime function of Diplomacy and Statesmanship is to check the contest for power and the means to be adopted, for its new balance of power.

SIX PRINCIPLES OF REALISM

Morgenthau developed his theory in the form of six principles of political realism.

Principle 1 Self preservation is the principle of human nature:-The first principle of Political realism is that Politics is governed by objective laws which have their roots in human nature. Man is a mixture of good and bad, selfishness and altruism. Loving and quarrelsome traits and possessive and sacrificial qualities. Above all this is the story of struggle for survival and human history is an account of war contest and peaceful settlements. The early theory of politics takes into account the story of human history as it has unfolded itself and tries to prevent it in a rational manner. A state's primary interest is self-preservation. Therefore, the state must seek power and must always protect itself

Principle2 Strong Power is only in existence:-Secondly, interest and power are no doubt the key concept in Morgenthau's Theory, but the meaning attached to them is not static and fixed once and for all. The states interests are fluid and change with the ever changing situation in the world at large. The world is a harsh and dangerous place. The only certainty in the world is power. A powerful state will always be able to outdo—and outlast—weaker competitors. The most important and reliable form of power is military power.

Principal3 Concept of National Interest: - Thirdly the main element of Political realism is the concept of national interest which Morgenthau defines in terms of power. His assumption is that statesmen think and act in terms of interest defined as power. Power is not only a tool of analysis but also a guide to policy. According to Morgenthau, a foreign policy should concern more with the political requirement of success rather than anything else. He guards against two popular fallacies. The concern with motives and the concern with ideological preferences. A student of international politics must not indulge in fining the motives of statesmen. For one thing such a task is difficult as motives are a complex psychological phenomenon and another it is unnecessary in political study. Another factor which we must guard against in the desire to find out ideological roots for statesman's act. Ideology very often provides an idealistic or philosophical cover for actions which are essentially nationalist and thus misguide the researcher. The Sino Soviet conflict had initially developed in ideological term. Mao had accused 'Khrushchev of abandoning the revolutionary mission of communism and of pursuing a policy of peaceful co-existence with imperialistic west. But by the beginning of the seventies. Mao himself had established ties with the US. He vehemently criticized Soviet Policy towards the non aligned world especially with India.

Principle4 Prudence is the supreme virtue:-Fourthly, political realism, though aware of the moral significance of political action, maintains that universal moral principles should not be applied to the action of states in their abstract universal formulation. It must be modified in accordance with the time and place. Realism, considers prudence to be the supreme virtue in politics. There can be no political morality without prudence.

Principle 5 No importance to Morality:-Fifthly, as political realism does not identify national interests with universal morality and defeats its own purpose, it does not treat what is right and justifiable for certain nation as good for all countries. It refuses to identify the moral aspirations of a particular nation with moral law that governs universe.

Principle 6 Autonomy in Political Sphere:-Finally political realism maintains the autonomy of the political sphere. It thinks in term of interest defined as power. It puts all other standards in subordination to political standard. It should not be mixed up with the legalistic moralistic approach to international politics;

PRACTICAL EVIDENCE OF REALIST THEORY

Politicians have practiced realism as long as states have existed. Most scholars and politicians during the Cold War viewed international relations through a realist lens. Neither the United States nor the Soviet Union trusted the other, and each sought allies to protect itself and increase its political and military influence abroad. Realism has also featured prominently in the administration of George W. Bush.

Machiavelli – A Ruler Of Realism

One of the best-known realist thinkers is the notorious Niccolo Machiavelli. In his book *The Prince* (1513), he advised rulers to use deceit and violence as tools against other states. Moral goals are so dangerous, he wrote, that to act morally will bring about disaster. He also gave advice about how to deal with conflicts among neighbouring states and how to defend one's homeland. Machiavelli's name has become synonymous with nasty and brutal politics.

Evaluation

Like any other general theory, Morgenthau's realist theory appears vague and abstract when subjected to detailed examination. Although he has termed his theory as realist, the rational statesman he has envisaged to exist more in theory than in reality.

As Stanely Hiffman has pointed out, irrational factors too influence Statesmen's decisions as it would be unrealistic to brush them aside as irrelevant intrusions or pathological deviations. History is replete with fanatic rulers who saw no other social good and morality except the one that they had cherished. To say that such fantasy was not rational is to admit the limitations of his realist model.

In conclusion we may say that Morgenthau made the study of international politics scientific. His two messages are (1) adopt that policy which enhances the power of a nation. (2) Know other's interest to avoid conflicts. So his approach is less open to risk.

(B) LIBERALISM

Liberalism emphasises that the broad ties among states have both made it difficult to define national interest and decreased the usefulness of military power. Liberalism developed in the 1970s as some scholars began arguing that realism was outdated. Increasing globalisation, the rapid rise in communications technology, and the increase in international trade meant that states could no longer rely on simple power politics to decide matters. Liberal approaches to international relations are also called *theories of complex interdependence*. Liberalism claims the following:

- The world is a harsh and dangerous place, but the consequences of using military power often outweigh the benefits. International cooperation is therefore in the interest of every state.
- Military power is not the only form of power. Economic and social power matter a great deal too. Exercising economic power has proven more effective than exercising military power.
- Different states often have different primary interests.
- International rules and organisations can help foster cooperation, trust, and prosperity.

Example: Relations among the major Western powers fit a model of complex interdependence very well. The United States has significant disagreements with its European and Asian allies over trade and policy, but it is hard to imagine a circumstance in which the United States would use military power against any of these allies. Instead, the United States relies on economic pressure and incentives to achieve its policy aims.

Tenets of Liberalism

Liberal and or neo-liberal theorists try to identify a common basis for international cooperation and interaction. Liberal theorists think that multiple actors are important to understanding outcomes in international system: states, MNCs, NGOs, etc. (these actors are not necessarily unitary or rational).

Economic, social and military goals motivate these actors to act and multiple means are used to achieve their goals. For liberals, the anarchic character of the inter-state system does not imply that policy makers face an unchanging situation of international conflict. The prospect of economic, technological, and cultural benefits may give policy makers reasons to cooperate with other states. These include asymmetries in interdependence, military or issue specific power (where different states have power on different issues, e.g. OPEC countries have power with respect to oil prices not political issues)

According to liberal theorists, the anarchic international system is mitigated by norms and rules of international law and trade. Governance without government is the ideal system for global organisation according to liberals. Liberals are particularly against the interference of the government in economic processes.

C) IDEALISM

Idealism is a specific school of liberalism that stresses the need for states to pursue moral goals and to act ethically in the international arena. Idealists believe that behaviour considered immoral on an interpersonal level is also immoral in foreign policy. Therefore, idealists argue that dishonesty, trickery, and violence should be shunned. In the United States, idealism has usually been associated with the Democratic Party since World War I.

Example: As he negotiated the treaty to end World War I in 1918, Woodrow Wilson worked to promote democracy and national self-determination. Wilson's idealism led him to push hard for the creation of the League of Nations, an international organization that would fight aggression and protect the weak from the strong, in 1919. Scholars use the term Wilsonian to describe a person or group who advocates promoting democracy overseas in the name of idealism.

D)SYSTEMS THEORY

Besides the idealist and realist approaches there are some other approaches which are more reasonable and realistic. The systems approach is one among them. Among the political scientists who made a significant contribution to this theory mention must be made of **David Easton, Gabriel Almond and Morton Kaplan** field of international politics.

Mortan Kaplan is one of the best representative of the system approach:- Kaplan believes that a system is most inclusive if it has such recognizable interest as are neither completely identical not necessarily opposed to each other. A political system should have specific areas of jurisdiction and should provide methods for settling conflicts of jurisdiction. To him force is necessary as a last resort to keep the political system intact. He believes that the most important system is the international system. But he does not regard international system as a political system is subordinate to their role of decision making with international system is subordinate to their role in the national actor system. He thinks that the behaviour of national actors in the field of international affairs is always governed by the basic consideration of national interests.

In other words to Kaplan actors on international scene belong to two categories: national actors and Supra national actors.

a) National actors are the nation states like Soviet Russia, U.S. India, and Saudi Arabia etc.
b) The Supra national actors are such international actors as the NATO, Warsaw pact, the U.N, etc.

Morton Kaplan suggests that six international systems may be identified the balance of power, the loose bipolar, the tight polar, the universal, the hierarchical and the unit veto systems. In a situation where too many actors influence international relations, it becomes difficult to strike a perfect balance of power position and loose bipolar system develops. The universal international systems grow when the universal actor like the U.N usurps many of the functions of powerful units in a loose bipolar system. In such a system the universal actor become powerful enough to prevent war among nations, but national actors, retain their individuality. In the Hierarchical international system, the universal actor becomes too powerful and the international community becomes a sort of world state. The unit

Veto system develops as a result of weapons development. This system corresponds to the state of nature described by Hobbes in which the interests of all are opposed and in which all are at war in with each other.

Evaluation :-Morton Kaplan's systems theory evoked more criticism than acclaim. His classification of international relations into six systems has been arbitrary and one can minimize or maximise such categories in another analytical frame work.

The Chief critique of Morton is Stanley Hoffman. He accused such theorists building models at the expense of our understanding in the field of political science

E)THE GAME THEORY

The approach suggested by the theory of game has also been used in the study of international politics. The theory of game has been developed mainly by mathematicians and economists. Martin Shubik, Oskar Morgenstern and Karl Deutsch were among the first to recognise the importance of game theory. It is a method of analysis and also of selecting the best course of action.

The theory has been defined as body of thought dealing with rational decision strategies in situations of conflicts and competition when each participant or player seeks to maximise gains and minimise losses. It is a mathematical model in which the player is placed in a certain fixed situation and tries to make maximum gains from his opponents.

Three principal kinds of game have been identified in the frame work of game theory. The first is called games with identical interests, the second games with opposite interests and the third games with mixed interests. The model which the game theory employs is that of a game strategy and not the game of chance. Game theory envisages several types of games (1) Zero-sum Two person's games. (2) Non-zero sum two persons games (3) Zero-sum persons games and (4) non-zero-sum persons games (In) (N) (1) the gain of one is equal to the loss of another. In 2nd and 3 the outcome is shared and the losses of one are not necessarily equal to the gain of another. In 4 the situation is extremely complex and gains and losses are shared by both sides to some extent.

The game theory has five important concepts. They are strategy, opponent, pay-off, rules and information. The strategy takes into account the potential behaviour of opponents. The Game theory assumes as opponent and this is the second important concept of game theory. The Third is pay off which refers what the game is worth at the end. The fourth is rules that govern a game. The fifth significant concept in Game theory is information.

Evaluation :-The theory is highly abstract and works only under assumed conditions. The players are rarely as rational as presented by this theory. It can be applied with some success only to cases of two person Zero sun games; but as Morton Kaplan has pointed out, there are few such situations in reality and the theory has only limited applicability to most problems of international politics.

F) COMMUNICATIONS THEORY.

Communication Theory has been developed mainly by Karl W Deutsch for understanding the national scene and has been applied to international politics by Charles. A. McClelland and others Deutsch's concern was to reduce the importance of the notion of power in Politics and highlight the importance of the flow of information in government decisions. The communications theory treats the Government as decision making system based on various information flows. The theory is equally important in international politics. Communications has indeed transformed human relation as well as relations between states to much greater extent than any other development. It has increased people's exposition to official and non-official and non-official propaganda and strengthened both totalitarian and regimes and democracies. The communication system has undoubtedly increased interdependence of international community. It has made functioning or an international agency likes the U.N much easier.

G)DECISION MAKING THEORY

This is another important approach that has been emphasised in the study of international politics during the last decades. The first major attempt at introducing the decision making analysis in the study of foreign policy was made by Richard Snyder and others after the II World war and is specially developed in the area of foreign policy making.

The decision making approach has two fundamental purpose. The first is the identification, crucial structure in the political realm where change takes place, decisions are taken and actions are indicated and carried out. The second is the systematic analysis of the decision making behaviour which leads to action. This approach focuses in query on action called decision makers and on the state defined as decisional units. The action of the state is seen through the action of decision makers.

Analysing the factor that operate on decision makers, Snyder divides them into three main sets of stimuli, the internal setting, the external setting and the decision making process. He studies the personality factor of the decision maker and the various agencies and processes involved in decision making. The theory takes the study of international politics to the real actor from the abstract states and collective situation.

The decision making theory has contributed a great deal to the understanding of the process of foreign policy making which all other theories has rejected. Snyder's scheme is most impressive as a detailed approach to the whole of international relations.

QUESTIONS

1. For some theorists the behaviour of the states is determined primarily by their internal characteristics. By contrast other theorists argue that state behaviour is shaped primarily by their position in the international system and especially by their relative power. Which view do you think is more accurate.
2. On a cold February morning, President Woodrow Wilson declares "states' internal values and norms should determine their foreign policy and the pattern of their international relations." Which theory of international relations does this statement support?
3. . In what ways do realism and liberalism differ?
4. Examine the uses of systems approach in international relations and examine the relevance of Kaplan 's system analysis?
5. How the decision making theory has contributed a great deal to the understanding of the process of foreign policy making which all other theories has rejected? Explain the Snyder Scheme in detail.
6. Morgenthau developed his theory in the form of six principles of political realism. Examine and evaluate the six principles of Political Realism
7. What are the traditional and modern approaches of international relations? Discuss its relevance in contemporary times?

CHAPTER 3

NATION-STATE SYSTEM

INTRODUCTION

In this section, we cover three of the most important terms in political science along with its historical background . The rise and decline of nation states plays an indispensable role in International Politics:

1. **Nation:** a large group of people linked by a similar culture, language, and history
2. **State:** a political unit that has sovereignty over a particular piece of land
3. **Nation-state:** a state that rules over a single nation

Because the nation-state dominates so much political discourse, many political scientists specialise in understanding how nation-states work internally, as well as how they relate to one another.

Nations

A **nation** is a large group of people who are linked by a similar culture, language, and history. Members of some nations share an ethnicity (almost everyone in South Korea is Korean, for example), whereas other nations consist of ethnically diverse groups of people (the United Kingdom, the United States, Australia, and Singapore, for instance). However, the members of a nation see themselves as connected. Fellow members are often regarded as part of an extended family. Many members of a nation take pride in being a part of something bigger than themselves as individuals, and they celebrate their nation.

Example: In common speech, we use the term nation to describe a collection of people with something in common. For example, some people refer to the "Red Sox Nation," consisting of all those who root for the Boston Red Sox. The term is used even more often as a synonym for country, which is technically incorrect.

People disagree about what counts as a nation. Nation-hood sometimes transcends geographical boundaries. Some groups consider themselves to be nations, even though much of the world does not consider them that way. Kurds, for example, live in Turkey, Iraq, and Iran, but many Kurds believe they belong to a Kurdish nation. Also, members of a nation frequently differ in a variety of ways, including speaking different languages and participating in different cultural practices.

In the end, determining what constitutes a nation is somewhat subjective. People may identify themselves as members of myriad nations, but even those identifications may change over time. And the strength of the identification also varies. The division between an ethnic group and a nation is a tricky one to make. To put it crudely, the moment that an ethnic group starts to view itself as a nation, it becomes a nation. The Kurdish people, for example, became a nation when they started thinking of themselves as an ethnic group with a common language, history, and culture that set them apart from the neighboring Turks, Arabs, and Persians.

States

A **state** is a political unit that has sovereignty over a particular piece of land. **Sovereignty** is the ultimate power within a territory. So the state has the power to make laws, defend its borders, and enact policies. The state also exercises a monopoly on the legitimate use of force: No group within its borders can use force legally without the permission of the state. In the United States, we use the word *state* to mean something more akin to the word *province* (the difference being that American states have more political autonomy and power than provinces in most other countries). But political scientists use the word *state* as a synonym for *sovereign governments.*

Who is Sovereign

A state is the ultimate authority within a territory. Smaller political units—such as city governments—exist within a state, but ultimately the supreme power rests with the state. The governments of the city of Chicago, for example, or Orange County, California, have some power to enforce rules within their territories. However, these governments do not have the final say: Local governments are not sovereign because they are subordinate to the federal government of the United States and must abide by the government's rules.

WHAT ARE NATION-STATES

Political scientists use the term **nation-state** to refer to modern countries and their political apparatuses. A nation-state is a *state* that rules over a single *nation.* France, for example, is a nation-state, as is Japan. The people in both countries overwhelmingly share a common language, history, and culture. The term *nation-state* reflects the situation in which the boundaries of a state coincide with the geographical area occupied by a nation. There are also states that are not nations—such as Switzerland, whose citizens speak four different languages and have varied cultures. And there are nations that are not states, such as Kurdistan, a region in the Middle East lacking firm borders that is occupied by Kurds, but it is not considered to be an independent state by its neighboring nations of Syria and Turkey.

In the age of internationalism, nation-state system can be regarded as the key stone of International Politics.

The nation state system in the words of Palmer and Perkins is *"the pattern of political life in which people are separately organised into sovereign states that interact with one another in varying degrees and in varying ways."*

In international Politics, the existence of these sovereign states is termed as nation state system". In order to protect that personal interests, they interact with one another. States have to engage in war if their interests are not protected. To secure their existence the states develop their national power.

One sign of the nation-state's prevalence in global politics is that nearly all states refer to themselves as nation-states, regardless of their national makeup. Every government works to build a sense of national identity among its citizens, and sometimes governments even carefully create or craft that identity. For this reason, some scholars argue that the concepts of "nation" and "nation-state" are more about perception and feelings of identity than concrete facts. Most nation-states have citizens of more than one nationality. For example, the small groups of Catalonians in Spain, Bretons in France, and Ainu in Japan differ in nationality from the majority of people in those nation-states. Usually, the minority groups are very small.

NATION-STATE MINORITIES

Often, people in the dominant nationality within a nation-state will mistreat those in the minority. For many years, the government of Australia, dominated by the ancestors of European settlers, enacted many harsh policies against the indigenous Australians, known as the Aborigines. These policies included taking over Aboriginal land and removing indigenous children from their families and placing them in special schools for socialisation.

NATION-BUILDING

In many nation-states, the government actively promotes the idea of common nationality. Children learn the same language and history in state-sponsored schools, and public events frequently invoke cultural heroes and icons. Citizens are often encouraged to work for the betterment of the nation. These practices, among others, are known collectively as **nation-building.**

Foreign governments also participate in nation-building. Sometimes a government will give money and advice to another country to help nation-building. At other times, a country will engage in nation-building after it militarily occupies another country. Before leaving, the occupying power seeks to build a nation that can govern itself. In the early years of the twenty-first century, the United States intervened militarily and participated in nation-building in Afghanistan and Iraq.

NEFARIOUS NATION-BUILDING

At times, nation-building has been undertaken using nefarious means. Nazi Germany, for example, sought to unite its people through a shared hatred of common enemies, most notably the Jews. The government of the former Soviet Union promoted national identity by forcing very different ethnic groups to learn the same language, going so far as to outlaw the use of some local languages.

Nation-States Around the World

Today, most of Europe consists of nation-states. But in Africa and the Middle East, states frequently do not coincide with nations, largely as a result of European colonialism. In the nineteenth century, during what is now known as "the Scramble for Africa," the Europeans divided up the continent without regard to indigenous national boundaries. When the Europeans left and the former colonies became independent states, they mostly kept the borders established by the Europeans.

Example: In 1947, the British government withdrew from what was then known as Palestine. Shortly thereafter, the United Nations established the state of Israel, unevenly splitting the land between the Jews and the Arabs and giving the state of Israel sovereign domain over such Palestinian areas as the West Bank and the Gaza Strip. The resulting tensions and violence among Jews, Arabs, and Palestinians continue to this day.

Colonial Boundaries

According to legend, the English set the boundaries of the Gambia, a small country in West

Africa, by firing a cannon from a ship on the Gambia River and then marking that nation's boundary according to where the cannonballs fell.

THE STRUGGLE FOR THE NATION-STATE

Throughout modern history, many groups have worked very hard to create nation-states. Sometimes, these efforts succeed, as with the unification of Italy in the late nineteenth century; the dissolution of the Austro-Hungarian Empire after World War I into the discrete nation-states of Austria, Czechoslovakia, Hungary, Poland, and Yugoslavia; and the independence of Eritrea from Ethiopia in the late twentieth century. In some cases, however, people have failed thus far in their attempts to create a distinct nation-state. Groups that continue to agitate for a nation-state include the Basques in Spain, as well as the Palestinians and the Kurds in the Middle East.

Empire

An **empire** is a state that governs more than one national group, usually as a result of conquest. One national group frequently dominates, giving members of that group a special place in the regime. Empires have existed in every era of human history, from the ancient empires of Egypt, China, Ghana, and Rome to the modern British Empire

HISTORICAL BACKGROUND

The state system is as old as the human history. It will be more correct to say that the history of the state system starts with the political consciousness of man. There are some of the examples of old state system.

1) Tigris Euphrates system existed in 600 BC
2) Warring state system of China (500-300BC)
3) Indian state system (1000 AD)

The Modern state system is the result of a long historical development. It originated in the renaissance and reformation period in Europe. They are different from older ones. In the modern state system the states are the epicentres of power while the medieval states lacked this characteristic. During the middle ages, the state power was not concentrated in the hands of the state. Feudalism and Catholicism had a great influence in the control of the states. Renaissance checked Feudalism and Reformation reduced the influence of Pope in state affairs.

FIRST STAGE OF NATION STATE SYSTEM :-

The Treaty of Westphalia in the year 1648 may be said to have established and formalized nation state system. By 1648 the state system was fully established in Europe. The result of Westphalia was very significant. It can be considered as the first stage in the evolution of the nation state system.

WESTPHALIA TO UTRECHT:

The second stage in the development of the state system lies in between 1648 to 1713. This period marked a conflict among France, Britain, Holland and Spain for colonial supremacy Louis XIV of France was determined to establish an empire. But, soon France had to face a coalition of Britain and Austria at the question of Spanish succession. France suffered heavy losses at the treaty of Utrecht. The agreement reached at Utrecht established such a balance to which Sweden, Russia and Poland could no longer resolve issued in the East with out involving West.

UTRECHT TO VIENNA

Another development was the rise of Frederick the great of Prussia, After the Utrecht treaty whenever a continental issued around France and Austria clashed. In order to check the threat of Frederick the great of Prussia, France and Austria form an alliance, which was joined by Russia. In order to establish a balance of power, Great Britain joined with Prussia. The result of these alliances and counter alliances was the 7 years war in which France, Austria and Spain were defeated. The third development was the French Revolution France under Napoleon become and important power. Britain, Prussia, Russia Austria and Sweden by combined efforts defeated France, War ended with Vienna meeting in which the old balance of power, was established again.

VIENNA TO VERSAILLES

The period between 1815 and 1914 is called the period of Pax Britannica. In cremean war (1854 - 56) Britain and France collectively checked the ambition to Russia to dominate Constantinople. As a result of the Franco- Prussian war Prussia unified empire under Bismarck and it became a leading power in the continent.

The decline of Turkish empire In the Balkans led to the rise of many sovereign states in Balkans. The states fulfilled their long cherished goals and nationalism became the basis of their Independence.

In the Western hemisphere the decline of Spanish power led to the rise of many independent states. These states today are known as Latin American states. In this period USA made tremendous progress. In the Far East, Japan came into conflict with China. At the beginning of the 20th century Japan achieved great credit by defeating one of the major powers Europe. Before the I world war European powers entangled themselves in such alliances and treaties which clearly divided European states into two groups. Triple Alliance and Triple Entente came into existence.

VERSAILES TO PRESENT

The treaty of Versailles contained the seeds of war. It humiliated the defeated nations. Moreover, it gave rise to Nazism in Germany and Fascism in Italy. Russia grew powerful under the communist rule. The modern state system which came into being with Westphalia basically continues to be the same. It is apterm in which the independent communities of the world, by organizing themselves into sovereign political entitles, act and react with one another. The state is sovereign externally and internally. Internal sovereignty means that the state can formulate laws at its own will and accept any method to secure its interest. The states manifest their sovereign political entity by adopting specific, currency and Flag.

CHRACTERISTICS OF MODERN STATE SYSTEM

The states the sovereign political entities – are different from one another in many respects. Infact, there are both similarities and dissimilarities among the states. The territorial basis gives the state legitimacy because the community inhibiting a specific territory evolves a language culture and religion. Almost all the states of the world are distinguished by their territory. After the II. World War many states in Asia and Africa came into being which do not possesses a natural geographical boundary or a distant territory. Whatever difference may be among the states as the basis of territory, population or culture, the states are considered legally equal to one another.

There is difference among states on the basis of Industrial development. They are as follows.

1. **Industrially developed :** Industrially developed countries have high rate of literacy. The use of luxurious goods is higher, death and birth rate is checked and balanced, political awakening is sufficient and its impacts can be seen in the foreign as well as domestic policy.

2. **Developing :** In the case of developing countries they are facing a lot of problems and it become some times very difficult for them to break and solve this problem. Their main problems are illiteracy, epidemics, political instability and lack of technical knowledge. India, Pakistan etc., belong to this category.

3. **Under developed:** In this category lives the major population of the world. These countries have to face problems of illiteracy, problems of transport and communication, rapid increase of population etc. Indonesia, Sudan are the examples.

Classification of states on the Basis of Power

The prominent writes of International politics classify the modern states on the basis of power. They are as follows.

1. **Great powers:** A great power is 'a power with general interest, and with such interest that it can attempt advance or protect those interests in every sphere". According to some, power is a changing factor. So a major power can become middle power and vice-versa.

2. **Middle powers:** It stands mid way between great power and small states.

3. **Small power**: It stands midway between middle power and no power. It is all power with the means of defending only limited interests."

BASIC FEATURES OF MODERN STATE SYSTEM

There are certain important features, with our which modern state system loses its sanctity Palmer and Perkins call them "corollaries of state system". They are as follows.

a) **Concept of Sovereignty:** In the words of Palmer and Perkins, 'Sovereignty is the legal theory that gives the state unique and virtually unlimited authority in all domestic matters and in relation to other states" In international Politics Sovereignty would mean the right of self government and promotion of national interest through foreign policy. It implies that states can make laws at its own will and has the right to make relations with other states.

b) **Doctrine of Nationalism:** Modern states cling to the idea of Nationalism. It is feeling of oneness among the people. Modern states are known as nation states. Aggressive nationalism, however, is harmful.

c) **Principles of National Power**: National power is the strength or capacity which a sovereign state can use to achieve its national interests. In the absence of national power, there is no existence to the nation states. Nation states in the International field is decided by the amount of national power.

DECLINE OF MODERN STATE SYSTEM

In the opinion of CAW Manning the western state system determined at the Treaty of Westphalia still continues to be the same. Even today the modern states are associated with 3 characteristics. But his view is not completely correct because modern state system has completely changed. The concept of sovereignty has changed a lot. Sovereignty does not exist in its ancient form of royal absolutism.

Scientific and technological advancement has completely changed the impermeability and territoriality of the states. Modern sophisticated weapons has completely changed the warfare. Ideology began to play an important role in International Politics. After the Second World War many states made alliances with powerful states. Supernational Institutions like NATO, SEATO, CENTO etc. are the result of this. As a result International Politics is not an inter action between two or more groups of sovereign states. Hence we can say that there is a decline of the nation state system. That is why the term 'International System' is used in place of national system.

THE FUTURE OF NATION STATE

Although the nation-state has been the predominant unit of political organisation for most of the last few centuries, its future is uncertain. Two trends point to the nation-state as receding in importance, but these trends sometimes contradict each other. Still, globalisation and devolution continue to occur at a rapid rate throughout the twenty-first-century world, and both will affect the future of nation-states.

RECENT TRENDS OF MODERN STATE-SYSTEM

GLOBALISATION

The first major trend is **globalisation.** Over the last few decades, national boundaries have broken down in a variety of ways, including economically. In today's truly global economy, money and goods travel across borders in huge quantities and at great speed. Many corporations build parts in a variety of countries, then assemble them in yet another country. Most goods are no longer "made in America," for example, because much of the manufacturing often happens in other places, whereas final assembly occurs in the United States. The rapid growth of international investing has further globalized the economy. Globalisation often leads to trans-nationalism, so should this globalizing trend continue, the nation-state might give way to the transnational government.

THE PERILS OF GLOBALISATION

Since the mid-1990s, people from around the world have attacked globalisation. Environmentalists see globalisation as a disaster for the environment, labour unions fear for their members' jobs in a global marketplace, and others see globalisation itself as a cause of poverty in developing countries. Most governments continue to favour globalisation, but anti-globalisation protesters have made their mark by demonstrating against meetings of the World Bank, the International Monetary Fund, and other international economic institutions. During the so-called Battle of Seattle in 1999, thousands of protesters swarmed the hotels and convention centers at which meetings of the World Trade Organisation were being held.

TRANS-NATIONALISM

Trans-nationalism has also occurred at the political level. International organisations, such as the United Nations and the World Trade Organisation, play an ever-increasing role on the political stage, and nations join them for such benefits as military protection and economic security. In the case of the European Union, national boundaries have very little meaning. All citizens can travel, live, and work freely throughout the European Union, and all internal tariffs and trade restrictions have been abolished. Some residents see themselves as citizens of a new European Union nation, not of their smaller countries. Transnational governments and groups literally transcend geographical and political boundaries.

Example: The World Trade Organisation, the United Nations, and the World Bank are just a few examples of international organisations that sometimes act like governments or play a substantial role in international relations. Other examples include the Organisation of American States, the North Atlantic Treaty Organisation, the Organisation for Economic Cooperation and Development, and the Organisation of Petroleum Exporting Countries.

The fact that increasing numbers of people around the world speak the same language demonstrates the transnational trend. English has become something of an international language, but other languages (such as French, Chinese, and Russian) are also spoken by many around the world. Overall, the total number of languages spoken is decreasing, while the total number of speakers of certain dominant languages is increasing.

DEVOLUTION

The second trend that marks the recession of nation-states concerns the increase in political power being given to local governments, sometimes to the point of autonomy. This trend is sometimes called **devolution** because states are said to devolve power back to local governments. In the United Kingdom, for example, Scotland has been granted a great deal of autonomy, as has Catalonia in Spain. Should this trend continue, local governments would replace national or central governments.

NEW FEDERALISM

Since the 1970s, a number of American presidents have pursued a policy sometimes called **new federalism.** Supporters feel that the federal government has gotten too powerful and that more power should be given to state and local governments. Although the federal government remains strong, more power has been given back to state and local governments. In the 1990s, for example, Congress created block grants that gave money to states with few strings attached. States were also given more freedom to experiment with policies, such as Wisconsin's experiment with welfare reform under Governor Tommy Thompson in 1996.

The table below summarizes the trends of globalisation and devolution.

GLOBALISATION AND DEVOLUTION TRENDS

	Globalisation	Devolution
Power flows	Outward, away from the state	Inward, down from the central government
Power belongs to	International organisations and transnational governments	Regional and local governments
Power is lost by	The state	The central government
Sometimes known as	Transnationalism	Subnationalism
Examples	The European Union, the United Nations, the World Trade	New Federalism in the United States, increased Scottish autonomy in the

Organisation	United Kingdom, in-creased study of local and regional languages (such as Breton in France)

SUBNATIONALISM

Accompanying devolution has been an increased identification with and interest in subnational groups. The prefix *sub* means "below" or "beneath," so the term *subnational* indicates a smaller division of a larger national group. Many people are working to preserve the language, culture, and history of subnational groups. Some in France, for example, are learning to speak Breton, a language that had largely disappeared. In a number of countries, local dialects that were suppressed under dictatorial governments have reemerged after a transition to a more democratic government.

Example: With the breakup of the Soviet bloc in Eastern Europe in 1989, a number of subnationalities emerged. In the Baltic states, for example, students learned native languages rather than Russian. Czechoslovakia went so far as to split into the Czech Republic and Slovakia. In the Balkans, the emergence of subnationalism turned violent as Serbs, Croats, Slovenians, and others fought over the remains of Yugoslavia.

CONCLUSION :- PREDICTING THE FUTURE

The future of nation-states is unclear. As trends, globalisation and devolution contradict each other, so it seems unlikely that both will continue in significant ways. On the one hand, if globalisation continues, then transnational governments or allegiances such as the European Union may eventually replace traditional nation-states. On the other hand, if devolution continues, powerful regional governments and subnational groups may come to dominate the political landscape. Then again, the nation-state has proven itself to be very durable throughout history. As the cliché goes, time will tell what the future holds for the nation-state.

QUESTIONS

1. Define the term Nation-State in the era of International Politics?
2. Why the Treaty of Westphalia was significant in the evolution of Nation State Sytem?
3. Nation-state has been the predominant unit of political organisation for most of the last few centuries, but its future is uncertain. Discuss the two trends which are responsible for its recession?
4. What are the major characteristics of Modern Nation State?
5. Differentiate between Nation and State?
6. Discuss the rise and fall of nation state system in the era of International Politics?
7. How the trend of Globalisation is responsible for the declining of Nation State System?
8. What do you mean by the concept of Nation- building and how it is different from Nefarious Nation Building?

CHAPTER 4

KEY CONCEPTS OF INTERNATIONAL REALTIONS NATIONAL INTEREST & NATIONAL POWER

INTRODUCTION

Origins of National Interest

The word interest is derived from Latin and means "it concerns, or it makes a difference to". In the 1930s, Charles Bear wrote the first book concerning national interest. In following years the notion of national interest in IR has been used to describe the underlying rationale for the behaviour of states in a threatening global environment, which preserves and protects one's values against another. Statesmen who are responsible for and to their separate publics, and who operate in an uncertain milieu, often have little choice but to put the interest of their own entity above those of others.

Meaning of National Interest

National interest is understood to mean a state of affairs valued solely for its benefit to the nation. National interest often becomes synonymous with national egoism, with its disposition of transferring self love onto the national group.

One cannot speak about national interest without reference to values, even if they are a culmination of those held by some or all members of a given society

What does Nation Interest include?

Scholars define national interest variously. Some put self-preservation (territorial integrity, political independence and fundamental government institutions) at the head of the list. Other categories of national interest focus on self-sufficiency, prestige, aggrandisement. Charles Bear focussed on the notion of territory and commerce as being the defining features of national interest.

Morgenthau says that a country's national interests should be proportionate to its capacities Britain and France after WWII had super-power ambitions, not consider to their capacities).

Criteria for Defining National Interest

- *Ideological criteria:* if one country's ideology is liberal-democratic, it will make policies supporting democratic governments and movements and oppose totalitarian ones.
- *Moral and legal criteria:* the imperative to act honestly and make decisions in accordance with international laws.
- *Pragmatic criteria:* unemotional, calculated decisions to deal with on ground realities.
- *Bureaucratic criteria:* each organisation tends to exaggerate its specific funding request and to argue in the name of the national interest rather than its own interest.
- *Partisan criteria:* to equate the success of one's own political party with an entire nation's success.
- *Racial criteria:* national interest defined in terms of interest of an ethnic or racial minority or majority
- *Class-status criteria:* a particular class will defend its interests while defining national interest.
- *Foreign-dependency criteria:* protector states define policy obligations of their dependencies.

National vs. Global Interests

Given the complexities of international politics, Morgenthau for e.g. opposes state action based on universal principles, instead he advocates a pragmatic approach of acting based on national interests. Yet, issues of global concern like growing inequalities and environmental problems require world leaders to think beyond the narrow ambit of national interests. The world is also becoming increasing interconnected due to which national interests often exert an influence on global interests and global interests to some degree also compel national interests.

The term national interest gained currency with the emergence of nation state system following the end of WWII, National interest become a tool to increase political control and the expansion of economic relations (Thompson, 1966).

National interest is the long term and continuing ends established by states for which they manoeuvre and acts. All and sundry states are bound to procure these goals. Some countries of west Europe in order to gain their interest pursued the White Man's burden policy. They regarded it their duty to uplift the deteriorated conditions of their brethren in yellow mans of Asia or in the black man's of Africa.

CLASSIFICATION OF NATIONAL INTERESTS

The political and strategic philosophers had classified national interest into diverse categories.

(1)Primary Interests:-The primary interests of a nation are the preservation of physical boundary, political system and cultural identity of the state against possible encroachments from outside powerful states. These interests are permanent and the state must guard them at all costs.

No state would compromise on it rather employ all possible means to defend it. Any state compromise on this point will immerse in the pages of history. The state would boost its defence so that no inimical state, whatsoever powerful, may cast a dirty eye. The state which could not solidify their defence disintegrated like the mighty power of United Kingdom, Union of Soviet Socialist Republic and Pakistan.

(2)Secondary Interests:-The secondary interest of state is the protection of their citizens in foreign countries. The state ensures the diplomatic immunities for the diplomatic staff (Krasner, 1978). The government of United State protected the Raymond Davis and secured his release from Pakistan manifested the way of protection of National Interest. Permanent interest of states refers to comparatively constant and long-term interests of the state.

The states frequently changes national interest when state deems it necessary to protect its vital interest. India supported Iran against US but caste vote against Iran in order to secure nuclear deal from USA. The China and Russia are supporting Iran to secure their strategic and economic interest.

(3)General Interests:-The general interests of nation refer to those positive conditions, which apply to a large number of nations in several fields such as economics, trade, and diplomatic intercourse.

(4)Identical Interest:-The identical interest refers to interest which are held in common by a number of states. The NATO pact, SEATO pact and Cento pacts are manifestation of identical approach to protect their national interest against an enemy state or group of nations (Frank & Weisband, 1971). The conflicting interests are not fixed and undergo changes due to force of events and diplomacy.

The question agitate the mind that how states achieve or secure their interests in complex world.

FOUR METHODS FOR ACHIEVING AND PROMOTING NATIONAL INTEREST

The states adopt three methods for achieving and promoting national interests.

(1) **Coercive Measures**:-The state adopts coercive measures to achieve national interest from other states or group of states. These measures are that measure which is taken within the state, which do not infringe directly upon the state against whom they are taken. These measures are of negative in character even though they may produce positive result. These are acts of non-intercourse, embargoes, boycotts, retaliation and reprisal, severance of diplomatic relations. These are non-violent in character and do not produce any international crisis. The US had taken coercive measure to woo the countries of South America. The USA is taken coercive measures through the UN to desist the Iran from pursuing nuclear technology.

(2)Alliances: - Alliances are concluded by two or more nations for the protection and promotion of common interest. Because of the alliances, the protection of these common interests becomes a legal obligation, which the member states are bound to discharge. The USA and countries of Western Europe formed a defensive alliance NATO against the threat of communism. The USSR and eastern European countries formed an alliance of Warsaw pact against capitalist countries (Ardent, 1958). The Muslim countries formed an alliance Organisation of Islamic Conference against the Israel. Currently countries are forming alliances to protect their economic interest rather than ideological interest.

(3) Diplomatic Negotiations:-The states pursue diplomatic negotiations for the protection of national interest. Diplomatic intercourse is used to reconcile the divergent interest of the state through process of mutual give and take (Urs, 1970). The UN has been encouraging diplomatic negotiation to defuse the tension between states. The regional organisations also adopt diplomacy to bring the warring states to table as SAARC did in post 98 nuclear explosion carried out by India and Pakistan. The United Nation has successfully maintained peace in the world through the process of diplomacy. In addition to national interest, states are trying to protect common interest in the larger interest of international community. For example, they are exerting pressure on nuclear states to avoid the use of nuclear weapon and divert their attention to combat environmental degradation and eliminating poverty.

(4) Formulating Foreign Policy:-The countries of world have collectively waged a war against global warming. It is a crystal fact that national interest is the predominant factor in the formulation of a country's foreign policy. In formulating, adopting and executing foreign policy, political leaders are confronted with a veritable spider's web of conflicting claims and values. The national interest must finally be established in terms of preferred goals and in relation to the power of other nations.

Limitations on promoting National Interest:-There is domestic and international limitation on the national interest. International organisation, International law, world community and reaction of other nations compel the states to formulate rational and accommodating foreign policy, which leads to world peace. Any foreign policy, which claims to operate in the national interest, must have some reference to the physical, political and cultural entity called the nation. The international environment also exercises a profound influence on the decision makers in the formulation of a country's foreign policy basically an important tool to achieve national interest. As a unit of the international community, the state is bound by certain regulations (conventional, customary, ethical, legal or institutional) and the framers of the foreign policy have to operate within these limitations (Solberg, 1968). The framers of foreign policy not only keep the national interests in mind but also consider the interests of world community who are equally determined to fight for their national interests. The national interest is compromised with the interest of world community in order to avoid conflict and reaction of other states. Above all, in formulating the foreign policy the political leaders must not lose sight of the factors like geography, natural resources, industrial capacity, demography, impact of various groups and interest in the society, strategic position of the countries.

B. NATIONAL POWER

Power has been the epicenter of human relations from the very inception of humanity. Power plays an important role in International relations and it is an essential element of politics. The status of state in the International sphere is determined not by its civilisation or culture but by its physical force.

National Power is a key component of International Politics. Basically International Politics is the process of struggle for power among Nations in which each nation seeks to secure its desired goals and objectives of National interests. Because of the absence of sovereign or of a fully powerful centralised international machinery making authoritative allocation of values among the nations and because of the sovereign status of each nation-state, the securing of national interest by each state is always done by the use of its national power

MEANING OF NATIONAL POWER

The dictionary meaning of the term Power is "that in a person or thing which enables them to act on other persons or things.

Morgenthau wrote this "when we speak of power, we mean man's control over the minds and actions of other man".

In International relations power may broadly, be defined as the capacity or ability of a states or to control their behaviour for the purpose of promoting its own vital interests.

Power in the formal sense, **according to Hartmann means**" the strength of capacity that a sovereign state can use to achieve its nation as interests.

George Schwarzenegger defined it as "the capacity to impose one's will on others by reliance on effective sanctions in case of non-compliance"

Palmer and Perkins observed "To the totality of states effectiveness in world politics, we apply the term power".

According to **Padelford and Lincoln,** *"National power is that combination of power and capacity of a state which the state uses for fulfilling its national interests and goals."*

ELEMENTS OF NATIONAL POWER

All the elements of national power cannot be satisfactorily determined. Morgenthau has divided the elements into two categories-permanent and temporary. Palmer and Perkins has divided the elements into tangible and intangible Organ ski has made a distinction between the natural determinants of power and social determinants of power.

The elements of National power are inter related. For example, oil without engineers is valueless and radio without ideas is fruitless. The following are some of the elements of National Power.

1. **Geography:** Napoleon once said that "The foreign policy of a country is determined by its geography". Geography has always been a determining factor of the national power of a state. Today states are inter dependent to each other. So geography has its role inthe relations of nations. Geography as an element of national power has the following sub elements.

a) Size: - The size of a state, whether small or great, is an important element of national power. But only size does not make a state powerful. Even a small country can exert its influence in International relations very much. i.e., Japan defeated Russia in 1905 in the Russia-Japanese. Big size creates problem for variety of reasons.

b) **Topography:** Topography gives certain advantages and disadvantages to a country. The rivers many provide ports, harbours and advantageous transport system. At the same time they may create obstacles in building road, play havoc through floods etc. Mountains cause rainfall, stops enemies etc. Russia is denied by topography access to the open seas.

c) **Climate:** Location, attitudes, rainfall and winds determine climate. Climate has an indirect effect on culture, economy natural resources, political organisations religion and direct on health and energy of people. Extreme heat and cold are unfavourable for strength.

d) **Location:** Diplomacy and war strategy has its impact on location. Nearness to sea will provide for good harbours and it will increase chance of trade. Insular position has its impact on its diplomacy. Great obstacles in the form of mountains etc. will decrease the chance of trade.

2. **National Boundaries:** Boundaries of the states are of two types – natural and artificial. Sea, mountains etc are natural boundaries. The contemporary tension in International relations is due to the boundary disputes. Boundaries often decide the fate of nations.

3. Natural Resources: Natural resources are the permanent factors of National power. Palmer and Perkins termed it as the Gift of Nature. Perhaps the natural resources are the most important elements of national power: The following elements constitute natural resources.

a) ***Food –Stuffs and Agriculture Products:***-The countries self sufficient in food stuffs have an advantage over other nations which lack it in times of war, It will become more clear, Scarcity of agriculture products limits the of power of a nation.

b) ***Minerals:*** For military strength, it is necessary to have highly developed industry, for which minerals are necessary. Possession of minerals will strengthen the industrial capacity of a nation. For example, Petroleum, an important mineral has created 'Oil Diplomacy' in the middle East.

4. Population: Prior to 20th century a large population was undoubtedly a significant and important source of national power. But in the 20th century, large population is a source of strength and weakness. It will be strength, if the state has the means to utilise its talent, energy and maintain a proper standard of living. A large population, has nothing to do with National power. For example China and India are the most populated states; but they are not the super powers. The age group, sex etc also must be taken into account. Too young and too old are not useful. Likewise if females outnumber males; it is also not useful for increasing power position.

5. Technology: Technology is the application of physical and biological sciences to engineering industry and other human activities. The technological advancement is a tremendous element of national power which has influenced the world affairs of recent times by increasing the technique of communications and inter dependence of states. Technology influenced strategic factors. Seas are now no barriers and hence the states separated by the seas do not remain attached to each other in any matter whatsoever. Technology has affected matter of foreign policy. Now Foreign policy includes the technological assistance. Increased emphasis on arms control, technological intelligence and communication satellites. Technology has sophisticated war methods. New inventions prove that the more technologically advanced is a nation the more is its capacity to influence other nations. All the factors can be made up by

6. Military Preparedness: - Military Preparedness require a military establishment capable of supporting the foreign policies pursued. The significant factors that make military preparedness one are follows.

a) ***War technology:*** The fate of nations and civilisation have always been determined by superior armies using sophisticated technology. The less sophisticated technology always has to face defeat.

b) ***Leadership:*** A military leader is the person, who makes best use of available resources in the appropriate time to reap the maximum fruits. Victory and defeat in war is associated with its leader.

c) ***Espionage:*** Today the success of military depends upon affective Espionage. Prior knowledge of enemies move, location and capacity of forces etc will open the way for easy success. The Radar and artificial satellites have played an important role in these filed.

d) ***Quality of armed force***: Military power is dependent upon the quality of men and arms. Modern developed arms will make the victory sure, Israel's victory over the Arab states can be cited as an example.

7. Ideologies: Ideology is a body of ideas concerning economic social and political values and goals with positive actions and programme for attaining these goals. The impact of Ideology in International relations is very wide. It has produced a new cohesiveness within nations and group of nations. Even the geographical boundaries fail to limit the extension of ideologies. However it can be said that the role of ideology as an element of national power is not as powerful as in the past.

8. National Morale: Morale is a healthy frame of mind characterized by fidelity to a cause. In the words of Palmer and Perkins, "Morale is a thing of spirit, made up of loyalty, courage faith and the impulse to the preservation of personality and dignity" National morale is an important aspect of national power. In the absence of which, the other factors will not work National morale is not static. There is a point where it breaks. National morale can be manufactured or stimulated by various factors. Factors like National character, culture, popular leadership popular government and circumstances make national morals

9. Quality of Leadership: - Leadership is the most important element of national power.

Without leadership people can't even constitute a state. Without it there can be no well developed technology and without it morale is totally useless. The functions of leadership are two fold, firstly it co ordinates other elements of national power and secondly, use all the resources for the maximum benefit of the state. The ups and downs in the history of a state can be related to its leaders. Leadership includes the fact of handling foreign affairs. A leader must be capable of conducting diplomacy successfully. A weak and under-developed nation can become a powerful nation under an effective leadership.

10. Quality of Diplomacy: Another effective factor of national power is the quality of diplomacy.

According to Morgenthau "Diplomacy of high quality will bring the ends and means of foreign policy with harmony with the available resources of national power. It will tap the hidden sources of national strength and transform them fully and securely. The quality of diplomacy is the most important of all the elements that influence the power base of a state as also its foreign policy.

National power is a relative one. The power of one state is to be measured in comparison with the power of other states. National power is also changing. A nation may be strong today, but tomorrow it may become weak. And the factors of power are inter dependent. This makes the measurement of power impossible. We shall conclude with the words of Palmer and Perkins" National power, like nearly everything else in this world of ours is relative. A man with a million dollars is not rich in a group of multi-millionaires, a man of forty is old to child of few and youthful to an octogenarian. Similarly, in the matter of power absolute has little meaning. 50 divisions, 300 war vessels 2000 planes all these may represent overwhelming might against one opponent one miserable inadequate against another".

METHODS FOR EXERCISING NATIONAL POWER

Having discussed the meaning of the term power, we will now turn our discussion to the methods by which one nation can make another nation to do what it wants it to do or to prevent another nation from doing certain acts considered undesirable.

Let us assume that Nation A wishes to influence Nation B. The question arises how can Nation A influence Nation B. How can it exercise power? Here we shall consider the ways or methods by which Nation A can influence the behaviour of Nation B.

Generally, there are four methods by which Nation A can make Nation B to do certain acts: it can persuade Nation B for doing what Nation A wishes. It can offer rewards to Nation B for doing certain things what Nation A wants, it can threaten Nation B with punishment if it does not do what Nation A wants, or it can use force to compel Nation B to do what Nation A wishes.

These four methods of exercising power are respectively called persuasion, rewards, punishment, and force. Let us now examine all these methods in detail.

1. Persuasion

Persuasion is the most effective and widely used method of exercising power. In this method, what Nation A does is to influence Nation B by way of argument or to redefine the whole situation so that Nation B changes its mind about what it ought to do.

In this, way, persuasion guarantees lasting results for Nation A. In fret most of the work of international organisations consists of the efforts of various delegates to persuade each other. Small nations, indeed, often use this method because they lack the power to use force, and also because it is cheap.

2. Rewards

Another method of exercising power is by offering rewards. Nation A can influence Nation B for doing what Nation A wants by offering it various rewards. Most of the rewards that Nation A can offer to nation B are psychological, material, economic and political.

The rewards may be only psychological, when a diplomat may change his State's policy to win the appreciation of his fellow diplomats from other nations. Most often the rewards are material in the shape of territory, military aid, weapons, troops and training facilities.

The rewards may also be economic in the form of loans or gifts. This has been the major method adopted by USA and USSR in recent years. Political rewards consist of freedom or support for another nation's position in international conferences etc.

3. Punishment

A third way of exercising power is punishment. As a matter of fact, rewards and punishment are very closely related. The most effective punishment is to withhold the reward, just as one of the most effective rewards is to refrain from some punitive actions which would otherwise be taken.

Acts of punishment, however, should be threatened in advance and not actually carried out. The most effective punishment is rarely meted out because the very threat of it succeeds in preventing the action of which the punisher disapproves.

If punishment is most likely to be carried out, it should be given in such a way that it can be withdrawn at once the offending party mends his way according to the satisfaction of the punishing party.

4. Force

The last method of exercising power is by using force. Punishment, however, is distinguished from force. Punishment implies threats to make another nation from doing or following particular course. But threat when actually carried out, assumes the shape of force.

The most extreme form of the use of force is war. As a method of influencing other nations, force is the last resort. It is only used when the other methods i.e. persuasion, rewards, punishment fail to exercise power over

LIMITATIONS OF NATIONAL POWER

- International Law and Treaties
- Balance of Power
- International Morality
- International Public Opinion
- International Organisations
- Collective Security
- Disarmament and arms and control

QUESTIONS

1. What are the different categories of National Interest?
2. What do you mean by National Interest and National Power? Differentiate between them
3. "The capacity to impose one's will upon others by reliance on effective sanctions in case of none compliance is known as Power" In the light of above given statement analyse the basic determinants and elements of National Power?
4. Give the four methods of promoting and achieving National Interest in International Relations?
5. What are the limitations in achieving the National Interest?
6. Is National Interest is above than the Global Interest?
7. Differentiate between the methods of National Interest and National Power?

CHAPTER 5

BALANCE OF POWER

There is a famous proverb to highlight diverse nature of international relations study.*"There is no permanent friend or permanent enemy in international politics but permanent interests, a friend of today may be the enemy of tomorrow and enemy of today may be the friend of tomorrow"*

INTRODUCTION

It is widely accepted that maintenance of balance of power is necessary for international peace and security. The political relations independent nations and especially of great powers traditionally have been explained by the theory of balance of power.

Palmer and Perkins suggest that the assumption of the theory of balance of power is that "the power alone can limit power".

Palmer and Perkins on balance of power remark them. "The essential idea is simple. When the weights in the scales are equal sented by a pair of scales. When the weights in the scales, the concept of the balance of power of power assumes that no one power or combination of powers should be allowed to grow so strong so as to threaten the security of the rest.

DEFINITION

The equilibrium of power among members of the family of nations as will prevent any one of them from becoming sufficiently strong to enforce its will upon the others. In other words ,The power equation between states is based on an assessment of each state's relative power capabilities and this assessment provides the basis for the conduct of relations between them.

Sideny .B.Fay maintains "Balance of power is just an equilibrium in power among the members of the family of nations as would prevent any one of them from becoming sufficiently strong to enforce its will upon others".

George Schwarzenegger defines it " as an equilibrium or a certain amount of stability in international relations that under favourable conditions is produced by an alliance of states or by other devices."

A HISTORICAL PERSPECTIVE

From 1648 (Peace of Westphalia) to 1789 (French Revolution) was a golden age of classical balance of power, when the princes of Europe began accepting (BoP) as the supreme principle of foreign policy. Evident use of BoP is also noted in the mid-17th cent., when it was directed against the France of Louis XIV. Balance of power was stated British objective for much of the 18th and 19th cent., and it characterized the European international system, for example, from 1815–1914. The Concert of Europe (from 1815 to1870) provides another good example of major European states striving to achieve balance power. The increasing the power of Germany began seeing bipolar set of alliances form, leading to the World Wars.

After World War I, the balance of power system was attacked by proponents of cooperation and a community of power. International relations were changed radically after World War II by the predominance of two superpowers, the United States and the Soviet Union, with major ideological differences between them. After the 1960s, with the emergence of China and the third world, a revived Europe and Japan, it re emerged as a component of international relations. With the collapse of the USSR in 1991, the United States, as the sole remaining superpower, has been dominant militarily and, to a lesser degree, economically.

FORMS OF BALANCE OF POWER

Balance of power is of two types. Simple balance and Complex balance.

1. **Simple balance:** If power is concentrated in two states or in two opposing camps, the balance or distribution of power is said to be simple. The important feature of the simple balance is that states or group of state are also divided into two camps like the two scales of the balance. In simple balance the power distribution between two opposing camps approximately equal. America and Russia individually and the western bloc and communist bloc collectively, are the examples of the simple balance. Such pattern of balance is called "Bi-polarisation", which has resulted in the cold war between the communist and the western bloc.

2. **Complex or multiple balance:** When there is a wide dispersal of power among states and a number of states or groups of states, balance each other, the balance is said to be 'Multiple of complex". A complex balance needs not have a balance. A simple balance may turn into a multiple or complex balance. Polycentrism has become a marked feature of politics. Within the communist as well as western block many new centre of power have come into existence. The uncommitted bloc is one of them.

Balance may in terms of their geographical coverage be spoken of as local, regional or worldwide. The balance of power is local if it operates between two neighbouring states for example India and Pakistan. The balance of power is regional if it involves in a number of states within a particular geographical area. The balance of power is worldwide if most of the countries of the world participate in the balance of power. The so called war between the communist and western bloc is the example of a global balance of power.

METHODS OF MAINTAINING BALANCE OF POWER:

The following are the ways or methods of maintaining the balance of power.

1. **Alliances and counter alliances:** Alliances is the necessary function of the balance of power operating with a multi-stage system. The rival groups in the balance of power system have three

choices in order to maintain and improve their relative power positions.

1. They can increase their own power, 2) they can add to their power the power of the other nations 3) they can withhold the power of other nations form the opponents. If they make the first choice, they embark upon an armament race. If they make second and third choices, they purpose a policy of alliance.

Alliances generally lead to counter alliances. When an alliance is specifically or indirectly directed against some states, it is quite natural that they will not remain as silent spectators. For example the triple alliance of 1882 between Germany, Austria, Hungary and Itlay led to a rival alliance, triple entente 1907 between Britain. France and Russia. Alliances may be both offensive and defensive. While an offensive alliance seeks to upset the balance in favour or its members a defensive alliance aims at restoring peace.

2. Armament and Disarmament: Power is a relative term which is determined in the context of a particular nation or a group of nations. In the event of an impending\ danger form the enemy, every nation tries to maximise its power. The direct way of maintaining the balance is to increase ones own power in relation to power of one's opponents. When there is a great disparity between power position of two nations, it is not possible for the weaker one to increase its own power to the level of its rival. This method of maintaining the balance can be resorted to only when there in a rough parity in the power position the rivals.

Like armament, disarmament can resolve a balance of power one can succeed in keeping its rival disarmed one preserves the balance in one's favour. But in practice disarmament as such has rarely been resorted to except in case of defeated powers on the conclusion of general war. For example the effort on the part of the allied powers after the first world war was to keep Germany permanently weak.

3. Acquisition of territory : Acquisition of fresh territories is also a method of balance of power. This is made possible either by occupying neighbouring territories by Israel is considered by the latter as essential for its security and the preservation of the balance of power.

4. Compensation and partition: A state increases its power by acquisition of new territories and thus balance is tilted in its favour. When such things occurs the other side also takes immediate steps to increase own power in compensation in order to preserve the balance. When some powerful nations occupy the territories of small nations, the powerful nations cannot tolerate this act. They place a condition either to share its under such conditions the powerful rival nations divide small nations swallow their share of prey.

The partition of Poland and later on its division between Russia, Prussia and Austria in a well known example of the Policy of compensation and partition. This principles is seen in the division of Germany, Korea and Vietnam. Each great power becomes a beneficiary and weak state their victim.

5. Creation of buffer states: The creation of a buffer state is also a technique of maintaining the balance of power. A buffer sate is a natural zone sandwiched between two powerful nations. It is usually a weak state. Its function is to keep two giants apart and thus reduce the chances of friction between them. Poland has been the traditional buffer between Russia and Germany. Tibet has been buffer between China and British India. Thus the buffer state acts as a balancing force between the two powerful rivals because neither of them can allow the other to absorb the buffer. But the balance can also be maintained if the two giants decide to decide the buffer zone between them. Buffer states have been often vanished this way.

HOW IS POWER BALANCED?

Often it is a matter of balancing threat rather than power, so distance, interdependence, and ideology matter.

(a) External balancing can take place through alliances but risks dependency on others and requires placing trust on them. This kind of trust and dependency was evident in NATO and Warsaw Pact during the Cold War.

(b)Internal balancing takes place by building up the capacity of the state, as occurred with the US-Soviet arms race, in which both super powers tried to balance power by becoming more powerful themselves.

DEGREE OF POLARISATION

Polarisation is the process that causes neutral parties to take sides in a conflict. It also causes individuals on either side of the conflict to take increasingly extreme positions that are more and more opposed to each other. As parties move toward these opposite "poles," they define themselves in terms of their opposition to a common enemy. Trust and respect diminish, and "distorted perceptions and simplified stereo-types emerge." Parties assume more rigid positions and may refuse to negotiate.

The study of polarisation first came to be identified with those realist writers who wrote about the structure of the international system, the impact of military alliances on war and peace, and the balance of power.

a) Tightness of poles - all states in one camp or other
b) Discreteness of poles – degree of interaction between states on each side
c) Level of animosity - degree of animosity

BALANCE OF POWER CAUSES WAR OR BRING PEACE

Truly uni-polar system would make major war less frequent, since one state can prevent others from arming for war. War is most likely during transitions in balance. Rising power gains strength, challenges previously superior state and, given newness of capabilities, war occurs because each side thinks it can win. So in order to maintain peace among the developed nations Mortan's Kaplan Rules of BOP is followed.

Morton Kaplan's Rules of Balance of Power

1. All states act to increase capabilities but prefer to negotiate rather than fight.
2. All states fight rather than pass up an opportunity to increase their capabilities.
3. All states stop fighting rather than eliminate an essential state.
4. All states act to oppose any coalition or single state which tends to assume a position of dominance within the system
5. All states act to constrain states who subscribe to supra-national organising principles
6. All states permit defeated or constrained states to re-enter the system as potential partners

OBJECTS OF BALANCE OF POWER

The advocates of the balance of power have suggested the following main purposes of the balance of power.

1. preservation of independence of states;
2. preservation of peace;
3. maintenance of International Law

1. Preservation of independent of states

The balance of power aims at such distribution of power among the state, that no single state or group of states becomes so powerful as to enforce its will upon the others. The balance of power helps to achieve stability nations to conquer or acquire control over small and weaker nations and they would probably be swallowed up of one ambitious state were allowed to achieve great superiority of power. But if there happen to be two or more powerful states none of them will tolerate the other to become more powerful. Each of the big powers will see to it that none of them commits aggression against the small and weak powers. Taylor remarks "No one state has ever been strong enough to eat up all the rest and the mutual jealousy of the great powers has preserved even the small states, which could not have preserved themselves". Thus the security and independence of all the states is assured.

2. Preservation of peace

Between peace and security, security will get priority over peace, because security is the first condition of peace. If security is in danger , peace shall have to be sacrificed. If big powers start absorbing small ones first and second world wars. Advocates of the balance of power believed that the balance of power causes peace and so long as the balance is maintained, peace is assured. If balance as maintained neither there will be aggressions, nor was and therefore peace would automatically be established.

3. Maintenance of international law

Balance of power is essential to the maintenance of international law. Regarding the relation between international law and balance of power Oppenheim writes "Balance of power is an indispensable condition of the very existence of international law. A law of nations can exist only if there can be an equilibrium , a balance of power between the members of the family of nations".

RELEVANCE OF BALANCE OF POWER TODAY

Although the concept of the balance of power has lost much its validity in the present day conditions, its operation is still meaningful. As long as the multi – nation state system exists, balance of power will remain as a relevant concept. The changes brought about in the international society have removed many of the conditions in which the balance of power. Since the balance of power is a devices of the management power it will remain relevant till some other device of managing power has not been found out.

If balance of power survives even today it is because of the fact that an effective substitute has not yet been possible such a substitute can probably be found out in the effective world organisation, world public opinion and worldwide acceptance of the obligations of international law. But this prospect is very remote. However,

Palmer and Perkins believe that balance of power will continue to operate, even if super- national world origination is formed . Any how that idea of balance of power is still the central theoretical concept in international relations.

But we cannot shut our eyes to realities. The rise of non- aligned countries on a large scale has adversely affected the importance of the principle of balance of power in the late twentieth century.

The non- aligned countries have became the largest group in the United Nations General Assembly and consequently have enhanced their position in world affairs. Since the non- alignied countries represent a force without a military power they have affected the principle of balance of power in its traditional sense.

With the increasing non- use of physical force against each other by the major nuclear power, the phenomenon global or world wars might vanish. But wars may persist at regional levels among non-nuclear powers or among the nuclear and non- nuclear powers with conventional weapons, and the concept may prove its validity also in the changes circumstance in regional affairs. All these local and regional wards have affected the balance of power position at the regional level. It would be safer, therefore to conclude that the balance of terror situation has reduced the validity of the principle of balance of power on a global scale but has retained it at regional level where wars are fought with conventional weapons.

At the global level balance of power has lost much of its reference but it continues to hold good at regional level relations among nations. In this way it continues to be an important controlling mechanism of international politics.

BALANCE OF POWER VS BALANCE OF TERROR

Now, it is important to make it clear that security analysts have coined a modern term for balance of power among nuclear states is 'Balance of Terror'. It is said to be a shift from conventional balance of power to a nuclear balance of power. Few of the security experts express their dissenting opinion on the very issue and they try to draw a line between both the terms i.e. 'Balance of power' and 'Balance of Terror'.

During 1950 a school of thought put forward that the advent of nuclear technology in international relations has made the notion of conventional balance of power as outdated. According to that school of thought nuclear deterrence works to regulate international hierarchy with different approach.But Snyder made argument in favour of balance of power theory declared it a valid theory to understand contemporary international relations. To him the revolution in military affairs has not dismissed balance of power politics but modified to an extent snyder further elaborated balance of power tendency in post 1945 era.

According to Snyder, a new system of equilibrium supplemented the Post World War II era, introducing new phraseology "Balance of Terror" in international relations to express balancing behavior between nuclear actors. **Both the systems, Balance of power(pre nuclear age) and balance of terror operate with different principles and were easily separable analytically but what's more important to examine is that they are inextricably amalgamated into a new kind of balance of power** in which the old balance of power system adjusts itself to coexist with the new system.

Some of the scholars assert that the classical balance of power among states came to an end with the outbreak of First World war and the innovative methods marked twentieth century with collective security and balance of terror to manage international system. That is indeed, false analysis about international system from 1945 to 1990, as the era starting from onset of cold war to the end of cold war was marked by the active pursuit of maintain balance of power between Superpowers and their respective allies.24

India and Pakistan from the early years after their independence got engaged in conventional balance. After India obtained nuclear bomb in 1974 and achieved superiority in military power over Pakistan. As a result of asymmetric balance of power, Pakistan felt threatened by Indian might and ultimately in May, 1998 became a 2nd nuclear power in South Asia. Pakistan's nuclearization restored the lost balance of power between India and Pakistan. The purpose to present a brief glimpse of Pakistan and India's shift from conventional balance of power to nuclear balance of power is that both states experienced peace during balance of power position and experienced war or otherwise skirmishes at border whenever balance of power got disturbed between them.

CONCLUSION

In sum, despite intense scholarly criticism, 'Realism', sticks around dominant theory in the field of international relations. States are continuously engaged in balancing against perceived threats. Balance of power among rival states can ensure relative peace. Cold war could not turn into hot war because of about balance between nuclear superpowers which was followed by policy of détente between them. Similarly India and Pakistan in post nuclear scenario initiated peace process to resolve outstanding issues between them. Indian Prime Minister, Atal Bihari Vajpayee visited Pakistan in Feb, 1999 and inaugurated bus service between New Delhi and Lahore to enhance people to people contacts between the two nations. Attempts to trigger war between India and Pakistan could not succeed but created hypertension. It can be concluded that balance of power, if does not bring peace but reduces the chances of war among rival states.

QUESTIONS

1. The equilibrium of power among members of the family of nations as will prevent any one of them from becoming sufficiently strong to enforce its will upon the others. In the light of given above statement discuss the different kinds of Balance of Power?
2. How far the concept of Balance of Power is relevant today?
3. "The power alone can limit power" What are the different methods to maintain balance between the developed nations?
4. Differentiate between Balance of power and Balance of Terror?
5. Do you think Balance of Power causes war or bring peace?
6. What do you mean by Balance of Power? Discuss its significance

CHAPTER 6

Diplomacy and War

INTRODUCTION

The term diplomacy has two principal meanings. Firstly, diplomacy is used in the sense of means or method of conducting the foreign policy of a nation. Secondly, diplomacy is also used to refer to the process of formulation and conduct of foreign policy of a nation. Thus diplomacy can be said to be a method and a process of conducting relations among nations. The essence of diplomacy consists in bargaining for a nations interest and securing it best by skilful and opportune use of the resources of the nation. Generally, diplomacy is supposed to secure the maximum advantage for a nation by means of negotiation and compromise.

DEFINITION

Diplomacy may be defined as the management of international relations by negotiation or the method by which these relations are adjusted and managed. In other words it is the process of representation and negotiations by which states customarily deal with one another in terms of peace.

Sir Ernest Satow has given a charming definition of diplomacy in his book "Guide to diplomatic practice". He writes "Diplomacy is the application of intelligence and tact to the conduct of official relations between the government of independent states".

E.A Johnson opines that diplomacy is an instrument and machinery which is used to influence and reduce misunderstanding to avert international crisis"

Morgenthau is of the opinion that diplomacy is the promotion of the national interests by peaceful means".

In the opinion of K.M Panikkar diplomacy is used in relation to international polices, is the art of forwarding ones interest in relation to other countries.

Quincy Wright observes that Diplomacy in the popular sense means the employment of task, shrewdness and skill in any negotiation or transactions. In the special sense used international relations is the art of negotiation, in order to achieve the maximum, of group objectives with a minimum of costs within a system of politics in which was is a possibility. In short, it is an application of tact and intelligence in international policies through negotiation, persuasion and compromise.

Diplomacy from a Historical Perspective

The ability to practice diplomacy is one of the defining elements of a state, and diplomacy has been practiced since the first city states were formed millennia ago (around 5th BC). For the majority of human history diplomats were sent only for specific negotiations, and would return immediately after their mission concluded.

Diplomats were usually relatives of the ruling family or of very high rank in order to give them legitimacy when they sought to negotiate with the other state. Envoys eventually became negotiators rather than being just messengers. During the Middle Ages (6th to 18th century), the scope of diplomacy did not grow much and diplomats were mostly confined to maintaining archives rather than negotiating them. In the late Middle Ages, in Genoa, the Duke of Milan established the first foreign mission. But this was still diplomacy of the court rather than that of the people.

After the American and French revolutions, diplomacy became more democratic and less aristocratic. The Congress of Vienna (1815) laid down procedures for diplomatic immunities and defined diplomatic hierarchies.

Functions of Diplomat:

A diplomat is the eyes and ears of his government. His primary duty is to execute the policies of his government report the major developments to his government and protect the interest of the nationals. Diplomacy functions through foreign office, embassies, consulate and special mission.

A diplomat is an agent of mutual adjustment between the ideas and forces upon which nation act. According to J.R. Childs a diplomat performs four basic functions.

1. **Representation:** A diplomat is the eyes and ears of his government. He is a link between his government and the Government to which he is accredited. He has to cultivate finest qualities of human behaviour and to make a lot of social contacts. He has to explain the policies and aspirations of his government and at the same time he has to take notice of undercurrents of the society its impulses, its reactions and its likings and disliking. Diplomatic representation is of three kinds-Symbolic, legal and political. He performed the symbolic function of the diplomatic ceremonial. He is the legal agent of the government he represents. His acts possess legal value. He may cast his vote at international conferences in the name of his government. He also contributes in shaping foreign policy of his state. This is his most important function. It is said that if foreign office is the nerve centre of foreign policy, the diplomatic representative are its outlying fibers maintaining the two way traffic, between centre and outside world. Upon the reliability of his report and soundness of his judgment the success or failure of the foreign policy of his government depends.

2. **Negotiations:** Negotiation is synonym and diplomats are by definition negotiators. Negotiation is the pursuit of agreement by compromise and direct personal contact. Their duty is to draft a wide variety of bilateral and multilateral agreements, Treaties conventions, protocols and other documents of a political, social and economic nature. The diplomat endeavours through negotiation to obtain certain privileges for the citisens, businessmen to win over the state to participate in regional organisations or security arrangements. It involves the presentation of views compromising differences search for areas of mutual interest and common agreement and to reach some agreement on accord.

3. **Reporting:** Diplomats are required to report to their governments developments in the appointed states. Their reports are the raw materials of foreign policy. These reports cover a wide range of subjects on current political, economic, social and military conditions technology achievements legislative programmes, public opinion, market conditions and trends of significance in the country which they are appointed. It is on the basis of the report that the governments shaped its foreign policy towards that nation in particular and to other nations in general. Hence a diplomat must be a man of keen observation, sound judgment and accurate description.

4. **Protection:** The primary function of the diplomat is to protect and advance the rights and interest of their country and its nationals abroad. They will have to watch that the honour of their country is not compromised. This responsibility is carried out through negotiations representations,

treaties, and executive agreements. They also have the more specific duty of attempting to assist and protect businessman, seamen and all other nationals of their own country who are living or travelling in the country in which they are stationed. Under disturbed conditions, this function of diplomats becomes much more heavy. They have to arrange for the safety of life of those nationals who are there and have to do everything in their power to help their nationals reach the places of safety. They also lodge protests or just appeal against the discriminatory treatment faced by their nationals.

DIFFERENCE BETWEEN DIPLOMACY & FOREIGN POLICY

Diplomacy should not be confused with foreign policy. The foreign policy of a state according to J.R.Childs is "the substance of foreign relations" whereas "diplomacy proper is the process by which policy is carried out". One is substance the other is method diplomacy is the agency through which foreign policy seeks to attain its purpose by agreement rather than by war. Diplomacy's methods are persuasion, compromise and threat of war.

INSTRUMENTS OF DIPLOMACY

- Most nation-states maintain state departments of Foreign Affairs or a Ministry of Foreign Affairs. Foreign office officials include career diplomats and political diplomats appointed by home governments.
- Ambassadors head foreign missions and serve as the personal representative of the home state in host country (they can be career diplomats or political appointees).
- Councillors of embassies rank second to the ambassador and are career diplomats.
- Secretaries, with first, second and third rankings are mid-career officials implementing foreign policies of their home countries.
- Attaches are junior career or non-career personnel focusing on specific areas (commercial, agricultural, naval, press attaches are common).

FORMS OF DIPLOMACY

There are two major forms of diplomacy. The simplest and the oldest is bilateral diplomacy between two states. Bilateral diplomacy is still common with many treaties between two states, and it is a main concern of embassies. The other form of diplomacy is multilateral diplomacy involving many states.

Formal multilateral diplomacy is normally dated to the Congress of Vienna in the nineteenth century. Since then, multilateralism has grown in importance. Today most trade treaties, such as the World Trade Organisation (WTO), arms control agreements, such as the Partial Test Ban Treaty and the Comprehensive Test Ban Treaty, and environmental agreements, such as the Koyoto Accord, are multilateral. The United Nations (UN) is the most important institution of multilateral diplomacy.

TYPES OF DIPLOMACY

1. Secret Diplomacy

Prior to World War I diplomacy was largely secret. The general public was not informed as to the nature of negotiations going on or told in full about the agreements reached. But after the war the belief began to circulate that the diplomacy should be open in the public. In old diplomacy the diplomats were responsible only to the executive and the executive being unaccountable, decided the guide-lines for diplomats. The general public was not informed as to the nature of negotiations conditions, attitudes and beliefs. It is undoubtedly true that the secret diplomacy was more successful than any other style as it made the diplomatic conduct more flexible and negotiations more successful. The diplomats were more confident and their area of activity was much wider.

The following arguments are generally forwarded in the favour of secret diplomacy.

1. Secret diplomacy is more successful as it is carried out in an atmosphere of realism. The concessions in the bargaining are flexible as the negotiations are free from the confusing noise of publicity.

2. In secret diplomacy the diplomacy, has the option to be more dynamic and realistic. His capabilities are respected and he commands much faith.

3. It never gets polluted by malicious propaganda.

4. In secret diplomacy, the negotiators may agree on certain points which they will never allow in an open diplomacy.

5. Secret diplomacy is conducted by professional diplomats.

2. Open (Democratic) Diplomacy

Open diplomacy is a reaction against the totalitarian and secret approaches to diplomacy. The attack on traditional diplomacy was led by Woodrow Wilson who specifically mentioned that "open covenant of peace openly arrived at, after which there shall be no private international understanding of any kind but diplomacy shall proceed always frankly and in the public view".

The arguments in favour of open (democratic) diplomacy run like this:

a) The people of a nation have a right to know what international commitments their governments make because it is they who will be called upon to sacrifice their wealth and lives to keep the pledge their diplomats have made.

b) In a democracy the government is responsible to the people. If the pledges and commitments are not conveyed to the people it runs against the democratic norms.

c) As open diplomacy is against the secret commitments and pledges no such treaty should be concluded which might ultimately prove disastrous to the people.

d) Open approach to diplomacy is not opposed to closed door negotiations. It is against only to secret provisions of the treaties and keeping the public uninformed about the agreements and their provisions

3. Diplomacy by Conference

Diplomacy by conference has now come to stay as a permanent factor of international relations. In a conference diplomacy the normal channels of diplomacy like diplomatic and councelling establishments are by passed and the conferences are made as an important diplomatic channel. The states through conference are able to postpone their hostilities for the time begin and thus succeed in avoiding the armed conflict.

The history of conference diplomacy is very old. Even before the world war I it became a very popular phenomenon in international relations and it was adopted and successfully tried. The treaty of Westphalia (1648) is one of the most glaring examples of conference by diplomacy. The league of nations had unsuccessfully tried to make conference diplomacy as one of the important means to maintain world peace and to iron out the misunderstandings among the member states. The UNO also attached much importance to such a diplomacy.

In conference diplomacy opposite camps can be brought around a table and open discussion can be conducted to dissolve the differences among nations. It is open and parliamentary in character and the procedure is flexible and there are very many possibilities for the representatives to establish personal friendship.

But there are some defects or limitations for the diplomacy by conference. The representatives who participate in a conference are the representatives of their sovereign government. They are assisted and watched by the experts of auxiliary services.

They are briefed by their respective governments on all those aspects where they have to agree and disagree. Nothing is left at their discretion. So the conference is merely show because the members are strictly controlled by the heads of the government the ideological differences between west and communist countries are so wide that no agreements by a way of conference can be dreamt of. But they convene conferences just to clarify their stand and to put all blame on other.

4. Personal Diplomacy

When the foreign ministers, prime ministers or heads of the states directly participate in diplomatic negotiations this termed as personal or summit diplomacy. Resort to such a diplomatic style is warranted in case the matters of serious concern are involved. During World War II this diplomatic style came to frequent use among the allied and axis powers. There were many personal meetings between Churchill and Roosevelt. The Atlantic charter (1941) was the result of the personal diplomacy.

Many conferences that have been held in post war period of nonaligned states were summit conferences. The Afro- Asian conference at Bandung (1955) is one of the most successful milestones of personal diplomacy in which the world saw a political awakening of high magnitude in the developing states.

Some of the examples of summit meetings are Bhuto- Indira Gandhi meeting at Shimla in 1972. Rajiv Gandhi- Gorbachev meeting at New Delhi in 1986 and Shaik Haseena- Devagowda meeting at New Delhi in 1996.

In personal diplomacy the representatives are assisted by a number of experts of different branches while the information rendered by experts makes the representatives upto date the presence of the head of the states or governments makes the experts confident. The agreements reached in such conferences are sure to be ratified as it has commitment of the highest officials of the states.

Personal diplomacy also suffered from some defects and they are:

1. The failure of personal diplomacy leaves no alternative to resume negotiations.
2. The presence of a high dignitary like head of the state or government arouses much public expectations and inspire the press. If the negotiations fail, public expectations and inspire the press. If the negotiations fail, public may cause embarrassment to the government. Whereas the presence of diplomats in foreign capital is a normal thing the failure of negotiations remains unnoticed.

5. Traditional Versus Modern Diplomacy

Traditional diplomacy assumed that major European powers had special responsibility for maintaining world peace and the colonies had no more significant diplomatic role than that of satellites. Traditional diplomacy was professional but secretive and relied on a limited cadre rather than extended diplomatic channels.

Modern diplomacy is more open and democratic; it requires reciprocal bargains and compromises so it is not possible for diplomats to spell out a given stance in advance.

LIMITATIONS OF DIPLOMACY

Limitations of diplomacy does not mean the complete failure of diplomacy as an instrument of national policy. It only conveys the ineffectiveness of diplomacy in resolving problems in international affairs. These diplomatic problems which have challenged diplomacy pose a great threat to the world peace. At the same time they indicate certain limitations of diplomacy also. The following causes may be attributed to the limitations of diplomacy.

1. Nature of Nations commitment to the issued concerned

Certain issues in international relations are so important to the states that they attach them with core interests and values of the Nation. They adopt an obstinate and non- compromising attitude in all negotiations. For example, the Kashmir problems is the question of India's core interests and values. Any compromise on this issue may create a turmoil internally and externally, harming the very ideals India is cherishing.

2. Role of a nation on the basis of ideologies

Nations pursue some specific ideologies through out their foreign politics. They take a rigid and a compromising stand in the negotiations which created problems and dims the possibility of diplomatic success. The communist and capitalistic blocs of the world are suspicious of each other. Diplomatic talks between these blocs has put diplomatic moves to light.

3. The nature of International System

Power relations and international law limit the impact of diplomacy on international system. Many problems in the field of international relations have remained unresolved as the states involved deem that any decision would affect the balance of power. The states in order to maintain status- quo took rigid stands in negotiations. In post 1945 period the observance of international law in international relations is one of the norms the world public opinion expects. It is significant because of the general support it has achieved. This phenomenon of international relations has made diplomacy a weak force in conducting negotiations and diplomatic tactics obsolete to some extent.

4. Equal power of the opponent

In a world of bipolarisation almost all the problems have become a sort of tug of war between the opponents of equal power. If, in negotiations a party is weaker, it is supported by super-power because of the ideological rivary to neutralise the pressure of a particular party. The frequent use of veto by the former Soviet Union in favour of India is a classical example to prove this contentions.

5. Weak Diplomatic Capabilities

The total effectiveness of a state in international politics is termed as diplomatic capacity. Whenever there occurs a diplomatic intercourse between two states, each tries to bargain for maximum advantages. If a state does not have the sufficient force military power to pursue its interests, economic strength to reward the counterpart and diplomatic skill to outwit others diplomacy will fail to achieve its objectives. The emergence of Asian and African states, with weak diplomatic capabilities have contributed to the failure of negotiations.

ESSENTIALS OF DIPLOMACY

- Diplomacy must be divested of crusading spirit. Those who try to achieve higher cause become impractical and impede negotiations. Instead it is necessary that foreign policy objectives must be defined in terms of national interest and supported by adequate power, to enable diplomats to negotiate effectively.

- Diplomats must be able to realise the objectives and interests of other nations as well. In turn, nations must be willing to show flexibility on issues not vital to them or else diplomacy will be in vain.
- Diplomatic recognition is perhaps the most important factor in determining whether a nation is an independent state. Receiving recognition has long been difficult, even for countries which are fully sovereign. For many decades after becoming independent, even many of the closest allies of the Republic of Netherlands refused to grant it full recognition.
- Today there are a number of independent entities without widespread diplomatic recognition, most notably the Republic of China. Almost all nations do not officially recognize the ROC's existence on Taiwan, but rather retain informal links. The United States, for instance, maintains relations through de facto embassies known as the American Institute of Taiwan and the Taipei Economic and Cultural Representation Office.
- Informal diplomacy has been used for centuries to communicate between powers. Most diplomats work to recruit figures in other nations who might be able to give informal access to a country's leadership.
- In some situations, such as between the US and China a large amount of diplomacy is done through semi-formal channels using interlocurs such as academic members of think-tanks. This occurs in situations where governments wish to express intentions or to suggest methods of resolving a diplomatic situation, but do not wish to express a formal position.

Diplomatic Procedures & Practices

- Presentation of credentials and assuming charge in host country involves interaction with host governments.
- *Agreation:* involves presenting credentials of diplomatic envoys, which are then approved by host countries where they are to be appointed.
- Diplomatic missions and personnel enjoy certain immunities and privileges like the rights of extra-territoriality and inviolability. Home states can dismiss diplomats or they can be declared *persona-nongrata* by host countries, due to different reasons, including rising tensions between the two states in question.

B. CONCEPT OF WAR

Introduction:- War has been far too common in human history and thus is the central problem of international relations. Many political scientists and foreign policymakers view war as the continuation of politics: When diplomacy fails, some states decide to use force. Others see war as the result of a breakdown of the modern international system because so many of the rules of international institutions were designed to reduce conflict among states.

The Geneva Conventions

In 1864, several states created an international agreement that regulated acceptable behaviour during war and armed conflicts. Since then, the Geneva Conventions have been amended in 1906, 1929, and 1949 as the nature of war and warfare has changed. The agreements prohibit torture, rape, genocide, mutilation, slavery, and other crimes against humanity. The conventions also state that prisoners of war must be treated humanely and that civilians may not be used as hostages.

CAUSES OF WAR

Political scientists have long debated the causes of war. These scholars have come up with the following list:

- **Human nature:** Humans are naturally violent and aggressive, making war inevitable.
- **Regime types:** Some regimes are more prone to waging war than others.
  Example: There has been extensive research on whether democracies are less likely to start wars than other regimes. Overall, it appears that democracies are less likely to fight other democracies, a phenomenon scholars refer to as the democratic peace. Democracies are, however, just as likely as other types of regimes to fight non-democracies.
- **Ideology:** Some political beliefs favour war more than others. Some scholars blame fascism, for example, for World War II.
- **Religion:** Religious belief has driven many states to war, either to spread the faith or to eradicate heretics.
  Example: During the early modern era, nearly every European country experienced numerous wars of religion as the Catholics sought to destroy the Protestants. The wars of religion culminated in the Thirty Years' War, which stretched from Spain and France to the eastern stretches of Germany during the seventeenth century. It was a brutal and horrific war, and the Catholics' failure to win the war marked the end of the major religious wars in Europe.
- **The global system:** Because the global system is anarchic, states must engage in war to protect themselves.
- **Economics and resources:** Disputes over resources often lead to war.

Just-War Theory

Debate has raged as long as wars have been fought as to whether a war can be morally just. Some prominent thinkers have proposed a **just-war theory,** which argues that wars should be fought for noble and worthwhile reasons. Just-war theorists also try to establish ethical rules for warfare. Of course, whether any war is justified is almost always a matter of debate. But most just-war theorists agree on some basic ideas:

- War must be the last option. All peaceful means to resolve the conflict must be exhausted before war breaks out.
- The cause of the war must be just (such as overturning aggression and righting a great wrong).
- The war must be winnable.
- The war's purpose must justify the cost in money and lives.
- The military must make every effort to prevent or limit civilian casualties.

"The Good War"

World War II is one of the few wars that nearly everyone believes was morally justified. Nazi Germany and Japan were dangerous regimes that committed atrocities against conquered peoples, and many nations felt that they needed to be stopped. For these reasons, some refer to World War II as "the good war." In contrast, the social and political turmoil caused by the Vietnam War was based, in part, on debate over whether that war was justified.

Types of War

Although all wars are violent, not all wars are the same. In fact, there are many different types of wars, which can be classified according to which people actually fight, the intensity of the conflict, and the extent of combatants' use of violence, among other factors.

Scholars generally describe five types of war:

1. Total war
2. Limited war
3. Guerrilla war
4. Civil war
5. Proxy war

Total War

A **total war** is a war in which combatants use every resource available to destroy the social fabric of the enemy. Total wars are highly destructive and are characterized by mass civilian casualties because winning a total war often requires combatants to break the people's will to continue fighting. World Wars I and II were total wars, marked by the complete destruction of the civilian economy and society in many countries, including France, Germany, the Soviet Union, Italy, Great Britain, and Japan.

Limited War

A **limited war** is a war fought primarily between professional armies to achieve specific political objectives without causing widespread destruction. Although the total of civilian casualties may be high, combatants do not seek to completely destroy the enemy's social and economic frameworks. The Persian Gulf War of 1990–1991 was a limited war in which the United States and its allies forcibly removed Iraqi troops from Kuwait.

Guerrilla War

A **guerrilla war** is a war in which one or both combatants use small, lightly armed militia units rather than professional, organized armies. Guerrilla fighters usually seek to topple their government, often enjoying the support of the people. These wars are often very long but also tend to be successful for the insurgents as evidenced by Mao Zedong's victory over Chiang Kai-shek in China in the 1940s, the Vietcong's victory over the United States in the Vietnam War, and the Mujahideen's victory over the Soviet Union in Afghanistan in the 1980s.

Civil War

A **civil war** is a war fought within a single country between or among different groups of citizens who want to control the government and do not recognize another group's right to rule. Civil wars are almost always total wars because each side feels compelled to destroy the enemy's political support base. Regional rifts, such as the American Civil War between the North and the South, characterize some civil wars, whereas other civil wars have been fought among ethnic rivals, religious rivals, and rival clans. Revolutions can spark civil wars as well.

Proxy War

A **proxy war** is a war fought by third parties rather than by the enemy states themselves. Many of the militarized conflicts during the Cold War, such as the Korean War and the Vietnam War, can be interpreted as proxy wars between the United States and the Soviet Union, neither of which wanted to fight each other directly.

Categorising Wars

A war can often be a limited war, a guerrilla war, and a civil war all at the same time. The Soviet invasion of Afghanistan in 1979 is a great example. The United States sent trainers, money, and weapons to Afghan rebels to fight against the invaders, making it a low-intensity, limited conflict from the U.S. point of view. The Afghan resistance mostly relied on guerrilla tactics. And the war split Afghanistan, so it was also a civil war.

INTERVENTION

Intervention is a fairly common way for a third-party state to get involved in a civil war or a war between two or more other states. A state intervenes when it sends troops, arms, money, or goods to help another state that is already at war. During the Cold War, the term *intervention* was used to describe one of the superpowers becoming involved in a smaller country's war (often a developing country).

But states sometimes intervene in order to bring peace. This type of intervention occurs when a country (or countries) sends military forces into another state to act as peacekeepers or to block other forces from attacking. Sometimes these interventions are organized or conducted by the United Nations or another international governmental organization.

Example: The United States, along with other NATO nations, sent troops into the former Yugoslavia on a number of occasions to protect people from war. A successful example of this peaceful intervention occurred during the 1999 U.S. bombing campaign in Kosovo, which helped stop a slaughter of Kosovars by attacking Serbs. A less successful example was the U.S. intervention in Somalia in the early 1990s, an attempt to provide humanitarian aid that ultimately achieved little at the cost of American lives. This failed intervention culminated in the Battle of Mogadishu (dramatised in the movie Black Hawk Down [2001]) October 3–4, 1993, which killed eighteen Americans and as many as a thousand Somalis

QUESTIONS

1. What do you mean by diplomacy? Discuss its various types.
2. When diplomacy fails, some states decide to use force Justify the statement
3. Discuss the various types of war ?What significant role played by the 'Intervention'?
4. Discuss the essentials of Diplomacy?
5. What are the main causes of war?
6. Diplomacy in the popular sense means the employment of tack, shrewdness and skill in any negotiation or transactions. In the special sense used international relations is the art of negotiation, in order to achieve the maximum, of group objectives with a minimum of costs within a system of politics in which was is a possibility. In the light of above statement discuss the major functions of the diplomat?
7. Examine the limitations upon the power of Diplomacy?

CHAPTER 7

IMPERIALISM AND COLONIALISM

INTRODUCTION

The aspiration for power is the distinguishing element of International Politics. Every nation possess the tendency to dominate and rule, and it tries to pursue the same policy by all means. Imperialism and colonialism are powerful instruments of national policy. Some nations tries to establish its dominance over others by conquering its territories or in other words, they want to expand their kingdom. Such expansionist policy has no limit and we generally call the expansionist policy as imperialism. The term 'imperialism' is used in a very vague way. It lacks any common definition. Imperialism like other 'isms' has been defined differently by different people. Imperialism remarks, Palmer and Perkins. "can be discussed. denounced, defended and died for, but can't be defined in any generally acceptable way. It means different thing to different people"

DEFINITIONS

According to Schuman, "Imperialism is the imposition by force and violence of alien rule upon subject people'

According to Morgenthau, "Imperialism is the expansion of a state's power beyond its borders".

According to Julius Bonn "Imperialism is a policy which aims at creating, organising and maintaining an empire."

METHODS OF IMPERIALISM

The following are the three general methods of imperialism.

1. Military Imperialism: In the words of Morgenthau, "The most obvious, the most ancient and also the crudest form of imperialism is the military conquest. By military conquest new territories are acquired and thus new power relations are established. Any change in this situation is only possible by another war instigated by the defeated nation. But in the new war, the change of victory goes to the victorious nation. Thus the use of this method is a great advantage to the imperialist nation. But it has a drawback. War is a gamble. Sometimes the imperialist nation may fall, Napoleons' example can be cited.

2. Economic Imperialism: Economic imperialism is concerned with controlling policies, domestic or foreign of the economically weaker nations by means of economic investment and economic assistance. The most modern Economic Imperialism does not change the power relation through the conquest of territory by way of economic control.

3. Cultural Imperialism: It is not at the conquest of territory or at the control of economic life, but the conquest and control of the minds of the man as an instrument for changing power relation. If a state conquest the minds of men of other nations and is able to impose its ideology it would be far more superior to economic mastery and military victory. The cultural imperialism would win a more complete victory than any military victory and economic master.

COLONIALISM

Colonialism is an elusive concept. It is a political, a legal, an economic, a cultural and a social phenomenon, which does not lend itself to a short and clear definition. While colonising states refrained from defining colonialism, many scholars of various disciplines have written about the subject. According to the Oxford English Dictionary, the mid-14th century "colonye" word was used to describe the Roman settling, creating out-posts, or occupying lands outside the Roman city-state. Colonialism emerged around the 19th century to rectify a European practice that was becoming prevalent across the world.

DEFINING COLONIALISM

The element of 'alien domination' appears to be at the heart of the colonial experience. Colonialism is foreign rule imposed upon a people. Colonialism is a system in which a state claims sovereignty over territory and people outside its own boundaries, often to facilitate economic domination over their resources, labour, and often markets.

Colonialism can be defined as a rule over people of different races living in separate lands by a single colonial power. Colonialism also refers to a set of beliefs used to legitimise or promote this system, especially the belief that the values and systems of the coloniser are superior to those of the colonised. Colonialism can thus be seen to imply domination of an alien minority asserting racial and cultural superiority over a materially inferior majority. Hobson describes colonialism 'in its best sense' as the natural outflow of nationality, its test is the power of the coloniser to transplant the civilisation they represent to a new social and cultural environment.

JUDGING COLONISATION

Defenders of colonialism argue that colonisation developed the economic and political infrastructure necessary for modernisation and democracy (they point to former colonies like Singapore as examples of post-colonial success). Post colonialist such as Franz Fanon argue that colonialism does political, psychological, and moral damage to the colonised as well.

Let us consider the case of British colonist for example. The British Empire, in the early decades of the 20th century, held sway over a population of 400–500 million people - roughly a quarter of the world's population - and covered roughly two-fifths of the world's land area.

The British Empire came together over 300 years through a succession of phases of expansion, inter-spersed with intervals of pacific commercial and diplomatic activity, or imperial contraction. Its territories were scattered across all parts of the world, and it was described with some truth as "the empire on which the sun never sets". The empire facilitated the spread of British technology, commerce, language, and government around much of the globe. Imperial hegemony contributed to Britain's extraordinary economic growth, and greatly strengthened its voice in world affairs. Even as Britain extended its imperial reach overseas, it continued to develop and broaden democratic institutions at the homeland.

From the perspective of the colonies, the record of the British Empire is mixed. The colonies received from Britain the English language, an administrative and legal framework on the British model, and technological and economic development. During decolonisation, Britain sought to pass parliamentary democracy to its colonies, with varying degrees of success.

British colonial policy was always driven to a large extent by Britain's trading interests. While settler economies developed the infrastructure to support balanced development, tropical African territories found themselves developed only as raw-material suppliers. A reliance upon the manipulation of conflict between ethnic and racial identities, in order to keep subject populations from uniting against the occupying power - the classic "divide and rule" strategy - left a legacy of partition or inter-communal difficulties in several parts of the world including the sub-continent.

Decolonisation

Decolonisation is the antithesis of colonisation. While anti-colonialist feeling first manifested in the 18th century (in the US), decolonisation is a product of the post-WW II period. Nationalism in Latin America, Asia and Africa, as well as the weakening of the colonial powers helped to achieve decolonisation.

The UN played an important role in ending colonial rule in Indonesia and certain African colonies. It particularly helped decolonise Liberia, Somalia and Eritrea from Italy. There is enough similarity between Imperialism and Colonialism and, therefore, the two terms are used almost interchangeably. They differ in the following respects.

1) Imperialism is comparatively older than colonialism. Colonialism is the modern form of Imperialism.
2) The purpose of Imperialism is basically to acquire political power, but the prime object of colonialism is economic.
3) Imperialism is the imposition of alien rule upon other people. It generally involves the use of military force. Colonialism is the natural outflow of alien nationality in the subject territory.

In Imperialism the control of the imperialist country is rigid and it establishes an autocratic rule over the subject people. In colonialism however, the control of the alien power is comparatively less rigid, and it also provides better opportunities for development and self government.

Imperialism and colonialism have common objectives today. A distinction, therefore, must be made. Colonialism is a form of Imperialism itself. Economic Imperialism is known as colonialism. Colonialism is the modern and economic form Imperialism

MOTIVES OF IMPERIALISM AND COLONIALISM.

1. **Nationalism:** Nationalism is one of the fundamental motives of Imperialism and Colonialism. Nationalism is charged for the evils of Imperialism Nationalism has an inherent desire to exalt a state and to further its interests of national territorial expansion. R.L.Buell remarks "Paradoxical as it may seem, pure nationalism has forced governments in the path of Imperialism." Every nation takes pride in its national expansion. Generations of Englishmen glorified in the boast that "the Sun never sets on the British Empire".

2. **Increase in National Prestige and National Power:** Every imperialist expansion adds to the prestige and power of the imperialist nation. Mussolini, Hitler and Napoleon etc. had the same in their mind.

3. **National Defence:** Imperialism also fulfils the objectives of National defence. It helps national defence by providing markets and essential raw materials. and by providing populations from which troops and labourers may be drawn. It also helps in the national defence by providing areas and bases for the defence of the state or its line of communications. Colonies have proved a good source of providing man power to the Imperialists. For example, England had nearly 4,00,000 troops from India alone, during the first world war.

4. **Adjustment of Balance of Power:** When a nation moves towards imperialist expansion, other nations also do not lag behind. France and Britain fell in the imperialist race for gaining control over more and more colonies to ensure the adjustment of Balance of power. When the imperialistic objectives of one nation is achieved, the rival nation also tries to pursue the same end by whatever means available to it. The so called American and Soviet Imperialism are example to this.

5. **Economic gain :** One of the fundamental motives of Imperialism is economic gain. The capitalist system also has motivated Imperialism. The grown industrialisation in Europe was very much responsible for imperialism and colonialism. The Imperialist nations for getting raw materials, market for their surplus goods and investment opportunities for surplus capital acquired colonies in the far of areas. Imperialist powers has always used colonies as means for economic exploitation.

6. **Surplus population:** Surplus population is also cited as one of the motives of Imperialism. Imperialism serve as an outlet of surplus population. When there is a rapid increase in surplus population., new areas are needed to emigrate surplus population, In the 19th century the European countries faced the problem of surplus population and the same has been adjusted by emigration to colonies. Actually populated states have found relief in emigrating to their colonies.

7. **Religious and Humanitarian Cause:** The advanced and developed western societies placed this argument that it was their obligation to carry the blessing of their religion and civilisation to backward people. The whole men felt that God has made them superior and therefore it becomes their duty to uplift the inferior race. For an example Joseph Chamberlion in 1893 declared that "it is our duty to take our share in the work of civilisation of Africa".

MERITS OF IMPERIALISM AND COLONIALISM

1. **White man's Burden:** The imperialist place this argument that God has imposed a moral obligation upon the advanced and cultured races to uplift the backward races. The white race of Europe claim that in the very discharge of their moral obligation they have assumed control over the backward races of Africa and Asia. It is indeed true that the modern and superior civilisation of Europe had made its effects upon Asia and Africa. Asians and Africans got an opportunity of learning European languages literature and modern science and they also came into contact with the superior and advanced race of Europe. This was an advantage of Imperialism to the subject people.

2. **Political Unity:** In Asia and Africa there used to be small states which lacked efficient and orderly government, The imperialist powers bound this areas in the threat of unity and centralised government. The political unity of India is an example.

3. **Economic Development:** With the establishment of European empires in Asia and Africa, economic development of the areas took place. These areas got the advantage of railway, transport and means of communication. The opening of new materials paved the way for industrialisation. Trade and commerce also developed.

4. **Training for self government:** The European established despotic and autocratic rule in the colonies. But gradually, they were given training for self government and ultimately got the rights of self-government. In due course they all become independent. It is also said the Imperialism is responsible for the resurgence of Asia and Africa.

8. **Promotes Inter- Nationalism** : Imperialism has given impetus to World brother-hood and internationalism. An empire comprises people of different nationalities, religion, races and languages and they come closer to each other. In this way world brother hood and inter-nationalism supersede nationalistic and parochial tendencies.

DEMERITS OF IMPERIALISM AND COLONIALISM

1) **Imperialism as symbol of Political subjection :** Imperialism is the imposition of alien rule upon the subject people. It is based on superior- subordinate relationship imperiatist power never consider the dependent people on equal status. It deprives the people of their political rights. Imperialism is established by force.

2) **Economic Exploitation :** Economic gain is one of the fundamental motives of imperialism. For their own interests the capitalist imperialist countries fully exploited the dependent countries. The Imperialist powers established factories in the colonies. But it was not for the development of the colonies, it was for the economic gain of the imperialists. Imperialist powers had exploited the colonies with all possible measures.

3) **Encourage racial discrimination:** Imperialism encourage racial discrimination. In India the Britishers created the problem of racial discrimination on the basis of religion. In Africa the policy of colour discrimination was pursued between whites and blacks.

4) **War and Rivalry:** Imperialist rivalries among the imperialist powers have become a source of war and inter-state conflicts. The first and second world wars were the results of the imperialistic rivalries among the big powers.

5) **Destroys native culture and morality:-** The imposition of western language, culture and dress etc. has destroyed completely the native language, literature and culture. It resulted in the decline of the prestige of national language and culture in the colonies. The Britishers even destroyed the morality of the colonies, by encouraging gambling and opium smoking in Far East.

NEW IMPERIALISM AND NEO – COLONIALISM

Definition of Neo Colonialism

Neo-colonialism implies political control of an underdeveloped people whose socio-economic life is directed by a former coloniser. Dependency theorists such as Andre Gunder Frank argued that neo-colonialism leads to net transfer of wealth from the colonised to the coloniser, inhibiting successful development.

The essence of neo-colonialism is that the state, which is subject to this phenomenon, is in theory independent and has all outward trappings of international sovereignty, but in reality its economic system and its political policy is directed from the outside.

The 3rd All Parties African People's Conference held in Cairo in 1961 described Neo-Colonialism as: "the economic infiltration by a foreign power after independence, through capital investment loans and monetary aids or technical experts, of unequal concessions, particularly those extending for long periods".

Why Neo-Colonialism Occurs

Weakness and growing resentment after WWII made direct colonisation impractical. Previously united colonial territories were divided into mostly unviable states, compelling them to depend on their former colonial powers for economic and defence needs

To fund welfare policies within their own countries, former colonial powers needed resources, which were easy to generate through former colonies still reliant on them, thus encouraging neo-colonial ties to develop.

Types of Neo-Colonialism

1) **Economic Dependencies :** An Economic Dependency is a politically independent and sovereign nation whose economic enterprises are control by a foreign country. They are economically under developed nations. If the major economic enterprises in the nations are run and controlled by foreigners the nation is an Economics Dependency. If a given percentage of national income, say 51/- is carned by foreigners the nation is an economic dependency.

2) **Satellites:** A satellite if formally an independent nation but it is controlled both politically and economically by some big powers. In communist nations major economic enterprises are run by the government. So it is not possible for one nation to control the economy of other with our dominating its political institutions. Thus a nation which is controlled to the politically and economically by some foreign power, becomes completely dependent to it and has to freedom of by a foreign power over satellite is much more complete than exercised over the economic dependencies.

CRITICISM

Critics of Neo colonialism allege that both nations and corporations have aimed to control other nations through indirect means; that in lieu of direct military or political control, neo colonialist powers employ economic, financial and trade policies to dominate less powerful countries. Those who subscribe to the concept maintain this amounts to control over targeted nations. They portray the choice to grant or to refuse granting loans, especially by international financial institutions such as the IMF and World Bank, as a decisive form of control. They argue that in order to qualify for these loans (as well as other forms of economic aid), weaker nations are forced to take steps favorable to the financial interests of the IMF/WB, but detrimental to their own economies, increasing rather than alleviating their poverty.

Critics of neocolonialism also attempt to demonstrate that investment by multinationals enriches few in underdeveloped countries, and causes humanitarian (as well as environmental and ecological) devastation to the populations which inhabit 'neo-colonies.' Thus, it is argued, results in perpetual underdevelopment; which cultivates those countries as reservoirs of cheap labour and raw materials, while restricting their access to advanced production techniques to develop their own economies. By contrast, critics of the concept of neo-colonialism argue that, while the developed world does profit from cheap labor and raw materials of developing nations, ultimately, it does serve as a positive force for development in developing countries of the Third World. With the time and age the form of Imperialism has also undergone or change. The age of military and political Imperialism has gone and its place has been taken by Economic Imperialism. As the form of Imperialism has undergone a change, Neo colonialism, has also taken the place of classical colonialism. After the II world war most of the Asian and African colonies got independence and they are free politically. But they are dependent economically. Actually they are under the influence of big powers. This is called Neo colonialism. The aim of Neo colonialism is to establish Economic dominance. According to Palmer and Perkins" Neo colonialism is a new and more insidious form of imperialism, widely prevalent and particularly pernicious and dangerous".

QUESTIONS

1. "Decolonisation is the antithesis of colonisation". Elaborate this statement
2. Define Imperialism and discuss the different methods of Imperialism?
3. Differentiate between Imperialism and colonialism?
4. One of the fundamental motives of Imperialism is economic gain. In the light of above statement discuss the basic motives behind **Imperialism and colonialism ?**
5. Discuss the merits and demerits of Imperialism and colonialism?
6. Neo colonialism is a new and more insidious form of imperialism, widely prevalent and particularly pernicious and dangerous". Define Neo- Colonialism and discuss the factors that led to the establishment of Neo-Colonialism ?
7. Critically analyse the concept of NEO- COLONIALISM ?

CHAPTER 8

Collective Security

INTRODUCTION

Collective security is commonly regarded as most effective method of maintaining peace and deterring aggression. Collective security was supposed not only to be the basis of the League of Nations but is also supposed to be the basis of the United Nations. Collective security is a device by which the security of all the nations in assessed. Under the system of collective security, aggression or war would no longer be the concern of any individual nation, but would be the concern of all nations.

MEANING AND DEFINITION

Collective security is a collective measure for security. The word security represents the goal while the word collective indicates the nature of the combined strength will face the aggression. The basic principle of collective security is that an attack on one state will be regarded as an attack on all states. Security becomes the concern of all nations and all will take care collectively of the security of each of them as if their own security were at state.

(a) According to Morgenthau "one for all and all for one is the watch-word for collective security."

(b) On collective security Palmer and Perkins observe "It clearly implies collective measure for dealing with threat to peace".

(c) George Schwarzenegger has defined collective security as machinery for joint action in order to prevent or counter any attack against an established international order".

(d) According to F.H Hartmann collective security in basically a mutual insurance plan against aggression anywhere and everywhere.

The basic principle of collective security is that if an aggression takes place it should be frustrated by an overwhelming force. It is therefore necessary that all nations must stand united against the aggression. So the principle of collective security is based upon the pre-ponderance of power in the hands of the protectors of peace and order and this is said to be the only basis of the success of the system. Its chief merit lies in the force may not at all be needed. A threat of collective action will be sufficient to deter the potential aggressor.

Development of collective security:- The Woodrow Wilson regarded as the enunciator of concept in modern time. The shock of first world war forced total reconsideration of the old ways of diplomacy, rival alliances and Balance of Power. James Bryce proposed the League shall under take to defend any one of its members who may be attacked by any other State who has refused to accept arbitration or conciliation. Under League of nation: Articles 10-16• UN Charter Chapter VII- Article 39-51

Nature of Collective Security:- Collective security recognises the relevance of power in international politics. It accepts the fact of war as a reality. Collective security is a device of a management of power, not that of the elimination of power. Collective security is something less than world government and more than balance of power or it can be considered to be an alternative of the world government, because latter is not feasible. A proper functioning of collective security system possible only through international organisation. It is different from balance of power and collective defence

CONDITIONS OF MAINTAINING COLLECTIVE SECURITY.

The principle of collective security in order to work successfully as an instrument for providing peace must fulfil the following conditions.

1. The basic requirement of collective security is that it should function impartially. If collective security is to operate impartially government and people must exhibit flexibility of policy and sentiments.
2. The system of collective security must be able to muster at all time such overwhelming strength against the potential aggressor that the later should not repeat the aggressor. The collective system must be able to meet any situation.
3. The nations which offer the combined strength to meet the threat of aggression under collective security system must have identical conception of security.
4. The nations must be willing to subordinate their political differences to the service of the world community by whole heartedly supporting collective action against the aggressor.
5. In the event of any aggression there should be unanimity among states in determining the aggressor.
6. Collective security must not be directed against any specific states group of states, but against aggression in general, that is against any aggression anywhere.
7. Collective security is incompatible with the traditional doctrine of neutrality in war. Neutrality strikes at the very root of collective security.
8. Collective security system necessitates the willingness of the nations to fight for the status-quo. Collective security does not accept a forcible change in the international order.

Objects of Collective Security

1. It aims at the preservation of peace by the collectivisation of force.
2. It focuses upon the ideals of world government and international cooperation.
3. Collective security aims at mutual co-operation in which the ideas of common out look, co-operation and trust are inherent.

RELEVANCE OF COLLECTIVE SECURITY TODAY

In its theoretical aspect collective security system appears to be logical but in its actual operation it reveals a number of short comings and drawbacks. The difficulties that come in the operation of the collective security system actually make the system itself unrealistic and unworkable. In reality collective security is an ideal which cannot be realized under the conditions prevailing on the international scene.

The collective security has no worked satisfactory under the league of nations and the united nations. In fact the machinery of collective security has never been satisfactorily developed.

Collective security is based upon wrong assumptions which are mostly hypothetical. The conflicting interests of the nations, the lack of common outlook, cold war and group rivalries and the threat of nuclear war are the factors which run counter to an effective system of collective security. Whatever failures might have been faced in creating a system of collective security, its value as theory is meaningful.

GULF WAR–AN EXAMPLE

The gulf war against Iraq in 1991 can be cited as the first example of the collective security measures undertaken by the UNO as conceived by the UN charter itself. This perhaps became possible as Soviet Union herself disintegrated during the same period and became dependent upon the United States for reorganisation of her economy. The world order had become unipolar and no country was in a position to challenge the US Act. The US too functioned in a responsible manner by consulting all other big powers in her war efforts, and the security council was transformed into a seat of collective action.

Thus, Iraq was defeated in proving the success of the collective security measures.

The success of collective security lies in the fact that today any aggression is condemned legally and morally by the international society, any aggression is everybody's business and aggression and problems of the disturbance of peace becomes the general concern of the international organisation. Moreover, it is a standing warning to the potential aggressor that is to be opposed by the combined and overwhelming force.

COLLECTIVE SECURITY UNDER THE LEAGUE OF NATIONS

The first effort for the enforcement of collective security on a world wide was made with the establishment of an international organisation, the League of Nations. For the first time in the history the convent of the League of Nations introduced the principle of collective security as a practical programme of action. However, the covenant nowhere used the word. "Collective security". The covenant contained three key articles on collective security- Article 10,11 and 16.

Article 10 provided for guarantee against aggression and stated " the members of the League undertake to respect and preserve as against external aggression the territorial integrity and existing political independence of all members of the League".

Article 11 provided for action in case of war or threat of war. It states "any war or threat of war, whether immediately affecting any of the members of the league or not is hereby declared a matter of concern to the while League and the League shall take any action that may be deemed wise and effectual to safeguard the peace of nations".

Article16 states that if a member resorts to war, all trade and financial relations with that members state will be cut and there will be prohibition of financial commercial or personal inter-course between the aggressor and the members of the League.

Despite the bold provisions in the covenant of the League of Nations, the scheme of collective security was never really implemented in fact; The members of the League were more concerned about their own security than a genuine and universal security system.

The failure of the United States to join, the rise of the Soviet Union outside the League system, the reluctance of great Britain to assume international obligation, and later the open defiance of Japan, Italy and Germany- all these combined to destroy any hopes that the League would be effective in major international crises.

In its short span of life, the League had to face two major crises involving open defiance of covenant but each time it proved unequal to the test and failed to take collective security measures. First was the Manchurian crisis in 1931-32 when Japan committed aggression against China. League branded Japan as aggressor and thereupon Japan with-drew form the League. The Principal members of the League were not prepared to use force against Japan. Thus the aggressor was left free and got what it wanted.

The principle of collective security was put to a very\ severe test in the Ethiopian crisis of 1935-36 when Italy invaded Ethiopia. The League powers were not prepared to apply military sanctions against Italy. However, the League Council voted to impose economic sanctions. In fact, the League members were not prepared to impose even economic sanctions sufficiently and efficiently. "The Italo-Ethiopian war the became the chief test case indeed, the only real one of the effectiveness of the League's security system;, says Palmer and Perkins. All the world knows the League failed in this crucial test. " The Italo- Ethopian war thus became the most important and the most decisive chapter in the history of the League of Nations. The failure of the League in this crucial test led to disastrous consequences. It followed the Nazi conquest of Austria, the surrender to Hitler at Munich and the invasion of Poland that started the second world war.

COLLECTIVE SECURITY AND UN

1. Provisions of the chapter: Like the covenant of the League, the Charter of the United Nations also made provisions for the collective security of its members. Article I of the Charter calls for "effective collective measures for prevention and removal of threats to the peace, and for the suppression of acts of aggression or other breaches of peace.

Charter VII makes detailed provisions regarding collective security measures. The Security Council can consider an act of aggression or a threat to the breach of peace and call upon member states to apply economic or military sanctions.

Article 39 of the charter says: The Security Council shall determine the existence of any threat to the peace, breach of the peace, or act of aggression and shall decide what measures shall be taken in accordance with Article 41 and 42 to maintain or restore international peace and security.

Article 41 makes provision for economic sanctions and for the Severance of diplomatic relations.

Article 42 provides for military sanctions, if economic and diplomatic sanctions prove inadequate. It may take such action by air, sea and land forces as may be necessary to maintain and restore international peace and security.

Article 43 makes it obligatory upon the member states to help the Security Council in such a task. Not only has the UN charter empowered the Security Council undertake necessary measure for collective security, but also has provided the permanent members of the security council with veto powers and thus it has deliberately exempted the permanent members form the application of the collective security measures. Since most of the breaches of peace resulted either from direct action by the veto possessing big powers or by others with a support from some such power, the Security Council in effect had become powerless in this respect. It was only when the General Assembly decided to break such a constitutional deadlock that the UN Could be activated for discharging its responsibility of collective security. Such an action arose in the case of the Korean war which merits our attention at this stage.

2. The Korean War experience: The Question of the North Korean attack on South Korea was referred to the Security Council. When the Security Council got seized of the matter, the Soviet delegation boycotted the council which thereafter passed a resolution recommending the members to furnish such assistance to the Republic of Korea as may be necessary to repel the armed Security Council the following month, the issue was deadlocked. Under these circumstances, the General Assembly took over the Korean issue and passed a historic resolution entitles Uniting For Peace. By this resolution the General Assembly empowered upon itself the responsibility of taking collective measures. The main features of the Uniting For Peace resolution were.

a) The General Assembly can meet within twenty four hours to consider breaches, or threats of breaches of peace, if the security council is deadlocked over this issue by the issue of veto.

b) The General Assembly can make recommendations to the member states for use of the armed forces to thwart aggression.

c) The member states should maintain elements of armed forces for use by the United Nations and make them available for collective security purposes.

3. The gulf war against Iraq in 1991: The United Nations was against Iraq in January, 1991 is another example of collective security in action. Saddam Hussain's Iraq invaded Kuwait on August 2, 1990.

The UN Security Council passed a resolution on November 29, 1990 authorizing the formation and the use of the UN forces to fight Iraq and liberate Kuwait. The gulf war began on 17 January, 1991. Unlike the Korean war of the fifties there was no other power, small or big, which had joined the Iraq side. Since there was no use of veto by any permanent member of the Security Council, it could form a UN force to fight the Gulf war. In this sense the gulf war against Iraq in 1991 can be ited as the first example of the collective security measures undertaken by the UNO as conceived so in the UN Charter itself.

This perhaps became possible as Soviet Union herself disintegrated during the same period and became dependent upon the United States for reorganisation of its economy. The world order has become unipolar and no country was in a position to challenge the US action. Although it was a war between the United Nations and Iraq on paper, in reality it was a war between the United States and Iraq. Iraq was defeated thus providing the success of the collective security measures.

C. PEACEFUL SETTLEMENT OF DISPUTES

One of the ways to avoid war is Peaceful settlement of disputes which is regarded as one of the important principles of International Relations. it is also included in the study of the controls of inter-state relations. A number of attempts have been made to settle disputes among nations form time to time. Among them peaceful settlement is regarded as one of the important attempts.

Quest for peace has been one of the major factors responsible for the formation of International Organisations. Before the dawn of the 20th century the problem of peace and security was mainly tackled through conventional diplomatic techniques or through occasional conferences convened to techniques or through occasional conferences convened to settle specific disputes which posed a threat to peace.

With the creation of the League of Nations, this world body was specifically entrusted with the responsibility of maintaining International peace by encouraging the settlement of disputes. According to elaude the peaceful settlement helps 'to inject into the dispute a disinterested party, with who negotiation may be conducted by states and to whom concessions can be made which either state would refrain, as a point of honour from making directly to the other"

Cohen regards "peaceful settlement and collective measures are inseperable part of the collective security". The first paragraph in the very first article of the UN charter says that the aim of the United Nations is "to bring about a peaceful settlement" of disputes among nations" In order to maintain International peace and security. Whenever a dispute arise between nations it may lead to war. To prevent war the concerned parties may follow peaceful methods to settle the dispute.

Methods

The important methods of peaceful settlement of disputes provided by the UN Charter are as follows.

1. Negotiation;
2. Good officers and mediation;
3. Enquiry;
4. Conciliation;
5. Arbitration and;
6. Judicial settlement

The above methods may be classified into two main groups a those based on persuasion with no birdirg for and (b) those which have a binding character. Good- office and mediation, negotiation. enquiry and conciliation-come with in the first category.

Disputes with political nature come under this category. They are considered as political methods. Arbitration and Judicial settlement come under the second category. They are legal methods and are concerned with legal disputes.

1. Negotiation

Direct Negotiation is the simple and common method of settling disputes.

"Negotiation is the legal and orderly administrative process by which governments, in the exercise of their unquestionable powers conduct their relations with one another and discuss, adjust and settle their difference" Negotiations are conducted through diplomatic respresentatives, foreign ministers or head of states or through conferences. The Indo-Pak Negotiation after the Indo pak war is an outstanding example of this method.

The conduct of Negotiation is a bargaining process. It is an attempt on the part of the contesting parties to settle the disputes by mutual discussions and deliberations.

Negotiation the claims of one party may be recognised by the other party and the dispute is settled. Another advantage of Negotiation is that the period of Negotiation allows an interval to let the tempers of the concerned parties cool down.

Good offices and Mediation

When the parties in the dispute are unable to reach an agreement through Negotiation a third country may offer its "good offices" or services to facilitate a settlement. If the disputing parties accept the offer of good offices of a third country, then the third country simply acts as a transmitting agency. If the third country offers its suggestions to settle a dispute, then it becomes a mediator. Good office imply that the third country tried to bring the disputant parties together and suggest a settlement without "a tender of good office is a polite inquiry as to whether the third state can be of any service preserving or restoring peace:. Tashkent agreement entered into by India and Pakistan in 1965 is cited as an example. Russia offered her good office and the agreement known as Tashkent Agreement was reached by President Ayub Khan of Pakistan and Prime –Minister Lal Bahadur Sastri of India.

Mediation on the other hand, is a method under which the third state whose good office is accepted, makes suggestion and assumes the responsibility to settle the dispute. The mediating state assume the role of a middle man. The mediator makes every attempt to reconcile the opposite claims of the disputing parties. However, the suggestions of the mediator are not binding upon the contesting parties.

The main difference between good offices and mediation is that under the former the third country tries to call negotiations and enter the latter the mediating party takes under an active part in negotiations.

2. Enquiry

Enquiry and conciliation are more effective than good offices and mediation. The first Hague conference of 1899 recommended the use of commissions of enquiry. It was renewed by the Second Hague Conference. Many treaties have made provisions for it . Even the convenant of the League supported this principle.

The duty of the commission of enquiry is to investigate the facts so as to clarify the issues and elucidate facts . It can hear both sides of the dispute, call witness and experts and on that basis presents its conclusions and recommendations. But it has no power to make the award binding on the disputant parties. Therefore, it investigates and makes suggestions when requested by the disputant parties.

3. Conciliation

Oppenheim defines conciliation as follows: "Conciliation is the process of setting a dispute by referring it to a commission of person whose task is to elucidate the facts and to make a report containing proposals for a settlement, but which does not have the binding character of award or Judgment' Conciliation is a method under which an outside party promotes an agreement between disputant states. The Conciliation Commission hear and ascertains facts and it may ask for compromises or concessions before advancing its proposals for settling a dispute.

Conciliation differ from Enquiry and mediation. The main object of enquiry is to clarify the issues and elucidate the facts leaving the parties to settle a dispute. Conciliation on the other hand aims at bringing the parties to an agreement oftering suggestions and recommendations. Conciliation differ from mediation because under it parties refer the issue to a committee or a council which ascertains the facts and makes suggestions for settling the dispute. Mediation, on the other hand, is a method under which the mediator assumes responsibility for the settlement of a dispute. Mediation is perfomed by an individual. Whereas conciliation is effected by a council, board, committee or commission.

Conciliation is constructive method and UNO use these methods frequently eg: The UN conciliation commission on Pakistan.

4. Arbitration and Judicial Settlement

Both arbitration and Judicial settlement are legal or Judicial in nature. Arbitration is a sort of semi-Judicial process and therefore a dispute is determined through a legal decision of one individual or of a tribunal chosen by the parties. The disputant parties bound to respect the award of the arbiter. Arbitration involves four important elements.

They are (1) settlement of disputes between nations through their voluntary action. (2) by Judges of their own choice. (3) on the basis of respect for law (4) obligation to accept the award as binding. Disputant Parties can demand reconsideration of the award. If the tribunal exceeds the authority given to them then their will be nothing like strikes. From time imemorial, Arbitration has been employed as an effective force for settling disputes. the Legue allowed a permanent court of arbitration set up under the first Hague Conference. Even UNO has so many commission.

Arbitration and conciliation differ from each other in the following respects.

1. Arbitration is Judicial process.

2. Arbitration is legal in nature. So the decisions are binding, conciliation is only recommendatory.
3. Arbitration is binding but conciliation is a friendly advise.

5. Judicial Settlement:

Judicial settlement, on the other hand is a form of arbitration. It is known as adjudication. Arbitration and adjudication differ from each other in the following respects.

a) Arbitration is more cheaper and simple than adjudication.
b) Arbitration is more clastic than adjudication.
c) Through adjudication, only legal disputes are settled. While arbitration tribunal settles both legal and politics issued.
d) Arbitration is performed by person or states while in adjudication the agency is a permanent body of court.
e) Arbitration has a character of voluntary Jurisdiction but there is no such thing in adjudication.

Adjudication of disputes obviously require the prior creation of a court to which disputes may be submitted. The central American Court of Justice (1907-17) was the first International court to handle legal dispute. League of Nations set up a permanent court of International Justice. It is continuing in the present UNO. The International court now decides all cases referred to it by the disputant parties.

Peaceful settlement and UNO

One of the major objectives of UNO as stated in article is to bring about by peaceful means and in conformity with the principles of Justice and International law, adjustment or settlement of International disputes or situations which might lead to a breach of Peace." By virtue of article 33 the Security Council can call upon the disputant parties to seek solution through peaceful means of their choice. approach UNO for a solution. Then the Security Council consider all possible means of solving such disputes by peaceful means. If the dispute is of a Judicial nature, UNO may refer the dispute to the International Court of Justice.

Difference between collective security and collective Defence

Collective defense is planned with a known opponent, and entails associated military preparations, whereas collective security is by its nature general. However, generally agreed that collective security will not deter all aggressors but may lead to punishment of aggressors. This delay leaves room for collective defense.

Collective defense and collective security are often considered identical and harmonious, esp as collective defense agreements allowed under the UN Charter, and non-democratic states are thought likely to threaten both. But can be tensions· eg. France called on to impose sanctions on Italy because of invasion of Ethiopia when Italy was ally versus major enemy Germany. Also US upholding collective security versus Fr and UK over Suez. US needs collective defence versus USSR.

PROBLEMS OF COLLECTIVE SECURITY

At the twilight of World War I, many political thinkers thought and hoped that the states of the world would make the League of Nations a collective security system that would maintain international peace and security, and some had the same hope after World War II in connection with the United Nations. Karen Mingst averred that collective security is borne out of some salient assumptions. These assumptions are that: wars are prevented by restraint of military action; aggressors must be stopped; the aggressor is easily identified; the aggressor is always wrong; aggressors know that the international community will act against them (Mingst, 1999). As asserted by Van Dyke (1957), "they wanted states to abandon narrow conceptions of self interest as a guide to policy and to regard themselves as units in a world society having an interest in preserving law and order everywhere." These ideas expressed by these scholars could not work out as a result of numerous problems associated with the concept of collective security. There are other scholars who feel that the concept of collective security is misguided. They see it as conceptually muddled and naively unrealistic. Although they are pledged to defend each other, many countries will refuse to do so, if such an act is not in their own best interests or thought to be too risky or expensive. In addition, they argue that collective security arrangements will turn small struggles into large ones, and prevent the use of alternative (non-violent) problem solving, relying instead on the much more costly approach of military confrontation. In addition, there is always a danger that alliances formed by the purpose of collective security can also serve as a basis for an aggressive coalition. Other problems associated with the collective security system are discussed as follows:

(i) States do not regard themselves as members of one society having a common vital interest in protecting and preserving each other's rights. Does it really matter to Japan if Paraguay and Bolivia destroy themselves in a war? Of what interest is it to Nigeria if Egypt should attack Tunisia and such attack is repelled or defeated? There is no doubt that states have demonstrated a willingness to ally themselves with certain other selected states and thus to pledge to defend certain selected frontiers in addition to their own, but the principle of "one for all and all for one" does not commend itself.

(ii) Another challenge to collective security is that its risks are great. Governments of nation-states can enforce law against individuals with little risk or fear. Internationally, however, the situation is quite different. Disparities of power are much greater. "Theoretically, it might be easy for a world society to defeat aggression by a smaller power like Nigeria, but what if one of the great powers turns aggressor?" It is one thing for a government to enforce a law against a hapless individual and another thing for the United Nations to try to enforce the law against a state which may be almost as strong as the rest of the world combined. The development of nuclear weapons makes the problem all the greater. An aggressor with such weapons could virtually wipe from the face of the earth a number of the members of the collective security system. Faced with such a possibility, a member whose own most vital interest was directly threatened might choose proud defiance rather than surrender. But a member whose own vital interests were not directly threatened would be unlikely to be so bold. Nor do states want to commit themselves in advance to undertake such risks, regardless of the identity of the aggressor and of his victim.

(iii) Jones (1985) and Rostow (1968) cited in Eke (2007) are in agreement that the principles of the United Nations veto is "a great inhibition to the smooth and effective functioning of the Security Council collective security system". In his observation, Rostow argued that "part of the problem is that the responsibility of world peace was resting on the shoulders of nations with preponderant military and political power." By this, he meant those nations that could become arrogant to ignore local wars, revolutions, or conquests on the assumption that they do not disturb the general equilibrium of power or endanger the sense of security of the system as a whole.The veto principle of the Security Council of the United Nations was originally meant to ensure commitment of the five permanent members to the United Nations. It was also meant that no superpower is against any UN action, which can lead to outbreak of hostilities (Butler, 1999). The superpowers were expected to exercise collective responsibility for the maintenance of global peace and security. But what we see today has been unilateral actions by some permanent members of the Security Council with veto powers, especially the United States and Great Britain against countries they perceive as threats to international peace and security. A good example is the invasion of Iraq by the United States and Britain, "this wave of American-styled security by domination in place of collective security creates both anxiety and curiosity over the weakness of the United Nations Collective Security as "sine qua non" for world peace and security.

(iv) The activities of powerful regional organisations have posed a serious problem to United Nations Collective Security System. "Experience has shown that members of such organisations demonstrate divided loyalty often times with more concern to the regional organisation than the UN." (Eke, 2007) Members of regional security have often abandoned the UN Collective Security System in preference to regional security system. Bulter observed that during the invasion of Iraq by the United States "the Security Council – the hub of collective security regime was bypassed, defied and abused. . . " (Butler, 1999). Palmer and Perkings agree that the United States and western powers, in their attitudes of placing more emphasis on national and regional defence than on collective security as the obligation to the Charter of the United Nations are fundamental problems of unanimity of the Council and by extension, the cause of failure of security regime. (Palmer and Perkins, 2007) In many instances of states and regional conflicts, members of regional security abandon the UN. For example, the North Atlantic Treaty Organisation (NATO) had helped to bury the optimism, which greeted the UN Collective Security System in the 78-day bombing of Yugoslavia, and of course Iraq, after the fall of Soviet empire. In these two crises situation, the Security Council which is the hub of collective security regime was bypassed. The double allegiance of members of the United Nations, especially by the veto-wielding ones, concretely depicts moral failure.

Evaluation/Criticism. The theoratical aspect of collective security system appears to be logical and flawless, but in its actual operation it reveals number of short comings and drawbacks(unrealistic and unworkable).The machinery of collective security system has never been satisfactory developed under League of Nations or United Nations. Most of the assumptions are hypothetical. It is an ideal assumption- not work in the contemporary world. In the age of nuclear age it became more irrelevant

FAILURE OF COLLECTIVE SECURITY UNDER THE LEAGUE OF NATIONS

Palmer and Perkings observed that the League of Nations was a complete failure as an instrument for enforcement of collective security. They cited the failure of the United States of America to join the League from the start and the rise of the Soviet Union outside the League as one of the major reasons why the League failed as instrument for the development and enforcement of collective security. They also believed that "the open defiance of Japan, Italy and Germany combined to destroy any hopes that the League would be effective in major international crisis." (Palmer and Perkings, 2007) This line of thought was also captured by Charles, Kegley. He posits that "the failure stemmed from the U.S. refusal to join the organisation; the other great powers' fear that the League's collective strength might be used against them. (Kegley, 2007)

Another example of the failure of the League of Nations' collective security is the Manchurian crisis when Japan occupied part of China. After the invasion, members of the League passed a resolution calling for Japan to withdraw or face severe penalties. Given that every nation on the League of Nations Council had veto power, Japan promptly vetoed the resolution, severely limiting the League of Nations' ability to respond. After two years of deliberation, the League passed a resolution condemning the invasion without committing the League's members to any action against it. The Japanese replied by quitting the League of Nations.

A similar process occurred in 1935, when Italy invaded Ethiopia. Sanctions were passed, but Italy would have vetoed any stronger resolution. Additionally, Britain and France sought to court Italy's government as a potential deterrent to Hitler, given that Mussolini was not in what would become the Axis Alliance of World War II. Thus, neither enforced any serious sanctions against the Italian government.

Karen Mingst argued that Collective Security does not always work. She observed that the inability of the international community to respond to Japan's invasion of Manchuria and Italy's assault on Ethiopia was the fundamental differences in state interests and ideologies. According to her, "Collective Security does not always work. In the period between the two world wars, Japan invaded Manchuria and Italy over/an Ethiopia. In neither case did other states act as if it were in their collective interest to respond.... In this instance, collective security did not work because of lack of commitment on the part of other states and an unwillingness of the International Community to act in concert. In the post-World War II era, Collective Security could not work because of fundamental differences in both state interests and ideologies." (Mingst, 1999)

Additionally, in this case and with the Japanese invasion of Manchuria, the absence of the USA from the League of Nations deprived the League of another major power that could have used economic leverage against either of the aggressors states. Inaction by the League subjected it to criticisms that it was weak and concerned more with European issues (most leading members were Europeans) and did not deter Hitler from his plans to dominate Europe.

FAILURE OF COLLECTIVE SECURITY UNDER THE UNITED NATIONS

While Article I of the UN Charter calls for "effective collective measures for the prevention and removal of threats to the peace, and for the suppression of acts of aggression or other breaches of peace," Article 43 of the Charter provides that members of the UN, in accordance with special agreements to be conducted, are to make available to the Security Council "armed forces, assistance and facilities, including rights of passage, necessary for the purpose of maintaining international peace and security." These shall take place "if the Security Council finds that an act of aggression or other threats to the peace has occurred, and if the parties concerned do not comply with such measures as the Council shall deem necessary. . . " (Palmer and Perkings, 2007)

The United Nations calls for necessary measures to maintain international peace and security, including the obligation of states to place at the disposal of the United Nations agreed power necessary for an international peace force to be equipped with agreed types of armaments. Rather than have an institutionalised collective security regime, under the U.N. regularised training, maintenance and command, loosely Collective Security mechanism took the force of multinational willingness to control troops to promote the U.N. peace agenda. Where there exists an aggressor, there is need to collectively counter the attacks of the aggressor and preserve the peace through a Collective Security system. In such a situation no member state of the United Nations can claim neutrality, and none would dare to support the aggressor. If the aggressor dares to use force, then the combined forces of all the other states should so overwhelm the aggressor that hostilities would terminate and would cause would-be aggressor to retrace its steps for fear of sanction.

One of the problems of the United Nations Collective Security system is the unwillingness of countries to subordinate their sovereign interests to collective action. "Thus far, governments have generally maintained their right to view conflict in terms of their national interest and to support or oppose UN action based on their nationalistic point of view. Collective Security therefore exists mostly as a goal, not as a general practice." (Rourke and Boyer, 1998)

Another problem which have resulted in the failure of the United Nations Collective Security system is the over-dependence of the Security Council on the member-governments for assistance, especially the United States, Britain, Germany, Japan, etc. This over-dependence has made these nations act unilaterally in conflict situations without approval of the Security Council of the United Nations. In some situations, they flout the orders of the Security Council not to act unilaterally. The Iraq crisis and the role of the coalition forces, which was molded by the United States and Britain is clearer example.

"Rather than seek the global interest of peace and security through stability in Iraq and the Middle East region, the domination oriented members amassed their vast economic, diplomatic and military resources, captured and brasenly subjugated Iraq to an unprecedented condominial regime serving their economic interest under Iraq Reconstruction Programme." (Eke, 2007)

This goes to show that the big powers of the world will only agree to cooperate with the United Nations in relation to collective security as long as it serves their interests.

"The larger powers (who, after all, must bear the major burdens of enforcing peace under a collective security system) have never been willing to give an unconditional commitment to carry out the commands of the world organisation; they have always reserved for themselves some escape hatch. They have never been willing to set up an international army of any significant strength, under direct control of the League of Nations or the United Nations without any strings attached."

Some scholars see the United Nations Collective Security as one sided system whereby lesser and medium powers are ignored during aggression. They argue that the United Nations has not completely applied the Principle of Collective Security on a universal scale. To them, collective security would be meaningful onlyif it applied to great as well as lesser powers. Thus these scholars have overly criticised the unrepresentative stature of the Security Council.

They question the non inclusion of any African country in the membership of the UN Security Council considering the fact that Africa makes about one third membership of the U.N. The lack of geographical spread of members of the Security Council, no doubt, has a negative effect on the function and strength of the Council on the role of maintenance of global peace and security. The major issue here is that such members that feel their voices are only heard but of no policy consequence in protecting their interest feel withdrawn in U.N. actions of Collective Security. According to George Schwarsenberger,

"Collective Security as understood at Dumbarton Oaks and San Francisco meant collective security against danger to peace from the middle powers and small states and collective insecurity in the face of aggression by any of the world powers."

The above observation is corroborated by Inis Claude who asserts that "in the final analysis, the San Francisco Conference must be described as having repudiated the doctrine of Collective Security as the foundation for a general, universally applicable system for the management of power in international relations.

The doctrine was given ideological lip service, and a scheme was contrived for making it effective in cases of relatively minor importance. But the new organisation reflected the conviction that the concept of Collective Security has no realistic relevance to the problems posed by conflict among the major powers (Claude, 1962).

On the other hand, the concerted action of the United Nations in the Korean Crisis of the 1950 proved that Collective Security under the United Nations was possible. The enforcement action undertaken by the United Nations against North Korea that invaded South Korea in 1950 marks the first time the organised community of nations in accordance with the principles of Collective Security, has employed armed forces against an aggressor.

When the United Nations found out that North Korea exhibited aggression against South Korea, it called upon members of the United Nations to send troops and other assistance to South Korea and it asked the United States President to designate a Supreme Commander of the UN Forces. Thus the United Nations demonstrated that even though it had no armed forces at its disposal, as provided for in Article 43 of the Charter, it was not impotent in the face of open aggression.

But critics argued that the enforcement of UN action against North Korea was possible only because the Soviet delegate at the time was boycotting the meetings of the Security Council. They argued that had he been present, he presumably would have vetoed any action against North Korea. To them, the action of the United States and of other United Nations members who supported enforcement actions does not necessarily reflect a commitment to resist aggression simply out of belief that the Principle of Collective Security deserved support. One of such critics is Arnold Wolfers who submitted that "instead of being a case of nations fighting any aggressor anywhere and for no other purpose than to punish aggression and to deter potential aggressors, intervention in Korea was an act of collective military defense against the recognised number-one enemy of the United States and of all countries which associated themselves with its action." (Wolfers, 1962)

These critics believed that, had South Korea been the aggressor, it seems unlikely that the non-communist states in the United Nations would have endorsed enforcement action for the benefit of the communist regime in North Korea.

CONCLUSION

Collective Security as an institutionalised mechanism for the maintenance of international peace and security has reduced tensions among states in the international community. It has done much by providing the framework for keeping conflicts from becoming major threats to international peace. As Palmer and Perkings pointed out, for Collective Security to be effective, it must be strong enough to cope with aggression from any power or combination of powers, and it must be invoked if and as aggression occurs.

The direction of the United Nations Collective Security system has always been dictated by the world big powers especially the five permanent members of the UN Security Council. Small and medium powers feel left out in the Collective Security arrangement as they can only benefit from the system only when the interests of any of the "big gives" especially the United States are at stake. However, its weakness does not dismiss the system as wholly unuseful. The UN Collective Security system remains relevant and needed, but its radical defects must be attended to by admitting the added duty to prevent the spread of weapons of mass destruction and terrorism, which were not initially conceived and by enlarging the Security Council to take care of political interests of states perceived as orchestrating these new security challenges "since collective security system has always remained an idealistic concept which has never been defined by treaty and, therefore, can be hijacked by the powerful nations in the lopsided United Nations Security Council.

It is of great importance therefore, to harp on the need to institute a confidence-building measure among the members of the United Nations so as to establish the requisite solidarity and cooperation for enduring global peace and security. To do this is to start genuine reforms as currently canvassed by member states of the United Nations; especially those of them from Asia, Latin America and Africa with enlargement and representation of the Security Council based on geographical location and power-relations.

QUESTIONS

1. What do you mean by Collective Security? What are the conditions essential for maintaining Collective security?
2. How far the concept of Collective Security is relevant today?
3. Discuss the major articles of Collective Security under League of Nations?
4. Analyse the various constitution provisions of Collective Security with United Nations? Are they successful in the fulfilment of their objectives?
5. The Gulf War against Iraq is the example of Collective Security. Elucidate the statement
6. Cohen regards "peaceful settlement and collective measures are inseparable part of the collective security". In the light of above statement ,discuss the various methods of peaceful settlement of disputes?
7. Differentiate between Collective security and Collective Defence?
8. Evaluate the concept of Collective Security in context of League of nation and United Nations?

CHAPTER 9

Revolution, Terrorism, Disarmament and Arms Control

INTRODUCTION

A **revolution** is any fundamental change in the social or political aspects of a state. Most revolutions are political, occurring when the citizens of a country try to oust the existing government and replace it with a new one. Political revolutions tend to be tumultuous, violent events. There is no clear-cut explanation as to why people revolt, but scholars believe that some or all of the following factors lead to revolution:

- **Injustice:** Aristotle argued that the cause of revolution was the perception of injustice. If the under classes feel that they are being treated unjustly, they will revolt.
- **Relative deprivation:** Some scholars have argued that revolutions occur after a period of good times has ended. The citizens began to expect a higher quality of life and feel cheated when they perceive a stagnation or decline in the quality of their lives.
- **State of the government:** Revolutions are more likely to happen in countries with corrupt governments. If citizens believe in the efficacy of their government, then revolution is unlikely. But if a regime appears to exist solely to enrich the rulers, then revolution is more likely.
- **The military:** As the strongest power in most states, the military frequently determines whether a revolution will occur and be successful. If the military backs the government, then revolution is unlikely. A turning point in many revolutions occurs when soldiers decide to stop obeying the government and decide to fight alongside the revolutionaries.

REVOLUTIONS IN HISTORY

Although people have always rebelled against their rulers and governments, the modern area witnessed many significant revolutions. Since the sixteenth century, most revolutions have been attempts to overthrow traditional regimes in the name of liberty. In the twentieth century alone, there were important revolutions in Russia, China, Egypt, and parts of communist Eastern Europe, as well as countless others in smaller countries. Revolutions, and countering revolutions, were a driving force of foreign policy in the twentieth century. However, three revolutions in particular have served as models for most of the world's revolutions in the nineteenth and twentieth centuries:

- **American Revolution** (1776–1783): Leaders of the American Revolution overthrew British colonial rule to establish an independent republic. These colonial leaders considered the revolution to be a necessary evil and restricted the use of violence. Although the revolution affected the lives of most Americans, there was little social upheaval.
- **French Revolution** (1788–1799): The French Revolution began much as the American Revolution had but quickly turned violent. Tens of thousands of French citizens were executed during Maximilian Robes Pierre's so-called Reign of Terror. Order was restored only when Napoleon Bonaparte seized control of the government.
- **Russian Revolution** (1917): Russian revolutionaries sought both the removal of the monarchy and the complete restructuring of civil society in accordance with Vladimir Lenin's version of communism. The second phase of the Russian Revolution served as the model for dozens of other communist revolutions.

Fostering Revolution

Some nations have encouraged and supported revolutions in other countries as a foreign policy tool. For most of its existence, the Soviet Union promoted communist parties and revolutions around the world, most notoriously through the Communism. Similarly, the United States fostered revolutions in such places as Iraq, Iran, Guatemala, and Nicaragua.

Major Revolutions in Modern History

Revolution	Place	Dates	Major Impact
English Civil War	England	1642–1653	Set the stage for limited monarchy, and eventually democracy, in England
Glorious Revolution	England	1688	Permanently ended absolute monarchy in England
American Revolution	United States	1775–1783	Created the first modern democratic state
French Revolution	France	1789–1799	Destroyed the old French monarchy, led to the creation of the French nation-state, and promoted nationalism around Europe
Haitian Revolution	Haiti	1804	Created the first free black republic
French Revolution of 1830	France	1830	Permanently ended French monarchy
Mexican Revolution	Mexico	1910	Overthrew the dictator Porfirio Díaz and created the modern Mexican state
Russian Revolution	Russia	1917	Ended czarist rule in Russia and created the first communist state
Spanish Revolution	Spain	1936	Turned Spain into a fascist state
Chinese Civil War	China	1949	Turned China into a communist state
Algerian War of Independence	Algeria	1954–1962	Ended French imperial control of Algeria
Cuban Revolution	Cuba	1959	Overthrew Batista and created a communist regime

Iranian Revolution	Iran	1979	Overthrew the shah and created an Islamic regime
Nicaraguan Revolution	Nicaragua	1979	Overthrew the despotic regime and brought Marxist Sandinistas to power
Revolutions of 1989	Eastern Europe	1989	Ended Soviet and communist rule of many Eastern European states

Success and Failure

Revolutions are extremely difficult to achieve. For a revolution to succeed, many people must agree that the government needs to be overthrown, and these people must be willing to put themselves in danger and prepare for the possibility of civil war. Moreover, revolutions usually fail. For example, in Europe in 1848, democratic ideas and the free market spawned a series of revolutions across the continent. Most of them failed miserably, and perhaps the main impact of the revolutions of 1848 was the strengthening of authoritarian rule.

The Industrial Revolution

Not all revolutions are political. A *social revolution* is a revolution that transforms society or the economy without drastically altering the existing political system. The Industrial Revolution of the late eighteenth and early nineteenth centuries had a major impact on every country in the world. Beginning around 1780 in England, industry started to replace agriculture, and machinery started to replace manual labour. By the mid-nineteenth century, new forms of production and transportation—including the invention of the steam engine, mechanical typesetting, and movies—had fundamentally altered the modern world. Consequently, the lives of Europeans changed drastically within just a couple of decades.

TERRORISM

Terrorism is the use of violence (often against civilian targets) to instill fear, generate publicity, and sometimes destabilise governments. Generally speaking, small groups fighting against powerful states practice terrorism, but governments also have the ability to practice terrorism. Throughout history, terrorism has taken many forms. Just in the last two centuries, for example, terrorism has been used by Russian nihilists, nationalists in Israel, Nazi forces, environmentalists worldwide, left-wing guerrillas in Europe, discontented radicals in the United States, Latin American death squads, and Islamic fundamentalists. Terrorism is not tied to any one particular ideology or group.

Types of Terrorism

Scholars generally classify terrorism into two types: terrorism practiced by governments and terrorism practiced by groups not affiliated with a government. **Ideological terrorism** aims to promote a particular belief system through acts of violence; it may be practiced by both governments and groups.

Types of Terrorism

Terrorism Practiced by Governments	• **State terrorism:** A government commits acts of terror against its own citizens. • **International terrorism** (also known as **state-sponsored terrorism**): A government supplies and trains terrorists to make attacks in other countries.	**Terrorism Practiced by Groups**	• **Anti-state terrorism:** Any terrorist act not committed by a government • **Domestic terrorism:** A group with no ties to another country or government commits terrorist acts within its own country.

Some types of terrorism fit into more than one of these categories. Suicide bombings in Israel, for example, are ideological (promoting a Palestinian state and sometimes also promoting Islamic fundamentalism), state-sponsored (a number of Arab governments fund the bombers), and domestic (many are carried out by Arabs living in Israel).

Guerrillas Versus Terrorists

Although guerrillas have been known to practice terrorism, guerrillas are not terrorists. Guerrillas fight against their governments, particularly against the military, in order to provoke a regime change. Terrorists, in contrast, target civilians and members of the military in order to create a social and political crisis of international proportions. Of course, those fighting a guerrilla group might label their opponents terrorists, and some terrorists may see themselves as guerrillas.

The Purpose of Terrorism Terrorist acts ultimately aim to undermine governments and disrupt societies. Many terrorists are young, frustrated men who feel that they have been treated unjustly. Sometimes terrorists try to destabilize a government directly, via assassinations, kidnappings, and the bombing of government buildings. Terrorists can also work to undermine governments indirectly by showing people that their leaders are too weak to prevent the attacks and that an active resistance movement exists. Sometimes, terrorists attack in order to provoke a strong response from the government, hoping that the response will alienate more people from the government and foster even more political discord.

Example: Many scholars and political analysts have argued that President George W. Bush played into al Qaeda's hands by passing the Patriot Act in 2001 and by invading Iraq in 2003. The Patriot Act gave the federal government more power to detain and question suspected terrorists—often without trial—and to monitor suspicious activity. The Iraq War, meanwhile, deeply divided Americans when it became clear that Saddam Hussein had no connection with al Qaeda and was not harboring weapons of mass destruction. The federal government's suspension of some civil liberties along with the specter of deceit has shattered much of the unity Americans felt in the wake of the September 11th terrorist attacks.

DISARMAMENT

President Eisenhower has said, "There is no alternative to peace. War in our time has been an anachronism. Whatever the case in the past, war in future can serve no useful purpose." War needs no documentation to prove its horrors. People have constantly been in the search of alternatives to war and approaches to peace. Despite two world wars in the present century and the impending horror of the nuclear holocaust, the frequency of war has not decreased. The two world wars have frightened man badly and in the very imagination of the Third World War one finds then end of mankind. Dr,

Gerald Weudt asserted, " If world War III comes, which we pray will never happen, it will be a war in which most people may die from silent, insidious, anti-human weapons that make no sound, give no warning, destroy no forts or ships or cities, but can wipe out human beings by the millions." It must be recognized that war today has potentialities for destruction beyond the range of human comprehension. President Kennedy predicated:

"A full scale nuclear exchange, lasting less than 60 minutes, could wipe out more than 300 million Americans, Europeans and Russians, as well as untold numbers elsewhere. "

Dr. Albert Einstein once remarked, "I do not know the weapons with which World War III will be fought, but I can assure you that World War IV will be fought with sticks and stones." Among the many ways by which the war may be prevented the most important is disarmament.

Palmer and Perkins put it: " If armaments are conductive to war, should it not follow that disarmament is road to peace?" In regard to approaches to peace, armament and disarmament, both are suggested as ways by which the war may be prevented. The supporters of the armament theory argue that the more frightful war became "the less likelihood there was of its becoming a reality." But this theory lands in very dangerous situation as " the creation of cast armament in itself calls for a condition midway between war and peace. "Moving in the direction of armaments will be going a long way on the path towards war. Morgenthu remarks, "Of the attempts to achieve peace through limitation, the most persistent has been that of disarmament."

Meaning of Disarmament

Disarmament literally means the reduction or elimination of armaments. The term ' Disarmament' is used in very general sense and as such it connotes the idea of limitation, or control, or reduction, or elimination of armaments. According to Morgenthau, "Disarmament is the reduction or elimination of certain or all armaments for the purpose of ending the armament race." Disarmament has become such a wide word that any matter relating to the regulation of armaments comes within its meaning

History of Disarmament

Disarmament attempts can be traced back to the Treaty of Westphalia in 1648, which stipulated against the need for building fortifications. In 1816, the Czar of Russia proposed to the British government the reduction of armaments, a call that was not well received however. In 1863 and in 1869, France made similar calls for disarmament in Europe, but it too was ignored. In 1898, the Tsar of Russia called on European powers to gather at Hague to discuss disarmament, a suggestion which was well received, leading to the First Hague Peace Conference attended by 28 states. In 1907, another conference was held at the Hague for the same purpose. Both conferences called upon military and naval experts to propose reducing military expenditures through disarmaments, but the major powers were not ready for such moves in practice.

Disarmament after WWI

The devastation caused by WWI impelled statesmen of the world to give serious thought to disarmament. Woodrow Wilson in one of his famous fourteen points asserted armament should be reduced to 'the lowest point consistent with domestic safety'.

The Treat of Versailles (1919) also recognized that 'the maintenance of peace requires the reduction of national armaments'. The League of Nations was given the specific duty to secure a general agreement on disarmament and the covenant of the League stated that only those countries will be allowed membership who accepted the proposed agreement.

A permanent advisory commission was established in the League, but being comprised of military personnel, it failed to make much progress in a path of disarmament.

The Council of the League appointed another commission in 1920, the Temporary Mixed Commission, with a fixed four year mandate and comprised primarily of civilians. This temporary commission of the League was asked to identify limitation of land and naval forces for various countries according to their national security needs, the commission also proposed compulsory arbitration and proposed international aid to victims of aggression.

Unfortunately, the commission's recommendations were not accepted by members of the League of Nations. In 1926, the League set up another preparatory commission for disarmament which prepared a draft of a treaty considered at the Geneva conference of the League in 1932 by 61 states. Discussions on this draft continued for 2 years but then the Japanese attack on Manchuria and the German withdrawal from the treaty in 1933, dashed the hopes for disarmament.

Disarmament after WWII

The devastation unleashed by WWII again led to calls for disarmament. The UN charter laid much emphasis on the need for disarmament. The UN established a Military Staff Committee to assist the Security Council to regulate armaments and explore means for disarmament.

Kinds of Disarmament

1. General and local disarmament: In General Disarmament , all or most of the great powers participate. Examples are the Washington Treaty of 1922 for the limitation of naval armaments, signed by all major naval powers, and the World Disarmament Conference of 1932. We refer to Local Disarmament when only limited number of nations are involved. The Rush – Baghot agreement of 1817 between the United States and Canada is an example of this type.

2. Quantitative and Qualitative Disarmament: Quantitative Disarmament refers to an over all reduction of armaments of most or all types. This was the goal of most nations represented at the world conference in 1932. Qualitative disarmament aims at the reduction or abolition of only certain special types of armaments as was discussed by the Atomic Energy Commission of the United Nations.

3. Total Disarmament: Total disarmament aims at complete elimination of armaments. There would be no weapon of any kind whatsoever.

4. Disarmament and Arms control : Disarmament is concerned with the reduction or elimination of armament, but this applies only to the control of existing weapons.

Arms control is concerned with regulating the armaments race in the future. As such, disarmament is concerned with the control of existing weapons and arms control with that of future weapons. Disarmament seeks to control armaments and arms control tries to check the armaments race.

Need for Disarmament

1. The prevention of War and the Establishment of Peace: According to Morgenthau, " It is believed that, by doing away with one of the typical manifestations of the struggle for power on the international scene, one can do away with the typical effects of that struggle"; International anarchy and war." Disarmament is considered to be the most effective means of preventing war and guaranteeing peace. It is commonly believed that unless there is disarmament, war and destruction cannot be checked. The only direct cause of war according to disarmament approach is the existence of armaments. It is argued that war results from armaments and, therefore, it can be checked only by disarmament. Thus the belief that arms cause war is fundamental to the theory of disarmament. The amassing of armaments and their instant availability make war probable and feasible or, as Clause asserts, even tempting for statement to plunge into war. The theory of disarmament proceeds on the assumption that by limiting armaments, the nations would be deprived of the very means of fighting. When a nation increases its military strength, other nationals develop feelings of fear and insecurity. This leads to belligerence on the part of other nations and they also seek to increase their military strength. I realms of arms, one nation's common-sense is another nation's high blood pressure." Thus develops a war hysteria. Sometimes, in anticipation of an attack a nation is acting in self defence. Armaments make the national outlook aggressive and militaristic. While the armaments encourage conflict and war, it would be incorrect to argue that it is the sole cause of war. Complete disarmament would, however, lead to peace by eliminating the very means to fight. According to Cohen, " Armaments aggravate tension and fear among nations. By releasing tension and fear disarmament should facilities and strengthen the process of peaceful settlement.

2. Nuclear Threat: The threat of nuclear weapons and even a very remote possibility of a nuclear war have made the problem of disarmament all the more important. A nuclear war will lead to total destruction. But at the same time the view has been expressed that the fear of total destruction is so great that a nuclear war would never occur. Any war may turn ultimately into a nuclear war and the very threat of a nuclear war has restrained the nations from going to war in the nuclear age. If disarmament, both of nuclear as well as conventional weapons, is possible, way may be prevented.

3. Economic : A very important argument in favour of disarmament is economic. The very important argument which are allocated for military purposes by the nations is the broad indication of what is denied to other avenues of public and private expenditure. If nations had not expanded their means for military purposes, they could obviously have put the resources so consumed to many other uses. The military expenditures affect both the immediate consumption as well as future economic growth. The path of economic growth is barred. The nations are deprived of the mutual economic aid they could otherwise receive form one another. International trade and exchange of technological "know- how" have been impeded. If there were no arms race, trade and other exchanges would almost certainly be easier. A halt to the arms race could by itself be an important stimulus towards the relaxation of other existing barriers.

4. Social" The economic case for disarmament is closely linked with the social case. Military expenditure also have profound social consequences. The problem of poverty, hunger, disease, illiteracy, housing and that of raising standard of living is not only confined to the developing countries. These problems in some measure are also present in the rich countries. Military expenditures absorb resources which would otherwise be released for providing social services. The military expenditure for the world as a whole is about two and half times the estimated total of the publicity financed health expenditure. A rough calculation suggests that all medical research in the world consumes only about 4000 million dollars as compared to some 25000 million dollars spent on military research and development. Nuclear tests and explosions are having their polluting effects on the physical environment and thus bring environmental devastation.

5. Political: Armaments cause international suspicious and fears and they poison relations in the political sphere. Political differences become sharpened by the fear and suspicion which the amassing of armaments generates. The amassing of armaments also increases the possibility that force might be resorted to as a means of dealing with international problems. Armaments, which are supposed to provide security, in fact, provoke the political difference. It should be borne in mind that war is not an answer to any of man's imminent problems. The spirit of militarism is opposed to the spirit of democracy and peaceful progress in the world.

6. Psychological: A war condition has a strange psychological influence over the minds of the people. Everybody feels that he lived in a world in which violence has become a commonplace, and which is stocked with sufficient lethal to create a psychological background of uncertainty, fear and anxiety. Some western social psychologists have expressed the view that the arms race and the horrors of war have developed a belief in the younger generation that world is a irrational place in which the improvement of society is a hopeless cause.

Hindrances in the way of Disarmament

1. Problem of Security:-The problem of disarmament is closely related to the problem of security. According to Palmer and Perkins. "There has long been a consciousness of an inverse relationship between disarmament and security. Unless some system can be evolved whereby nations will actually be more secure with less armed strength, disarmament will indeed remain a 'pipe dream'. International tension and the mutual fear among the nations develop in them a feeling of insecurity. So long as the nation are not assured of their security, any effort for disarmament would meet with failure. No guarantee can be provided to nations in view of the nature of the present international society. In the conditions like this, every nation is bound to depend upon its own power for its security.

2.Fear and Mutual Distrust:-Another hindrance in the way of disarmament is the fear and mutual distrust. As a result, every nation views with suspicion the disarmament proposals put forth by others. Every nation feels suspicious about the intentions of others nations that while it way effect a reduction in it's armaments, other may not do so. This mistrust functions in two ways, " it hampers initial agreement and it might lead to the breakdown should a disarmament scheme be put into operation." But as Prof. Schleicher observes. "If there were perfect trust between nations, arms would be unnecessary and disarmament would but be the problem." So the basic problem of disarmament is that there is lack of mutual trust among the nations.

3. Failure of Disarmament Conferences:- No nation express itself against disarmament as such, but it views any disarmament plan from the point of view of its national interest. During disarmament negotiations such conditions are placed by some of the participants, which are not acceptable to others. As a result, the disarmament conferences fail. In fact, the nations lack the real desire for disarmament and that is why they put such condition which may not be acceptable to others.

4. Cold War:-The developments after the second world war divided the world into two blocs, and that gave birth to so- called cold war. Every nation is concerned about its security because of unstable balance of power. Armaments are the result of certain psychological factors. So long as these factors persist, disarmament seems to be a distant possibility. And disarmament proposal is, therefore, considered by the nations only in the contest of present international system.

5. Overkill capacity of super Powers:-In the realm of armaments, the super powers have achieved the maximum limit. In other words, they have gained such a potential capacity in armaments that it would not be worthwhile to go any further. Today both the U.S.A and the U.S.S.R are in the possession of overkill capacity. It is now in their interest to put a halt to arms \race. But the nations which are much behind in the arms race want disarmament only when they have reached a rough parity in arms with the super powers. They consider the power- equality as the ideal situation for disarmament. Since this situation is highly improbable, disarmament also appears improbable in the near future.

6. One important hindrance in the way of disarmament is with regard to the ratio among the armaments of different nations after a reduction in the armaments has been effected. Every nation wants to be superior in the race of disarmament to others. This questions is always the first on the agenda of disarmament to others. This question is always the first on the agenda of disarmament conference and commissions as so what should be the nation among the armaments of different nations and within that ratio how different types and quantities of armaments are to be allotted to different nations.

Justifications for Armament

Weapons are not the causes but the consequences of conflictive relations. A historical survey of the arms race indicates that during the past two centuries this form of international competition often ends peacefully in recognition of the military superiority of one side or the other. Countries which have no adequate defence tempt aggressors and therefore preparing for war is the best way to achieve peace.

Arguments for disarmament

Arms and arms races are costly and potentially very bloody. Arms reduction can curtail defence burden and allow economic investment for more productive purposes.

The unchecked growth of armaments without economic means can lead to internal repression and external aggression.

ARMS CONTROLS

Arms reduction implies partially disarmament based on mutually agreed set of arms levels between given groups of nation states. Arms limitation includes a wide variety of international accords to limit impact of potential wars or to prevent their accidental outbreak (exchange of information to prevent misunderstanding or banning acquisition of particular types of weaponry).

Disarmament efforts by the UN

The UN established the *Atomic Energy Commission* consisting of all five Security Council members and Canada. The Commission was meant to explore mechanisms for peaceful transfer of nuclear technology, to identify safeguards by way of inspections for compliant states to prevent hazards of violation and to eventually work towards elimination of nuclear weapons.

While both superpowers agreed to co-operate, their divergent stances (the US arguing that control take precedence over disarmament and the USSR arguing the reverse) on the Commission goals led to its ineffectiveness. The General Assembly of the UN also established a Commission on Conventional Armaments, which also felt victim to Cold War divergences, ultimately the USSR pulled out of both Commissions due to China's representation on them.

Atoms for Peace Plan

In 1953, President Eisenhower of the US proposed establishment of a pool of fissionable materials donated by declared nuclear states to the Atomic Energy Commission, which could be provided to other countries strictly for peaceful purposes.

The Soviets opposed this plan arguing that an agreement on prohibiting nuclear weapons was first necessary prior to disseminating nuclear technology.

Other Disarmament Efforts

Many disarmament and arms control efforts were undertaken through bilateral means between the two superpowers, the biggest proliferations of armaments in the post-WWII period (NTBT, NPT, SALT I and II).The six nation summit held in New Delhi in 1985 is indicative of the growing concern amongst developing countries about arms race, particularly nuclear weapons (Ironically, India too is now a declared nuclear state).

CTBT

The NTP review conference was held in Geneva in 1995 which recommended infinite extension of the NTP. Israel, Pakistan and India were criticized for not acceding to the NPT nor to the subsequent CTBT, which even forbids tests required for developing nuclear weapons. Even France signed the CTBT after conducting its last nuclear test in the South Pacific. India and Pakistan remain reluctant and argue that the advanced nuclear states can keep their weaponry safe and updated by tests stimulated in lab settings.

QUESTIONS

1. Do you think the concept of Revolution and Terrorism led to the development of armament race? Justify the interrogation
2. What do you mean by Disarmament ? What are its essentials.
3. What are the basic hindrances in the way of Disarmament?
4. Justify the major revolutions of modern history? What are those factors that are responsible for revolution?
5. What are the efforts undertaken by UN in controlling the arms race among the super powers of the world?
6. Discuss the historical evolution of the concept of Disarmament after WWI and WWII?

CHAPTER 10

Relevance of International Law in International Relations

INTRODUCTION

International laws are rules which relate to the functioning of individuals, institutions and states in an international arena. International law has various ingredients including general principles of law and justice, which are equally suited to regulate the conduct of individuals, organisations within a state and states themselves.

A. DEVELOPMENT OF INTERNATIONAL LAW

Formulation of international law can be traced back to the third and fourth millenniums B.C. Early rulers had made international rules to safeguard emissaries, initiation and cessation of hostilities and arrangement of truces, and maritime laws.

To aid governance, the Romans devised principles of just laws of the people. By the time the Roman Empire fell, application of these laws was widely accepted. European states also contributed to international laws at a later stage in history. By the 14th century, scholars were writing about international law. Hugo Grotius, for example, produced a momentous work on laws concerning war and peace, emphasising the independent nature of law. In the past century, the League and the UN system, and subsequently the International Court of Justice have made important contributions to international law. Other institutions like IMF or WTO influence laws concerning trade economic laws.

B. NATURE AND DEFINITION

The laws which regulate the dealings of the states with one another are called international laws. It is a law which governs the conduct of the states. It is a law among nations. International law is the most important factor to preserve order and to prevent abuse of power in international area. Among the controls of inter-state relations, the more general and continuous one is the international law. As Robert A Tatt observes, "peace in this world is impossible unless nations agree on a definite law to govern their relations with each other".

The term international law was coined by Bentham in 1780. International law has been defined in different ways by different writers.

Oppenheim define international law as "the body of customary and conventional rules which are considered legally binding by civilised states in their inter-course with each other".

Lawrence defines International law as "the rules which determine the conduct of the general body of civilised states in their mutual dealings".

Briefly defines it "as the body of rules and principles of action which are binding upon civilised states in their relations with one another".

C. DIFFERENT TYPES OF INTERNATIONAL LAW

- Private and Public Laws: private law concerns individuals, whereas public law concerns the behaviour of organisations and even states.
- *Procedural and Substantive Laws:* Procedural laws define types of permitted behaviour whereas substantive laws concern territorial rights of states.
- *Laws of War and Peace:* There are laws governing behaviour of states in a state of war (concerning rights of prisoners of war) and those meant to prevent outbreak of violence and promote peace.
- *Particular and General Laws:* General or universal laws are applicable to all sovereign states, whereas particular laws are defined by bilateral or regional agreements.

D. SOURCES OF INTERNATIONAL LAW

It refers to the methods or procedures by which international law is evolved. Following are some of the important sources.

1. Roman Law: Roman law formed a complete and general code of dealings "the jusgentium". The jusgentium was applied to the dealings of citizens belonging to different nations. From this general code most of the continental countries in Europe derived their legal principles. Roman law provided a positive basis for international law in two ways.

1) By the idea of the law of nations, 2) By contributing the nation of equality of citizens before the law. This notion got extended to the equality of sovereign states intonation law.

2) Customs: This is another source of international law. As a matter of fact international law is customary. Certain customs and conventions which particular states adopted have been accepted and followed so generally that they have come to constitute a definite body of rules. Customs may be defined as "the rules evolved after a long historical process which in due course find place in their recognition by international community. Many rules of international law relating to maritime warfare the right of aliens freedom of the seas etc. have been greatly determined by international customs.

3) Decisions of League of Nations and UNO: League of nations and UNO have been very important international institutions of 20th century. The UNO lays stress on direct legislation, Mediation, Arbitration and International Court of Justice at Hague. Decisions of the court at Hague and the resolutions passed by UNO proved very fruitful in the growth and development of International law

4) Opinions of Diplomats and Statesman: The written opinions of statement and lawyers and diplomatic correspondence have helped much in the growth and development of international law, These opinion are often confidential but in democracy there is greater tendency to publish them. The important portions of these opinions are published in England and USA. States also issue instructions for the guidance of their foreign service representatives and commanders of armed forces. These play a great role in the growth and development of international law.

5) Works of Eminent Jurists: The views of greet jurists are taken into consideration while deciding international cases. For example Hugo Grotius's famous book "on the law of war and peace" published in 1625 is regarded as the Chief source of international law. Kent, Wheaton, Manning, Woolsey, Westlake, Lawrence and Hall are known as modern authorities on international law.

6) Treaties and Alliances: Treaties, alliances and conventions for commercial or for political purpose are important sources of international law. When most of the states become parties to such a treaty, convention or alliance they tend to create an international law

7) State Laws: Municipal law or slate laws also form a source of international law. For example the rules and regulations of citizenship, nationalisation etc. are some of the rules and regulations which have international bearings. These rules and regulations have helped a lot in the development of international law.

E. INTERNATIONAL LEGAL PERSONALITY

International legal personality refers to the entities or legal persons that can have rights and obligations under international law.

1. States

A *State* has the following characteristics: (1) a permanent population; (2) a defined territory; (3) a government; and (4) the capacity to enter into relations with other States. Some writers also argue that a State must be fully independent and be recognised as a State by other States. The international legal system is a horizontal system dominated by States which are, in principle, considered sovereign and equal. International law is predominately made and implemented by States. Only States can have sovereignty over territory. Only States can become members of the United Nations and other international organisations. Only States have access to the International Court of Justice. .

2. International Organisations

International Organisations are established by States through international agreements and their powers are limited to those conferred on them in their constituent document. International organisations have a limited degree of international personality, especially vis-à-vis member States. They can enter into international agreements and their representatives have certain privileges and immunities. The constituent document may also provide that member states area legally bound to comply with decisions on particular matters.

The powers of the United Nations are set out in the United Nations Charter of 1945. The main political organ is the General Assembly and its authority on most matters (such as human rights and economic and social issues) is limited to discussing issues and making recommendations. The Security Council has the authority to make decisions that are binding on all member States when it is performing its primary responsibility of maintaining international peace and security. The main UN judicial organ is International Court of Justice (ICJ), which has the power to make binding decisions on questions of international law that have been referred to it by States or give advisory opinions to the U.N.

3. Nationality of individuals, companies, etc.

Individuals are generally not regarded as legal persons under international law. Their link to State is through the concept of *nationality,* which may or may not require *citizenship. Nationality* is the status of being treated as a national of a State for particular purposes. Each State has wide discretion to determine who is a *national*. The most common methods of acquiring nationality at birth are through one or both parents and/or by the place of birth. Nationality can also be acquired by adoption and naturalisation.

Companies, ships, aircraft and space craft are usually considered as having the nationality of the State in whose territory they are registered. This is important because in many circumstances States may have international obligations to regulate the conduct of their nationals, especially if they are carrying out act activities outside their territory.

Under the principle of *nationality of claims*, if a national of State A is injured by State B through internationally unlawful conduct, State A may make a claim against State B on behalf of its injured national. This is known as the doctrine of *diplomatic protection*.

F. SOVEREIGNTY OF STATES OVER TERRITORY

Sovereignty is the exclusive right to exercise supreme political authority over a defined territory (land, airspace and certain maritime areas such as the territorial sea) and the people within that territory. No other State can have formal political authority within that State. Therefore, sovereignty is closely associated with the concept of political *independence*.

Classical international law developed doctrines by which States could make a valid claim of sovereignty over territory. The doctrines included *discovery* and *occupation* and *prescription*. During the period of Western colonial expansion new territories and islands were subject to claims of sovereignty by discovery and occupation. Sovereignty could also be transferred to another State by *conquest* (use of force) or by *cession* where the sovereignty over the territory would be ceded by treaty from one State to another.

Since a State has sovereignty over its territory, the entry into its territory by the armed forces of another State without consent is a *prima facie* breach of international law. Among the attributes of sovereignty is the right to exclude foreigners from entering the territory, which is traditionally referred to as the right to exclude aliens.

Since a State has sovereignty within its territorial sea (with some exceptions such as the *right of innocent passage*), it has the exclusive authority to exercise police power within its territory sea.

For example, if foreign ships are attacked by "pirates" in the territorial sea of a State, the only State that can exercise police power and arrest the pirates in the territorial sea is the coastal State.

G. ROLE OF THE INTERNATIONAL LAW COMMISSION (ILC)

The ILC was established by the UN in 1948. The 34 members of the ILC are elected by the General Assembly after being nominated by member States. They possess recognized competence and qualifications in both doctrinal and practical aspects of international law and the ILC reflects a broad spectrum of expertise and practical experience.

The mandate of the ILC is the progressive development and codification of international law. The ILC usually spends many years studying areas of international law before presenting draft articles to the General Assembly for adoption as a draft convention. The primary written products of the ILC aside from the draft articles themselves are the detailed periodic reports prepared by the Special reports on each subject and the official commentary for each draft article.

H. JURISDICTION AND IMMUNITIES OF STATES UNDER INTERNATIONAL LAWS

1. Principles of Jurisdiction

(a)Territorial Jurisdiction: The concept of *jurisdiction* refers to the power of a State to prescribe and enforce criminal and regulatory laws and is ordinarily based on the *territorial principle*, under which a State has jurisdiction over activities within its territory.

(b)National Jurisdiction: Some states also claim jurisdiction over activities outside their territory which affect their territory. States can also claim jurisdiction based upon the *nationality principle* by extending jurisdiction over their nationals even when they are outside the territory. For example, civil law countries extend their criminal law to cover their nationals while abroad while common law countries usually only do so in exceptional cases.

(c) Universal Jurisdiction: There is also a very narrow category of crimes – including genocide and war crimes - over which States may assert jurisdiction based upon the *universality principle, which gives* all States have jurisdiction irrespective of nationality or location of the offence.

(d)Protective Jurisdiction: Almost all States claim jurisdiction under the *protective principle*, under which a State asserts jurisdiction over acts committed outside their territory that are prejudicial to its security, such as treason, espionage, and certain economic and immigration offences.

(e)Passive Personality Principle: The most controversial basis for jurisdiction – followed by very few States - is the *passive personality principle*, which establishes jurisdiction based on the nationality of the victim. In recent years States have asserted jurisdiction over terrorist acts outside their territory directed against their nationals, thereby basing jurisdiction on a combination of the protective and passive personality principles. Modern counter-terrorism treaties establish jurisdiction among State Parties based on the *presence of the offender* within their territory. If a persons who are alleged to have committed the offence established in the treaty (e.g, hijacking of an aircraft) is present in their territory, a State Party to the treaty is under an obligation to take the persons into custody, and to either prosecute them or extradite them to another State Party that has jurisdiction over the offence.

(f) Concurrent Jurisdiction:-If two or more States have jurisdiction over a particular offence, they are said to have *concurrent jurisdiction*. In such cases the State which is most likely to prosecute the offender is the State which has custody over him. No State may exercise jurisdiction within the territorial sovereignty of another State. The police of State A cannot enter the territory of State B to arrest a person who has committed a crime in State A. Also, if a crime takes place in the territorial sea of a coastal State, no State other than the coastal State my intercept and arrest the ship carrying the offenders.

States enter into bilateral treaties to provide for the *extradition* of alleged offenders. Sending an alleged criminal to another State for investigation or prosecution in the absence of an extradition treaty is referred to as *rendition*.

The high seas and outer space are outside the territorial jurisdiction of any State. The general principle of jurisdiction in these common areas is that ships, aircraft and spacecraft are subject to the jurisdiction of the "flag State", or State of registration. The general principle is that ships on the high seas are subject to the exclusive jurisdiction of the flag State, and cannot be boarded without its express consent. The most notable exception is piracy. All States have a right to board pirate ships on the high seas without the consent of the flag State.

IMMUNITIES FROM JURISDICTION

(a) **Soveriengn Immunity:**-The principle of *sovereign equality of States* requires that the official representatives of one State should not be subject to the jurisdiction of another State. For example, the law of the sea provides that warships are subject only to the jurisdiction of the flag State. Even if warships commit acts contrary to the right of innocent passage or the laws and regulations of the coastal State, the coastal State's only remedy is to escort the offending warship out of the territorial sea. The principle of *State immunity or sovereign immunity* provides that foreign sovereigns enjoy immunity from the jurisdiction of other States.

(b) **Diplomatic Immunity:-**The principle of *diplomatic immunity* provides that the diplomatic agents of the sending State have complete immunity from the criminal jurisdiction of the receiving State. Since this immunity belongs to the sending State and not to the diplomat, it can be waived by the sending State. Also, the receiving State has the right to expel any diplomatic agent from its country by declaring them *persona non grata*. The premises of an embassy or diplomatic mission as well as its records and archives are also inviolable. The authorities of the receiving State cannot enter a foreign embassy without the express permission of the head of mission, even in the case of an emergency.

I. DIFFRNTIATE BETWEEN INTERNATIONAL LAW FROM MUNICIPAL LAW/NATIONAL LAWS/ INTERNATIONAL AGREEMENTS.

(a)Differences between international Law and Municipal Law

1. Municipal laws are framed by the competent legislative machinery. In other words state laws are framed by a sovereign legislature whereas international laws are not the product of any sovereign legislature.

2. Municipal law is definite and precise. But international laws are not definite. They are very vague and uncertain that they can be interpreted by the states in the manner they like.

3. There is a definite agency to enforce state laws. International society has no central executive for the enforcement of international law. UN in that respect is a weak agency.

4. Violation of law is punishable by the state. Law courts give punishment to those who violate it, That is Municipal law enjoys compulsory jurisdiction. International law lacks compulsory jurisdiction.

5. Municipal laws are within the territory of a state and that differs from state to state. But international laws are common to all states of the world even if it lacks compulsory jurisdiction

(b) International Agreements and International Law

In order to make the global system less chaotic and unpredictable, states often make agreements with one another to modify their behavior. **International agreements** are treaties signed by a number of states that establish global rules of conduct. Some agreements focus on single issues, whereas others cover many areas. Theoretically, international agreements benefit the states that sign them States that break these rules—sometimes called **rogue states**—are usually treated with wariness by the rest of the world.

Example: The United States has identified North Korea, Iran, Syria, and Cuba as rogue states because they have continually threatened international security by harboring terrorists and fostering the development of weapons of mass destruction. Afghanistan and Iraq were considered rogue states before the American invasions in the early twenty-first century. As soon as a state begins cooperating and participating in the international community, it loses its status as a rogue state. In 2002, the U.S. Department of State removed Libya from its list of rogue states after the Libyan government voluntarily agreed to renounce terrorism and violence.

International law is the collection of rules and regulations that have evolved over the past few centuries. These rules define the rights and obligations of states. Sometimes treaties codify and formalize international law, but just as often, international law arises from custom and habit. The International Court of Justice, in the Netherlands, is the judicial body of the United Nations and is responsible for resolving disputes among states.

Example: In 2006, the International Court of Justice heard testimony relating to a boundary dispute between Nicaragua and Colombia. Another case on its docket concerned charges of genocide brought by Bosnia against Serbia; in early 2007, the court ruled in favor of Bosnia, deciding that Serbia had failed to prevent genocide in Bosnia.

The Effectiveness of International Law

A key dispute among political scientists concerns the effectiveness of international law. Realists argue that because there is no international police force to enforce international law, the law has no real power. States only obey international law when it is in their interest to do so. Liberalists, however, dispute this idea, contending that there are real consequences to breaking international law—such as sanctions and even military occupation—and that international organisations have a measurable impact on global relations.

International Treaties

International treaties serve as an important part of international law. States sign treaties to end wars, protect their interests, and make international law. The treaties listed in the chart below have significantly contributed to the structure of the international systems.

SIGNIFICANT INTERNATIONAL TREATIES

Treaty	Date Signed	Purpose/Effect
Sykes-Picot Agreement	1916	Set boundaries that still exist today for nations in the Middle East
Treaty of Versailles	1919	Ended World War I; its punitive treatment of Germany set the stage for World War II
Munich Agreement	1938	Gave the Sudetenland (part of Czechoslovakia) to Germany in exchange for a promise of no more expansion; its violation led to World War II
United Nations Charter	1945	Created the United Nations
General Agreement on Tariffs and Trade	1947	Greatly reduced tariffs and boosted trade
North Atlantic Treaty	1949	Created the North Atlantic Treaty Organisation (NATO), an alliance of Western powers dedicated to preventing communist expansion
Convention on the Prevention and Punishment of the Crime of Genocide	1951	Made genocide a crime punishable by the international community
Warsaw Pact	1955	The communist response to NATO; created an alliance of Eastern

		European communist states
International Atomic Energy Treaty	1957	Regulates the use of atomic energy
Nuclear Non-Proliferation Treaty	1968	Made it illegal for states without atomic weapons to acquire them
Anti-Ballistic Missile Treaty	1972	Prevented the United States and the Soviet Union from developing antiballistic missiles
Camp David Accords	1978	A peace treaty between Egypt and Israel
Kyoto Protocol	2005	Regulates greenhouse emissions to reduce global warming

(c) International versus National Laws

National laws have much greater legitimacy than international laws. While individuals rarely have recourse to self-help within nations, states rely on self-help as a matter of norm lest they are bound by a treaty of some sort. With the passage of time, international laws are becoming more accepted and complex and sanctions and international censure ensure states to oblige to them.

J. PRINCIPLES GOVERNING RELATIONS BETWEEN STATES

The general principles governing friendly relations between States are set out in UN General Assembly Resolution 2625. It states that the progressive development and codification of the seven principles below would secure their more effective application within the international community and would promote the realisation of the purposes of the United Nations. Therefore, the resolution sets out the consensus in the international community on the content of the following seven principles:

1) States shall refrain in their international relations from the threat or use of force against the territorial integrity or political independence of any State, or in any other manner inconsistent with the purpose of the United Nations
2) Peaceful settlement of disputes
3) Non-intervention in matters within the domestic jurisdiction of any State, in accordance with the Charter
4) Co-operation with one another in accordance with the Charter
5) Equal rights and self-determination of peoples
6) Sovereign equality of States
7) States shall fulfil in good faith the obligations assumed by them in accordance with the Charter

K. RESPONSIBILITY OF STATES FOR WRONGFUL ACTS

The 2001 ILC Articles on the Responsibility of States for Internationally Wrongful Acts set out the principles in this important field of international law. The ILC Articles is the combination of codification and progressive development. Even though the ILC Articles have not been adopted as an international convention, some of the provisions have been referred to by international courts and tribunals as reflective of customary international law.

States are responsible to other States for their *internationally wrongful acts*. A State commits *internationally wrongful act* when conduct consisting of an act or omission (a) is attributable to the State under international law; and (b) constitutes a breach of an international obligation owed by that State to the injured State or the international community. Therefore, if a dispute arises between two States, the first question is whether the offending State owed an international obligation to the injured State under either a treaty or under customary law. The second question is whether that obligation was breached by conduct consisting of either an act or an omission that is attributable to the offending State.

The rules on attribution are based on common sense. The conduct of an organ of the State is attributable to the State because a State acts through its official representatives, such as its Head of State, Minister of Foreign Affairs, Ambassadors and government ministries and departments. The official acts of these persons and organs are attributable to the State. The conduct of private persons or private entities is generally not attributable to the State unless the State knew of the conduct and failed to act in relation to that conduct when it had an international obligation to act. However, the conduct of a person or entity empowered by the law of the State to exercise elements of government authority is attributable to the State and a State may also ratify and adopt the conduct of private persons or control their conduct in such a manner that it can be attributed to the State.

A State is in breach of an international obligation when conduct attributable to it is not in conformity with what is required by the obligation. A State may not rely on provisions of its internal or domestic law as justification for failure to comply with an international obligation. The responsible State is under an obligation to *cease the wrongful act* if it is continuing. It is also under an obligation to offer appropriate *assurance and guarantees of non-repetition*, if circumstances so require. In addition, the responsible State is under an obligation to make full *reparation* for the injury – both material and moral - caused to the other State by the internationally wrongful act.

The *forms of reparation* under international law are *restitution, compensation and satisfaction*. The preferred form of reparation is *restitution*, which requires the State to re-establish the situation which existed before the wrongful was committed. In so far as the damage is not made good by restitution, the State much pay *compensation* to cover the financially assessable damage, including loss of profits insofar as it is established. If the injury cannot be made good by either restitution or compensation, the State must provide *satisfaction*, which may consist of acknowledgement of the breach, an expression of regret, a formal apology or another appropriate remedy.

There are defences available to the responsible State which preclude the wrongfulness of an act, including valid consent by the injured State, self-defence, force majeure, distress, necessity and valid countermeasures. The ILC Articles set out the requirements which must be met before these defences can be invoked. Some of the provisions of the ILC Articles on these "defences" can be classified as "progressive development" rather than a codification of customary international law.

L. THE ROLE OF THE ICJ

The ICJ is the chief judicial organ of the United Nations. All members of the UN are automatically parties to the Statute of the International Court of Justice. The jurisdiction of the ICJ in "contentious disputes" between States is subject to the principle of consent. It can obtain jurisdiction in three ways.

(a) First, the States parties to a dispute may enter into an *ad hoc* agreement to refer a particular legal dispute to the court.

(b) Second, States can submit an "optional clause declaration" to the UN Secretary-General declaring that they accept the jurisdiction of the ICJ over certain categories of disputes with other States which have also filed an optional clause declaration. This category of disputes is quite rare, as many States are not willing to accept the jurisdiction of the ICJ in advance for wide categories of disputes.

(c) Third, many international conventions contain dispute settlement clauses called "co promissory clauses" allowing disputes between States parties to the convention to refer disputes concerning the interpretation or application of provisions of that convention to the ICJ by one of the parties to the dispute. Some conventions allow States to "opt out' of such co promissory clauses.

If a dispute between two States is decided by the ICJ, the decision is final and binding as between the parties to the case. It is not binding on other States. However, to the extent that the ICJ pronounces on issues of customary law or treaty law, its judgment will be treated as an authoritative interpretation of international law by many States.

(d) The ICJ also has advisory jurisdiction. The UN Security Council and the UN General Assembly may request advisory opinions on any legal question. The UN General may also authorise other UN organs or specialised agencies to request advisory opinions on legal questions arising within the scope of their activities.

M. LIMITATIONS OF INTERNATIONAL LAW

International law operates in the international society based upon non-state system consisting of sovereign states. It is a law among the states and not over them. International law has the following limitations and short comings.

1. No legislative machinery:

International law is not the product of any sovereign international legislative, where as state laws are the product of a sovereign legislature.

2. No Executive Machinery:

International society has no central executive machinery for enforcement of international law.

3. No effective Judicial machinery

International law and international judicial system lack compulsory jurisdiction.

International Court of Justice has no compelling jurisdiction over the states and the states, are not obliged, to submit their disputes to the court.

4. Uncertainty of International law:

The main instrument through which international law is created are international treaties. They are so vague and uncertain that they can be interpreted by the states in the manner they like to suit their interest. The UN charter itself is vague and uncertain. For example the word 'self defence' can be defined differently in different circumstances and each stat is its own judge in the matter.

5. Domestic affairs outside the jurisdiction of international law.

Domestic affairs of a state lies outside the jurisdiction of international law. UNO cannot interfere in matters which are essentially within the domestic jurisdiction are brought under the purview of international law, it would fail in performing its effective role.

CONCLUSION :-RELEVANCE OF INTERNATIONAL LAWS

Despite its limitations, international law helps give shape to international order. It influences and channels bilateral or even multilateral economic, social and political cooperation. It provides the normative background based on which independent states can make their decisions. Today international law is given great importance and it is regarded as the law in the true sense of the term.

But during the 19th century John Austin said that international law is not true law but only positive international morality. According to Austin every law must be backed by the authority of the state and if that element is lacking it cannot be called law. In that sense there is no political authority over and above the states of the world to implement international law in the true sense. Another jurist Holland calls international law as law only by courtesy. Kelson is also of the view that the so called international law cannot be classed law in the same sense as state law, because it is not supported by the coercive authority of the state.

QUESTIONS

1. The body of customary and conventional rules which are considered legally binding by civilized states in their intercourse with each other. Describe the evolution of these international rules along with its various methods and procedures through which they are evolved?
2. What are the different types of International Law? Differentiate International laws from Municipal and National laws?
3. Examine the close relationship between International laws and International Agreements?
4. What are the principles of Jurisdiction and Immunities of state under the obligation of International Law?
5. Justify the role of International Court of Justice(ICJ) and International Law Commission(ILC) ?
6. What is the role of International Legal Personality in International Law?
7. What do you mean by international Law ? Discuss its nature with its limitations?
8. Do you think International Laws are relevant for contemporary times?

CHAPTER 11

New International Economic Order (NIEO)

INTRODUCTION

Since WWII, the world economy has undergone drastic changes brought about by changing political circumstances, industrial and technological changes, and changing trade patterns. The dominant economic order which prevailed for four decades after WWII is referred to as IEO.

IEO Subsystems

- *North-West System*: referred to financial and trade linkages between developed nations of Western Europe, Japan and North America.
- *North-East System*: referred to centrally controlled economies of the Soviet Union and Eastern Europe
- *South System*: referred to developing countries of Africa, Asia and Latin America

Economics based on nationalistic grounds has received a lot of criticism. It failed to function in the case of the North-east, leading to the collapse of the USSR. The control of capital and use of neo-colonial and imperialistic tendencies in terms of trade resulted in large disparities around the world. The North-West system donated money to the South System, but it was not enough to remove wide-spread poverty. Many developing countries and segments of the population within the developed world called for a revision of the prevailing IEO. Reacting to the inequitable economic situation, countries of the South articulated a strategy to alter the structure of international economic systems. The NIEO called for economic justice and balanced economic growth which could be sustainable in the future.

(1) UNITED NATION DECLARATION OF NEW INTERNATIONAL ECONOMIC ORDER(NIEO)

The United Nations, at its Special General Assembly on Natural Resources held in April, 1974, adopted "A Declaration and a Programme of Action on the Establishment of a New International Economic Order". The Declaration stated that the present international economic order is a product of the age of colonialism and is designed to help.

New International Economic Order and International Economic Laws the industrially advanced countries only to gain profits. It stressed the need to establish a NIEO to achieve fairness and equality for all the countries of the world, including the developing countries. As the fundamental principles, it advocated the equality of national sovereignty, self-determination by all peoples, disapproval of acquisition of territory by force, non-interference in the affairs of other countries, permanent sovereignty over natural resources, adoption of special measures for the most seriously affected countries, promotion of producer cartels, restrictions on activities of multinational corporations, and so on. As the action plan, it called for the formation of an overall program for raw materials and primary products, extending loans to the developing countries for their development programs, helping promote industrialisation and transfer of technology, restricting activities of multinational corporations, promoting cooperation among the developing countries, and so on. This is an outline of the NIEO.

In December, 1974, the General Assembly of the United Nations adopted by an absolute majority a Charter of Economic Rights and Duties of States (generally known as the Echeverria Charter), a codified version of the New International Economic Order Declaration and a Programme of Action. The Charter lays down concrete rights of the developing countries to be for improvement of their economic and social position. Specifically, it calls for, among others, (1) guarantee of permanent sovereignty over natural resources, (2) right to restrict and supervise foreign capital investments and principle of non-interference in the affairs of other countries by foreign business enterprises, (3) right to nationalise and appropriate foreign assets, (4) right to form producer cartels for primary products, and (5) unlimited expansion of preferential trade agreements for the developing countries.

The basic spirit of the NIEO is outlined in the above-mentioned "Declaration and Programme of Action" and Charter of Economic Rights and Duties of States. The Western industrial nations, however, are not necessarily willing to accept these resolutions of the United Nations so readily, because they do not have legal binding power. The Third World countries voted for the Algeria Declaration in February, 1975 on the strength of the Group of 77 and once again demanded the establishment of the NIEO. In March of the same year, they passed the Lima Declaration at the Second General Assembly of the United Nations Industrial Development Organisation. In this Declaration, they touched on not only economic affairs involving permanent sovereignty over natural resources, producer cartels, price indexation, multilateral trade negotiations, and transfer of technology, but also political matters including apartheid, and neo-colonialism in an attempt to pressure the industrially advanced countries. The ideas set forth in these declarations are the essence of the NIEO.

(2) HISTORICAL BACKGROUND OF NEW INTERNATIONAL ECONOMIC ORDER DECLARATION

The New International Economic Order Declaration is a challenge to the existing international economic order. What then is the existing international economic order?

(i) IEO System:-An international economic cooperation system came into being for the first time in the 20 th century, particularly after the end of the World War I. Former United States President Wilson, in his Fourteen-Points Declaration, stated that the elimination of all economic barriers and the creation of equality of trade terms are indispensable to' world peace. At the world economic conference held at Geneva in 1927, proposals were made for liberalisation of international trade and elimination of tariff barriers, but with no concrete results. As for international cooperation, the International Labour Organisation (ILO)assumed a concrete form under the Covenant of the League of Nations, but international cooperation in the economic field made little progress. In the 1930's, following the world-wide depression, the major powers of the world adopted a policy of forming their own economic bloc. The international economy became an isolated and closed system aptly described by such terms as regionalism, bilateralism or discrimination Economic confrontations among individual blocs were heightened and gradually developed into political confrontation and eventually war.

(ii) Emergence of International Organisations with Undeclaration:-With the World War II marking a turning point, international cooperation in the economic field made rapid progress. From 1943 to 1944, the United Nations Relief and Rehabilitation Administration, Food and Agriculture Organisation of the United Nations (FAO), International Monetary Fund (IMF), International Bank for Reconstruction and Development (IBRD), etc. came into existence one after another.

This was the reflection of the deep recognition among individual countries, stemming from the experience of the World War II, that the promotion of international cooperation is closely related to the preservation of peace. A manifestation of this is the Charter of the United Nations which declares the need to promote social progress and better standards of life in larger freedom, and to employ international machinery for the promotion of the economic and social advancement of all peoples. Thus, the United Nations termed international economic cooperation as equally important as security for the preservation of world peace. Important problems relating to politics and safety are handled by the Security Council, while important economic and social problems are handled by the General Assembly which has the Economic and Social Council and Trusteeship Council. Various specialised international organisations handling international economic and social problems function in close cooperation with the Economic and Social Council. Among the specialised organisations of this kind are International Finance Corporation, International Development Association, IMF, F AO, ILO, ITU, ICAO, International Atomic Energy Agency and so on. In this way, international cooperation in the economic field made rapid progress after the World War II, with the formation of a variety of international organisations which now function under the auspices of the United Nations.

(iii) Emergence of Financial International Organisations IMF and IBRD :-Most important among the international economic organisations formed after the World War II are IBRD (World Bank), IMF, GATT (General Agreement on Tariffs and Trade). IMF and IBRD were established on the basis of the Bretton Woods Agreement concluded at an allied currency conference held in 1944, while the International Trade Organisation (ITO) was formed on the basis of the International Trade Charter adopted at an international trade and employment conference held in 1947. The objectives of these three organisations closely related with problems of international currency, international finance and international trade were to ensure cooperative development of the international economy after the end of the World War II.

The IMF started functioning in March, 1947 with the aim of promoting currency stability and assisting member countries to service temporary deficits in their international current accounts. IBRD began functioning in June, 1946 with the prime objective of providing long term loans to member countries for reconstruction and development of production facilities and resources. ITO, however, did *not* materialise because the United States refused to ratify the International Trade Charter. As a substitute for ITO, 23 countries which took part in drafting the International Trade Charter signed the GATT in October, 1947.

(iv)Regional International Economic Organisations:- Besides the international organisations under the United Nations, there also appeared various regional international economic organisations. A representative example is the European Economic Community. Other organisations include the Latin American Free Trade Association (LAFT A), the Central American Common Market (CACM) and the East Africa Common Market (EACM). The Association of South East Asian Nations (ASEAN) is now taking shape as a regional economic organisation.

(3) LIMITATION TO FUNCTIONS OF INTERNATIONAL ECONOMIC ORGANISATIONS

As the political and military confrontation which ensued after the World War II in the form of the cold war between the East and West and the struggle for independence of colonies became more serious, international economic cooperative organisations began to reveal their limitations. The international cooperative organisations mentioned above, oblige member countries to perform their duties within the scope of the respective agreements. But even the Economic and Social Council does not have any binding power over the member countries, and its activities are limited to study, research and making recommendations. As the clash of interests among individual countries becomes more serious, each country has tried to make use of organisations for international cooperation for its own ends, thereby preventing the formation of really effective international organisations. In the 1960's, an increasing number of Asian and African colonies gained their independence, and the number of the Third World countries increased. These countries began to raise increasingly strong voices of criticism that the specialised organisations under the United Nations paid less attention to the benefits of the developing countries. They thus demanded the establishment of an international economic organisation which will give priority to the problems relating to the developing countries. The world economy after the World War II expanded rapidly along the principles of freedom, non-discrimination and multilateralism under the leadership of the United States. This was the free economy system based on the theories of free trade and international division of labour. In the early stage, there inevitably existed the vestiges of the colonial economic system. There was indeed a system for international economic cooperation, but this system was more for the benefit of the industrially advanced countries. Consequently, the disparity between the industrially advanced countries and the Third World countries tended to expand further.

4. NECESSITY OF NEW INTERNATIONAL ECONOMIC ORDER FROM STANDPOINT OF THE THIRD WORLD

In order to understand the inevitability of the demands by the Third World countries for the establishment of a NIEO, let us follow the process of their efforts under the Bretton Woods system. From around the middle of the 1950's, the developing countries carried out a policy of promoting their industrialisation through assistance from foreign countries rather than through foreign trade, but this policy ended in failure. At the first United Nations Conference on Trade and Development, the developing countries sought foreign trade rather than assistance and shifted emphasis toward promotion of their own industrialisation through increasing exports. Some of them succeeded in their new policy, but most other countries suffered setbacks. At the second UNCTAD, they sought both assistance and trade. They then realised that economic development needs both capital and technology, and began to welcome direct investments which bring about capital and technology at the same time. Free entry of foreign capital, however, could eventually lead to control of domestic industry by foreign capital. Thus, the developing countries found they had to place restrictions on direct foreign investments and multinational corpo· rations. They also tried to expand their trade through economic cooperation among themselves, but this attempt, too, ended in failure. The only results of their efforts were the widening of the gap between the North and South and an accumulation of debts to the industrially advanced countries. In view of these developments, they realised that it is impossible for them to achieve political and economic independence, equality with the industrially advanced countries, and fair distribution of profits under the existing international economic system, and began to demand the revision of the existing system. This is the background factor behind the Third World's demand for the NIEO.

It may be true that such a movement was stimulated to some extent by the successful strategy of OPEC, but there were undeniably some circumstances which urged them to resort to political settlement in order to solve their accumulated economic problems.

5. SUBSTANCE OF NEW INTERNATIONAL ECONOMIC ORDER

As stated above, the developing countries demanded the expansion of assistance and trade after the 1960's so as to rectify the disparity between the North and South. Specifically, they sought preferential treatment and opening of markets in the field of foreign trade. Against a background of the growth of this new resources nationalism, they found it absolutely necessary to reform the international economic system in order to solve the problems between the North and South. They made it clear that they would use their natural resources and their solidarity as weapons in the struggle to that end. Thus, as time wore on from the 1960's to the 1970's, the focus of the North-South problems changed toward a demand for reformation of the modern international economic system. The Third World adopted the Dakar Declaration in February, 1975 and the Lima Declaration in March, 1975,following the New International Economic Order Declaration and the Charter of Economic Rights and Duties of States in December, 1974.

The main points of the NIEO as demanded by the Third World are as follows:

(a) The existing international economic order which exists solely for the benefit of the industrially advanced countries must be abolished.

(b) The Third World should be granted their justified rights and establish sovereignty in the field of the international economy using their natural resources and solidarity as the main weapons.

(c) The existing international trade structure based on neo-colonialism must be replaced by a new international economic order based on the principles of justice and fairness. In order to reform the free trade system after the war, the developing countries should intervene in, and regulate the markets for primary products and, thereby, organise the markets. This would be the best method of solving the North-South problems.

(d) The Third World is determined to claim the principle of permanent sovereignty over. natural resources. This is based on the concept that the natural resources of the developing countries are essential for economic development and should be used for a long period in a planned way for the economic development of the developing countries themselves. This concept originates in the resources nationalism which takes the position that the countries possessing natural resources should regain control from huge multinational corporations which now command control over the entire aspects of development, production and distribution of natural resources, and they should make the decision on production and pricing of natural resources.

(e) The Third World should form producer cartels with respect to copper, bauxite, mercury and iron ore, following the pattern of the Arab oil products. In view of the worsening economic conditions on the part of the non-oil-producing developing countries and the decline in market prices of primary products since the oil crisis, international buffer stocks of primary products should be established, and countries possessing natural resources should be allowed to intervene in the pricing mechanism and regulate the markets.

The above-mentioned concepts, that is, the principle of permanent sovereignty over natural resources, restrictions on multinational corporations and direct investments, formation of producer cartels based on their solidarity, and market control and its reorganisation, represent a firm rejection of the conventional capitalistic market principle. The capitalistic market mechanism and market principle may admittedly bring about an expansion in the disparity between the North and South, but it is still questionable whether the denial by the NIEO of the free market principle will really help develop the economies of the developing countries without causing any friction.

6. CRITICAL EXAMINATION OF NEW INTERNATIONAL ECONOMIC ORDER

The industrially advanced countries are not willing to readily admit the concept of the NIEO. Some economists are of the view that such an idea is not acceptable in itself from the standpoint of international economic theories. Will an idea that is scientifically unacceptable be able to survive the current of history? This makes it necessary to critically analyse the concept of the NIEO.

Following are some important views about the proposed NIEO from the standpoint of economics:

(a) Some economists consider that the NIEO is one of the methods of redistribution of income. They take the stand that the NIEO is acceptable if it serves to foster the income creating ability on the part of the developing countries, but, if not, it can be taken only as a form of intimidation and blackmail by the developing countries against the industrially advanced countries. However, there is no guarantee that redistribution of income in the form of expanded aid and a moratorium of debts will help strengthen the income creating ability of the developing countries. Even if it is urgently necessary to settle debts for some specific countries, the economists in this group hold, the concept of a new international economic order will not conform with economic theories unless the developing countries with accumulated debts show some positive attitude toward solving the problem. As long as the developing countries make no efforts, income redistribution forming the core of the NIEO will become no more effective than an international social security system or a price support system, and can hardly help the developing countries to promote their own economic development. The greatest defect of the NIEO, they argue, is that the developing countries have failed to present a detailed and convincing schedule of how they can strengthen their income creating ability, while demanding a redistribution of income. According to them, it is highly questionable whether the denial of the existing market mechanism by the NIEO will help develop the economies of the developing countries without any frictions. They also point out that the NIEO requires the developing countries to reform their own policies through their own self-help efforts on the one hand, and for the industrially advanced countries to revise their economic policies so as to adapt the free trade system to the NIEO, on the other hand.

(b) Some other economists take the view that the aim of the NIEO is to ensure equality, and it is a little harsh to connect the new idea directly with income creating ability. It is well-known, they say, that the market pricing mechanism does not necessarily guarantee equality. To say that the essence of economic development under the NIEO lies in the self-help efforts on the part of the developing countries tends to ignore the viewpoints of the development of events leading to the birth of the concept of the NIEO and its true aims. The developing countries actually made efforts in the past in accordance with the guidance of the industrially advanced countries. Sometimes they asked for more aid. Sometimes they tried to step up their exports.

Sometimes they welcomed direct foreign investments. The end result, however, was a widening of the disparity between the North and South and an accumulation of their debts. It is only natural, they say, that the developing countries should no longer sit silent if they are simply asked to make self-help efforts alone.

(c) Still other economists are of the opinion that the developments leading up to the NIEO should not be taken from the viewpoint of the conventional economics alone. They say that there are still many problems left unsolved with respect to future global industry distribution under the NIEO, the division of labour among individual countries, and how the transfer process under the new concept will end. These problems are of an international political and economic nature. The North-South problems should not be approached from the viewpoint of economics alone, but should be studied from the comprehensive viewpoints of world history, politics and international economy as a whole. An attempt will inevitably have to be made to change the world system toward the concept of the NIEO.

NIEO CONSTRAINTS AND CHALLENGES

NIEO does not pay sufficient attention to environmental concerns. This focus on the environment is vital since growth that ignores environmental costs is not sustainable.

Achieving NIEO requires real shifts of power and privileges in the world order, which will have serious political implications. It must be kept in mind however, that economic development does not necessarily guarantee for human development.

What the Third World, or at least the driving element among the nonaligned, meant by a new international order was very different. Revision of the international division of labor along the lines described was intended to accompany and implement the establishment of a self-reliant industrial national economy.

The strengthening of the national state and the active role of state policy were, in this strategy, to ensure that industry was not made up of discrete fragments, but of every stage of the production process. The resort to importation of the ingredients of these production lines (the purchase of turnkey factories) entailed a high level of exports, whether of 'traditional' raw materials or new industrial products. Hence the success of the strategies was largely dependent on the capacity to win concessions, which was in turn the program for the new international economic order.

The conflict of these two 'interpretations' of the new order has appeared in all the negotiations on the industrial international division of labor and relocation. The points of discussion were the character and options of establishment, the degree of decentralised decision-making, and the methods of financing the transfers, issues of personnel training and management, and access to external markets. The Third World states generally pressed for: the establishment of as complete industries as possible, with upstream and downstream links, agreed rules subjecting the management of industrial units to the state's industrial policy, an option for management of units by local staff, access to international distribution networks for manufactured goods to localised firms (as the lowering of protectionist barriers by the developed countries was not regarded as a sufficient guarantee of access to these markets), support for national technological research, regulated financing (to avoid, for example, a subsidiary of a multinational financing its investment by calling on local banking sources without bringing in new capital), regulation of transfers (a sharing of risks, ceilings on exportable profits, obligations to invest part of the profit in the national economy) and so on.

These demands were regarded as unacceptable by the multinationals whose sole interest was in partial relocation through subsidiaries under their virtual control.

Gradually, most of the Third World states have had to come to terms with the redeployment strategy. The only states in a position to negotiate are those that refuse the direct establishment of subsidiaries and seek an alternative in the purchase of turnkey factories within the framework of their overall industrialisation policy.

The strategy of these states counted on the possibility of successful change of the international order through unilateral joint action, and through further action from North-South collective negotiations. The idea, it should be remembered, was to organise cartels of Third World producers who could insist on price revisions for raw materials. National control over natural resources should allow scope for negotiation not only on supply, but also and above all on exploitation of the resources that took into account long-term national interests and halted the rates of exploitation governed entirely by the needs of the developed world.

With this new-found strength, the Third World countries hoped to enjoy a genuine negotiating power that would oblige the North to make concessions: for instance, access to its markets, a code of conduct for transfers of technology. Co-operation between Third World countries ('collective self-reliance') was part of this bid for strength.

This is the essential context for discussing the use of oil surpluses. On some views the NIEO was to be no more than the rise in oil prices alone and the relocation of export industry a minor operation. On this view the oil revenue surpluses should be made available to the developed financial markets to supply their own policies of intervention in relations between developed countries, and marginal support for the 'survival' of the old international division of labor in the developing countries. This rescued the attitude of 'aid' as a permanent safety-valve ensuring the perpetuation of a system that was increasingly unjust day by day. The actual use of oil surpluses has in fact served this purpose.

In the mid-1970s there was still the hope that the Third World would reject this narrow view. The nonaligned movement and the group of 77 were seeking a strategy for collective battle for across the board increases in raw materials prices, as the resolution on the solidarity fund and producers associations taken at Dakar in February 1977 showed. This strong and valid approach was not sustained. Under the pressure of the developed countries and the bias of UNCTAD and endless 'negotiation' and 'dialogue', the 'stabilisation' fund strategy replaced that of producers associations for collective unilateral intervention where such was required.

QUESTIONS

1. The basic spirit of the NIEO is outlined in the "Declaration and Programme of Action" and Charter of Economic Rights and Duties of States. Describe the United Nations declaration of NIEO?
2. The New International Economic Order Declaration is a challenge to the existing international economic order. What then is the existing international economic order? Examine the historical perspective of NIEO with the context of IEO SUBSYSTEMS
3. Examine the role of IMF and IBRD in the establishment of New International economic order with special reference to Bretton woods agreement?
4. What are the basic reasons for increasing disparity between the industrially advanced countries and the Third World countries ?
5. What were the main points of the NIEO as demanded by the Third World in the Dakar Declaration in February in 1975?
6. The industrially advanced countries are not willing to readily admit the concept of the NIEO. Some economists are of the view that such an idea is not acceptable in itself from the standpoint of international economic theories. Will an idea that is scientifically unacceptable be able to survive the current of history?
7. Discuss NIEO basic constraints and challenges in maintaining international relations?

CHAPTER 12

New International Economic Order and International Law

INTRODUCTION

The NIEO is not only a challenge to the old international economic order but also a challenge to the traditional international law as well as international economic laws. Specifically speaking, what points of modern international law is the NIEO challenging?

(i) Characteristics of Modern International Law:-

(i) Throughout the 18th and 19th centuries, Western European countries became modern nations through their awareness of national sovereignty founded on racial unity. They adopted the form of a constitutional state with government based on the principles of independent legislative, executive and judicial powers. Furthermore, they built up capitalism as their economic system based on the principles of private ownership and freedom of contract. Modern international law (hereinafter referred to as "the law"), therefore, was a legal system upheld by modern states which were supported by the aforementioned awareness of national sovereignty. Again, modern international society which supported "the law" was formed by modern European nations with a common social foundation. Accordingly, this international society was stamped with the mark of the European heritage, Christianity and capitalism.

(ii) The second characteristic of "the law" was that it was tied closely to modern colonialism from the beginning. Among nations comprising European populaces only, it was believed that all Europeans possessed equal rights and duties since they were mutual equals. Non-Europeans and non-Christians, however, were not recognised as equal human beings with the right of the protection of the international law. Europeans regarded the land on which non-Europeans lived as "unclaimed land" and based on the legal logic of "prior occupation", therefore these territories became the target of colonisation. The expropriated colonies were exploited wholly for the benefit of the colonizing countries through the plundering of resources, harsh treatment of the natives bordering on slavery and exploitative business management. It is said that "the law" was established as a tool to justify these ends. This is the aspect of colonialism found in "the law."

(iii) The third characteristic of "the law" is that it is a law of nations and a manifestation of national sovereignty founded on the modern concept of sovereign power. Since the concept of sovereignty was a theory to justify the concentration of power in the hands of modern nations, no international machinery was set up to pass judgement on any violations of the international law and, consequently, no organ to apply sanctions against offenders were established.

As noted from the foregoing, "the law" was a manifestation of the policy of the strong and advanced nations to acquire new territories and conduct international transactions. It did not function as a law to protect the weak. If the mutual restrictions which bind the strong can be prescribed as the "merkmal" of law, it is doubtful whether "the law" can be called an international law.

(ii) Challenge to Modern International Law

The challenge to "the law" originated in the resistance against the aforementioned three characteristics of "the law."

(a) The first opponent appeared in the form of socialism. The new socialist nation, Russia, born after the World War I, rejected the principles of capitalism and liberalism contained in the law and opposed it by introducing altogether foreign elements into the international society. This socialist State was established as a result of the opposition to the principles of liberalism and capitalism as well as their off. shoot, imperialism. Accordingly, it emerged as a doctrine which rejected the principles of liberalism and constitutional government embodied in the law. In other words, the international law of socialist States prescribes that the existing international law is a bourgeois law and a tentative legal system to remain in effect only during the transition from capitalism to socialism. That is, territorial acquisition through prior occupation, prescription, cession, and conquest etc. are rejected on the grounds that these are the principles of imperialism.

Conversely, self-determination of peoples is emphasised as a right incorporated in the international law. Furthermore, the recognition of national sovereignty, inviolability of territory, equal rights of nations, and non· intervention are stressed as democratic principles and any restrictions imposed on or abolishment of sovereign power are opposed.

Since the World War II, the number of socialist countries emphasizing the above doctrine has increased greatly and the trend to reject "the law" is growing stronger.

(b) After the World War II, the peoples living in the vast regions of Asia and Africa who had been satisfied by wholly playing subservient role under the international law became independent and joined the international society as legal entities (persons) on an equal footing with their former European rulers. Their independence was won as a result of the battle against the traits of colonialism found in the law.

(c) In short, this means that socialist and developing countries have challenged the law, which possesses the characteristics of liberalism and capitalism as well as the tendency to recognise only Christian nations practicing colonialism as equitable and legal entities, and are gradually achieving their goals. After the oil crisis, specifically, this challenge of the developing nations against the existing international legal order became stronger as they were inspired by the oil strategy of the Arab countries and they began to employ their solidarity and natural resources as weapons. Judging from the demands and aspirations of developing nations which won their independence and became a majority in the United Nations,it can be said that the international society has now reached a worldwide scale in the true sense of the word.

(iii) United Nations as a Place for the Development of the NIEO

Along with the internationalisation and wider expansion of the world economy, the international law has clearly emerged as a law of the international society. It first appeared as a world-wide organisation in the form of the League of Nations. In the era of the United Nations, the organisation was further consolidated and separated into the

organ for maintenance of peace (Security Council) and the organ for the economic and social development. Even in the United Nations, however, many systems were established which functioned advantageously for advanced nations at the outset. Since 1960, when the majority of the A nations won their independence, the situation has gradually changed.

By relying on the UNCT AD and other organs of the United Nations which operate on the "one vote, one nation principle", these countries began to fight for the rights of developing nations. Thus, the law which was established as a legal system of advanced countries is being forced to undergo a significant change.

(iv) Impact the NIEO against the International Law

The new nations consisting of the group of AA countries which won their independence in the 1960's wielded a serious impact on the existing international legal order. This is because they began to act in concert to confront colonialism, to abolish racial discrimination, and to demand the closing of the economic gap between the nations of the

North and South. They also began to fight for their aims in cooperation with socialist States. It was inevitable, therefore, that these new forces should have influenced the existing international law. At this point, a study will be attempted confined to the impact on several fundamental principles of the international law.

(a) Impact on the Concept of National Sovereignty

Under the NIEO, the concept of sovereignty of the modern state developed along the lines of permanent sovereignty over wealth and natural resources (1962). That is, the natural resources of developing countries were valuable assets in their economic development and should be utilised for the economic developing of the owner country based on long-term planning (the Declaration and Programme of Action on the Establishment of a New International Economic Order, 1974).This belief in permanent sovereignty over wealth and natural resources developed parallel with the concept that restrictions should be placed on giant foreign multinational enterprises which exercised control over all aspects of the development, production and distribution stages of natural resources, and that the right to control these development activities should be returned to the nations which own the natural resources so that they can make their own decisions on production and prices.

(b) Principle of Self-Determination

The anti-colonialist nations, which had already won their independence, assisted other peoples in the remaining colonies to achieve their political freedom based on the principle of the traditional (national) self-determination. 1960 was acclaimed as the "year of Africa" in view of the impressive results achieved in this field (17 new nations joined the United Nations in this year). It was in the same year (1960) that the "Declaration on Granting Independence to Colonies" which confirmed the rights of self-determination, was adopted by the United Nations General Assembly. The NIEO was effective in promoting the application of the self-determination principle to natural resources and international economic issues.

(c) Criticisms against the Binding Power of Traditional International Legislation

As a result of the independence won by AA countries, the weight of influence among the constituent groups of the United Nations was reversed. Today, the AA countries are the largest of the main groupings in the United Nations. By becoming members of the

international society, the AA countries are demanding the revision of the traditional international law by raising questions as to why they should be automatically bound by the international law which functions to their disadvantage and which they did not participate in forming. In regard to the international economic order, they cast serious doubts on the basis for the existence of the old international law. In addition, they have made new declarations and demands in succession in order to achieve a new international economic order.

(d) Impact on the Theory of National Obligation

Supported by the theory of "permanent sovereignty over wealth and natural. resources" and the principle of "self-determination", many AA States which had achieved independence, expropriated or nationalised foreign property in their countries (e_ g., the nationalisation of the petroleum industry by Iran, similar measures taken by Indonesia and Cuba, the nationalisation of the Suez Canal by the Egyptian government). The international legal theory on national obligations covers a wide field of which the conflict of opinions between the advanced and developing countries regarding nationalisation is notable. For example, in regard to the pros and cons on the need for suitable compensation, the NIEO is demanding the revision of the traditional international law in respect to national obligations. This is because if the traditional international law is maintained, it will result in protecting the assets plundered from the former colonies.-

As to national obligations, this is a serious issue confronting new States in terms of overseas investments, especially, in connection with attracting foreign investments to their countries in the future. If they insist on alleviation of their national obligations, investments from advanced nations for economic development cannot be expected and the necessary capital and technology required by new States cannot be obtained. As a result, the NIEO is forcing a change in the concept of overseas investments as they are conducted today. That is, overseas investments should be made on the understanding that the economic development of lesser developed countries will eventually work to the advantage of the entire international society. In other words, foreign investments should be provided in the form of international aid until the lesser developed countries are able to function as independent participants in the international economic market. Therefore, an Investment guarantee system on a national or international basic should be set up to promote private overseas investments.

QUESTIONS

1. Discuss the three major characteristics of Modern International Law? Later Examine how these characteristics prove to big challenge for NIEO?
2. Examine the impact of NIEO against the international law?

CHAPTER 13

Non Alignment Movement – Historical Perspective

INTRODUCTION: MEANING AND NATURE

Non alignment has been regarded as the most important feature of Indian foreign policy . Non alignment aimed at maintaining national independence in foreign affairs by not joining any of the two military alliances formed by USA and soviet Union. Non alignment was neither neutrality nor non involvement nor isolationism . It was a dynamic concept which meant not committing to any military bloc but taking an independent stand on international issues according to the merits of each case. The policy of non alignment won many supporters in the developing countries as it is provided an opportunity to them for protecting their sovereignty as also retaining their freedom of action during the tension ridden cold war period. India as the prime architect of non-alignment and as one of the leading members of the non-aligned movement has taken an active part in its growth. The Non-aligned movement is providing all member states regardless of size and importance an opportunity to participate in global decision making and world politics.

ORIGINS

The Non-Aligned movement was never established as a formal organisation, but became the name to refer to the participants of the *Conference of Heads of State or Government of Non-Aligned Countries* first held in 1961. The term "non-alignment" itself was coined by V.K. Krishna Menon in 1953 remarks at the United Nations. Menon's friend, Animesh Aggrawal used the phrase in a 1954 speech in Colombo, Sri Lanka. In his speech in Colombo, Nehru described the five pillars to be used as a guide for Sino-Indian relations, which were first put forth by Chinese Premier Zhou Enlai. Called Panchsheel (five restraints), these principles would later serve as the basis of the Non-Aligned Movement. The five principles were:

- Mutual respect for each other's territorial integrity and sovereignty
- Mutual non-aggression
- Mutual non-interference in domestic affairs
- Equality and mutual benefit

- Peaceful co-existence

A significant milestone in the development of the Non-Aligned Movement was the 1955 Bandung Conference, a conference of Asian and African states hosted by Indonesian president Sukarno, who gave a significant contribution to promote this movement. Bringing together Sukarno, U Nu, Nasser, Nehru, Tito, Nkrumah and Menon with the likes of Ho Chi Minh, Zhou Enlai, and Norodom Sihanouk, as well as U Thant and a young Indira Gandhi, the conference adopted a "declaration on promotion of world peace and cooperation", which included Nehru's five principles, and a collective pledge to remain neutral in the Cold War. Six years after Bandung, an initiative of Yugoslav president Josip Broz Tito led to the first *Conference of Heads of State or Government of Non-Aligned Countries*, which was held in September 1961 in Belgrade. The term *non aligned movement* appears first in the fifth conference in 1976, where participating countries are denoted as *members of the movement*.

At the Lusaka Conference in September 1970, the member nations added as aims of the movement the peaceful resolution of disputes and the abstention from the big power military alliances and pacts. Another added aim was opposition to stationing of military bases in foreign countries.[6]

The founding fathers of the Non-aligned movement ere: Sukarno of Indonesia, Jawaharlal Nehru of India, Josip Broz Tito of Yugoslavia, Gamal Abdul asser of Egypt and Kwame Nkrumah of Ghana. Their actions were known as 'The Initiative of Five'.

The criteria of NAM membership were as follows:

1. The country should have adopted an independent policy based on the coexistence of States with different political and social systems and on non-alignment or should be showing a trend in favor of such a policy.
2. The country concerned should be consistently supporting the Movements for National Independence.
3. The country should not be a member of a multilateral military alliance concluded in the context of Great Power conflicts.
4. If a country has a bilateral military agreement with a Great Power, or is a member of a regional defense pact, the agreement or pact should not be one deliberately concluded in the context of Great Power conflicts.
5. If it has conceded military bases to a Foreign Power the concession should not have been made in the context of Great Power conflicts

HISTORICAL PERSPECTIVE

The Non-Aligned Movement (NAM) was created and founded during the collapse of the colonial system and the independence struggles of the peoples of Africa, Asia, Latin America and other regions of the world and at the height of the Cold War. During the early days of the Movement, its actions were a key factor in the decolonisation process, which led later to the attainment of freedom and independence by many countries and peoples and to the founding of tens of new sovereign States. Throughout its history, the Movement of Non-Aligned Countries has played a fundamental role in the preservation of world peace and security.

While some meetings with a third-world perspective were held before 1955, historians consider that the Bandung Asian-African Conference is the most immediate antecedent to the creation of the Non-Aligned Movement. This Conference was held in Bandung on April 18-24, 1955 and gathered 29 Heads of States belonging to the first post-colonial generation of leaders from the two continents with the aim of identifying and assessing world issues at the time and pursuing out joint policies in international relations.

The principles that would govern relations among large and small nations, known as the "Ten Principles of Bandung", were proclaimed at that Conference. Such principles were adopted later as the main goals and objectives of the policy of non-alignment. The fulfillment of those principles became the essential criterion for Non-Aligned Movement membership; it is what was known as the "quintessence of the Movement" until the early 1990s.

In 1960, in the light of the results achieved in Bandung, the creation of the Movement of Non-Aligned Countries was given a decisive boost during the Fifteenth Ordinary Session of the United Nations General Assembly, during which 17 new African and Asian countries were admitted. A key role was played in this process by the then Heads of State and Government Gamal Abdel Nasser of Egypt, Kwame Nkrumah of Ghana, Shri Jawaharlal Nehru of India, Ahmed Sukarno of Indonesia and Josip Broz Tito of Yugoslavia, who later became the founding fathers of the movement and its emblematic leaders.

Six years after Bandung, the Movement of Non-Aligned Countries was founded on a wider geographical basis at the First Summit Conference of Belgrade, which was held on September 1-6, 1961. The Conference was attended by 25 countries: Afghanistan, Algeria, Yemen, Myanmar, Cambodia, Srilanka, Congo, Cuba, Cyprus, Egypt, Ethiopia, Ghana, Guinea, India, Indonesia, Iraq, Lebanon, Mali, Morocco, Nepal, Saudi Arabia, Somalia, Sudan, Syria, Tunisia, Yugoslavia.

The Founders of NAM have preferred to declare it as a movement but not an organisation in order to avoid bureaucratic implications of the latter.

The membership criteria formulated during the Preparatory Conference to the Belgrade Summit (Cairo, 1961) show that the Movement was not conceived to play a passive role in international politics but to formulate its own positions in an independent manner so as to reflect the interests of its members.

Thus, the primary of objectives of the non-aligned countries focused on the support of self-determination, national independence and the sovereignty and territorial integrity of States; opposition to apartheid; non-adherence to multilateral military pacts and the independence of non-aligned countries from great power or block influences and rivalries; the struggle against imperialism in all its forms and manifestations; the struggle against colonialism, neocolonialism, racism, foreign occupation and domination; disarmament; non-interference into the internal affairs of States and peaceful coexistence among all nations; rejection of the use or threat of use of force in international relations; the strengthening of the United Nations; the democratisation of international relations; socioeconomic development and the restructuring of the international economic system; as well as international cooperation on an equal footing.

Since its inception, the Movement of Non-Aligned Countries has waged a ceaseless battle to ensure that peoples being oppressed by foreign occupation and domination can exercise their inalienable right to self-determination and independence.

During the 1970s and 1980s, the Movement of Non-Aligned Countries played a key role in the struggle for the establishment of a new international economic order that allowed all the peoples of the world to make use of their wealth and natural resources and provided a wide platform for a fundamental change in international economic relations and the economic emancipation of the countries of the South.

During its nearly 50 years of existence, the Movement of Non-Aligned Countries has gathered a growing number of States and liberation movements which, in spite of their ideological, political, economic, social and cultural diversity, have accepted its founding principles and primary objectives and shown their readiness to realise them. Historically, the non-aligned countries have shown their ability to overcome their differences and found a common ground for action that leads to mutual cooperation and the upholding of their shared values.

The ten principles of Bandung

1. Respect of fundamental human rights and of the objectives and principles of the Charter of the United Nations.
2. Respect of the sovereignty and territorial integrity of all nations.
3. Recognition of the equality among all races and of the equality among all nations, both large and small.
4. Non-intervention or non-interference into the internal affairs of another -country.
5. Respect of the right of every nation to defend itself, either individually or collectively, in conformity with the Charter of the United Nations.
6. A. Non-use of collective defence pacts to benefit the specific interests of any of the great powers. B. Non-use of pressures by any country against other countries.
7. Refraining from carrying out or threatening to carry out aggression, or from using force against the territorial integrity or political independence of any country.
8. Peaceful solution of all international conflicts in conformity with the Charter of the United Nations.
9. Promotion of mutual interests and of cooperation.
10. Respect of justice and of international obligations.

IDEOLOGY OF NAM

Secretaries General of the NAM had included such diverse figures as Suharto, a corrupt and militaristic anti-communist, and Nelson Mandela, a democratic socialist and famous anti-apartheid activist. Consisting of many governments with vastly different ideologies, the Non-Aligned Movement is unified by its commitment to world peace and security. At the seventh summit held in New Delhi in March 1983, the movement described itself as "history's biggest peace movement". The movement places equal emphasis on disarmament. NAM's commitment to peace pre-dates its formal institutionalisation in 1961. The Brioni meeting between heads of governments of India, Egypt and Yugoslavia in 1956 recognised that there exists a vital link between struggle for peace and endeavours for disarmament.

During the 1970s and early 1980s, the NAM also sponsored campaigns for restructuring commercial relations between developed and developing nations, namely the New International Economic Order (NIEO), and its cultural offspring, the New World Information and Communication Order (NWICO). The latter, on its own, sparked a Non-Aligned initiative on cooperation for communications, the Non-Aligned News Agencies Pool, created in 1975 and later converted into the NAM News Network in 2005.

The Non-Aligned Movement espouses policies and practices of cooperation, especially those that are multi-lateral and provide mutual benefit to all those involved. Many of the members of the Non-Aligned Movement are also members of the United Nations. Both organisations have a stated policy of peaceful cooperation, yet the successes the NAM has had with multilateral agreements tend to be ignored by the larger, western and developed nation dominated UN. African concerns about apartheid were linked with Arab-Asian concerns about Palestine and multilateral cooperation in these areas has enjoyed moderate success. The Non-Aligned Movement has played a major role in various ideological conflicts throughout its existence, including extreme opposition to apartheid governments and support of guerrilla movements in various locations, including Rhodesia and South Africa.[5] The Non-Aligned Movement has become a voice of support for issues facing developing nations and it still contains ideals that are legitimate within this context.

Evolution

The creation and strengthening of the socialist block after the defeat of fascism in World War II, the collapse of colonial empires, the emergence of a bipolar world and the formation of two military blocks (NATO and the Warsaw Pact) brought about a new international context that led to the necessity of multi-lateral coordination between the countries of the South .

In this context, the underdeveloped countries, most of them in Asia and Africa, felt the need to join efforts for the common defence of their interests, the strengthening of their independence and sovereignty and the cultural and economic revival or salvation of their peoples, and also to express a strong commitment with peace by declaring themselves as "non-aligned" from either of the two nascent military blocks.

In order to fulfill the aims of debating on and advancing a strategy designed to achieve such objectives, the Bandung Asian-African Conference was held in Indonesia in April 1955. It was attended by 29 Heads of State and Government of the first post-colonial generation of leaders and its expressed goal was to identify and assess world issues at the time and coordinate policies to deal with them.

Although the Asian and African leaders who gathered in Bandung might have had differing political and ideological views or different approaches towards the societies they aspired to build or rebuild, there was a common project that united them and gave sense to a closer coordination of positions. Their shared program included the political decolonisation of Asia and Africa. Moreover, they all agreed that the recently attained political independence was just a means to attain the goal of economic, social and cultural independence.

The Bandung meeting has been considered as the most immediate antecedent of the founding of the Movement of Non-Aligned Countries, which finally came into being six years later on a wider geographical basis when the First Summit Conference was held in Belgrade on September 1-6, 1961. This gathering was attended by the Heads of State and Government of 25 countries and observers from another three nations.

This First Summit of the Movement of Non-Aligned Countries was convened by the leaders of India, Indonesia, Egypt, Syria and Yugoslavia. On April 26, 1961, the Presidents of the Arab Republic of Egypt (Nasser) and Yugoslavia (Tito) addressed the Heads of State and Government of 21 "non-Aligned" countries and suggested that, taking recent world events and the rise of international tensions into account, a Conference should be held to promote an improvement in international relations, a resistance to policies of force and a constructive settlement of conflicts and other issues of concern in the world.

The Movement played an important role in the support of nations which were struggling then for their independence in the Third World and showed great solidarity with the most just aspirations of humanity. It contributed indisputably to the triumph in the struggle for national independence and decolonisation, thus gaining considerable diplomatic prestige.

As one Summit after another was held in the 1960s and 1970s, "non alignment", turned already into the "Movement of Non-Aligned Countries" that included nearly all Asian and African countries, was becoming a forum of coordination to struggle for the respect of the economic and political rights of the developing world. After the attainment of independence, the Conferences expressed a growing concern over economic and social issues as well as over strictly political matters.

Something that attested to that was the launching at the Algiers Conference in 1973 of the concept of a "new international economic order." By the end of the 1980s, the Movement was facing the great challenge brought about by the collapse of the socialist block. The end of the clash between the two antagonistic blocks that was the reason for its existence, name and essence was seen by some as the beginning of the end for the Movement of Non-Aligned Countries.

The Movement of Non-Aligned Countries could not spare itself difficulties to act effectively in an adverse international political situation marked by hegemonic positions and unipolarity as well as by internal difficulties and conflicts given the heterogeneity of its membership and, thus, its diverse interests. Nevertheless, and in spite of such set-backs, the principles and objectives of non-alignment retain their full validity and force at the present international juncture. The primary condition that led to the emergence of the Movement of Non-Aligned Countries, that is, non-alignment from antagonistic blocks, has not lost its validity with the end of the Cold War. The demise of one of the blocks has not done away with the pressing problems of the world. On the contrary, renewed strategic interests bent on domination grow stronger and, even, acquire new and more dangerous dimensions for underdeveloped countries.

During the 14th Summit of the Non-Aligned Movement in Havana, Cuba in September 2006, the Heads of States and Governments of the member countries reaffirmed their commitment to the ideals, principles and purposes upon which the movement was founded and with the principles and purposes enshrined in the United Nations Charter.

The Heads of States and Governments stated their firm belief that the absence of two conflicting blocs in no way reduces the need to strengthen the movement as a mechanism for the political coordination of developing countries. In this regard they acknowledged that it remains imperative to strengthen and revitalise the movement. To do so, they agreed to strengthen concrete action, unity and solidarity between all its members, based on respect for diversity, factors which are essential for the reaffirmation of the identity and capacity of the movement to influence International relations.

They also stressed the need to promote actively a leading role for the movement in the coordination of efforts among member states in tackling global threats.

NAM -14 TH SUMMIT IN HAVANA (Purposes & Principles)

Inspired by the principles and purposes which were brought to the Non-Aligned Movement by the Bandung principles and during the First NAM Summit in Belgrade in 1961, the Heads of States and Governments of the member countries of the Non-Aligned Movement adopted in their 14th Summit in Havana the following purposes and principles of the movement in the present International juncture:

I. Purposes

a. To promote and reinforce multilateralism and, in this regard, strengthen the central role that the United Nations must play.

b. To serve as a forum of political coordination of the developing countries to promote and defend their common interests in the system of international relations

c. To promote unity, solidarity and cooperation between developing countries based on shared values and priorities agreed upon by consensus.

d. To defend international peace and security and settle all international disputes by peaceful means in accordance with the principles and the purposes of the UN Charter and International Law.

e. To encourage relations of friendship and cooperation between all nations based on the principles of International Law, particularly those enshrined in the Charter of the United Nations.

f. To promote and encourage sustainable development through international cooperation and, to that end, jointly coordinate the implementation of political strategies which strengthen and ensure the full participation of all countries, rich and poor, in the international economic relations, under equal conditions and opportunities but with differentiated responsibilities.

g. To encourage the respect, enjoyment and protection of all human rights and fundamental freedoms for all, on the basis of the principles of universality, objectivity, impartiality and non-selectivity, avoiding politicisation of human rights issues, thus ensuring that all human rights of individuals and peoples, including the right to development, are promoted and protected in a balanced manner.

h. To promote peaceful coexistence between nations, regardless of their political, social or economic systems.

i. To condemn all manifestations of unilateralism and attempts to exercise hegemonic domination in international relations.

j. To coordinate actions and strategies in order to confront jointly the threats to international peace and security, including the threats of use of force and the acts of aggression, colonialism and foreign occupation, and other breaches of peace caused by any country or group of countries.

k. To promote the strengthening and democratisation of the UN, giving the General Assembly the role granted to it in accordance with the functions and powers outlined in the Charter and to promote the comprehensive reform of the United Nations Security Council so that it may fulfill the role granted to it by the Charter, in a transparent and equitable manner, as the body primarily responsible for maintaining international peace and security.

l. To continue pursuing universal and non-discriminatory nuclear disarmament, as well as a general and complete disarmament under strict and effective international control and in this context, to work towards the objective of arriving at an agreement on a phased program for the complete elimination of nuclear weapons within a specified framework of time to eliminate nuclear weapons, to prohibit their development, production, acquisition, testing, stock-piling, transfer, use or threat of use and to provide for their destruction.

m. To oppose and condemn the categorisation of countries as good or evil based on unilateral and unjustified criteria, and the adoption of a doctrine of pre-emptive attack, including attack by nuclear weapons, which is inconsistent with international law, in particular, the international legally-binding instruments concerning nuclear disarmament and to further condemn and oppose unilateral military actions, or use of force or threat of use of force against the sovereignty, territorial integrity and independence of Non-Aligned countries.

n. To encourage States to conclude agreements freely arrived at, among the States of the regions concerned, to establish new Nuclear Weapons-Free Zones in regions where these do not exist, in accordance with the provisions of the Final Document of the First Special Session of the General Assembly devoted to disarmament (SSOD)1) and the principles adopted by the 1999 UN Disarmament Commission, including the establishment of a Nuclear Weapons Free Zone in the Middle East. The establishment of Nuclear Weapons-Free Zones is a positive step and important measure towards strengthening global nuclear disarmament and non-proliferation.

o. To promote international cooperation in the peaceful uses of nuclear energy and to facilitate access to nuclear technology, equipment and material for peaceful purposes required by developing countries.

p. To promote concrete initiatives of South-South cooperation and strengthen the role of NAM, in coordination with G.77, in the re-launching of North-South cooperation, ensuring the fulfillment of the right to development of our peoples, through the enhancement of international solidarity.

q. To respond to the challenges and to take advantage of the opportunities arising from globalisation and interdependence with creativity and a sense of identity in order to ensure its benefits to all countries, particularly those most affected by underdevelopment and poverty, with a view to gradually reducing the abysmal gap between the developed and developing countries.

r. To enhance the role that civil society, including NGO´s, can play at the regional and international levels in order to promote the purposes, principles and objectives of the Movement.

II. Principles

a. Respect for the principles enshrined in the Charter of the United Nations and International Law.

b. Respect for sovereignty, sovereign equality and territorial integrity of all States.

c. Recognition of the equality of all races, religions, cultures and all nations, both big and small.

d. Promotion of a dialogue among peoples, civilisations, cultures and religions based on the respect of religions, their symbols and values, the promotion and the consolidation of tolerance and freedom of belief.

e. Respect for and promotion of all human rights and fundamental freedoms for all, including the effective implementation of the right of peoples to peace and development.

f. Respect for the equality of rights of States, including the inalienable right of each State to determine freely its political, social, economic and cultural system, without any kind of interference whatsoever from any other State.

g. Reaffirmation of the validity and relevance of the Movement's principled positions concerning the right to self-determination of peoples under foreign occupation and colonial or alien domination.

h. Non-interference in the internal affairs of States. No State or group of States has the right to intervene either directly or indirectly, whatever the motive, in the internal affairs of any other State.

i. Rejection of unconstitutional change of Governments.

j. Rejection of attempts at regime change

k. Condemnation of the use of mercenaries in all situations, especially in conflict situations.

l. Refraining by all countries from exerting pressure or coercion on other countries, including resorting to aggression or other acts involving the use of direct or indirect force, and the application and/or promotion of any coercive unilateral measure that goes against International Law or is in any way incompatible with it, for the purpose of coercing any other State to subordinate its sovereign rights, or to gain any benefit whatsoever.

m. Total rejection of aggression as a dangerous and serious breach of International Law, which entails international responsibility for the aggressor.

n. Respect for the inherent right of individual or collective self-defense, in accordance with the Charter of the United Nations.

o. Condemnation of genocide, war crimes, crimes against humanity and systematic and gross violations of human rights, in accordance with the UN Charter and International Law.

p. Rejection of and opposition to terrorism in all its forms and manifestations, committed by whom so ever, wherever and for whatever purposes, as it constitutes one of the most serious threats to international peace and security. In this context, terrorism should not be equated with the legitimate struggle of peoples under colonial or alien domination and foreign occupation for self-determination and national liberation.

q. Promotion of pacific settlement of disputes and abjuring, under any circumstances, from taking part in coalitions, agreements or any other kind of unilateral coercive initiative in violation of the principles of International Law and the Charter of the United Nations.

r. Defense and consolidation of democracy, reaffirming that democracy is a universal value based on the freely expressed will of people to determine their own political, economic, social, and cultural systems and their full participation in all aspects of their life

s. Promotion and defense of multilateralism and multilateral organisations as the appropriate frameworks to resolve, through dialogue and cooperation, the problems affecting human kind.

t. Support to efforts by the countries suffering internal conflicts to achieve peace, justice, equality and development.

u. The duty of each State to fully and in good faith comply with the international treaties to which it is a party, as well as to honor the commitments made in the framework of international organisations, and to live in peace with other States. v. Peaceful settlement of all international conflicts in accordance with the Charter of the United Nations.

w. Defense and promotion of shared interests, justice and cooperation, regardless of the differences existing in the political, economic and social systems of the States, on the basis of mutual respect and the equality of rights.

x. Solidarity as a fundamental component of relations among nations in all circumstances.

y. Respect for the political, economic, social and cultural diversity of countries and peoples.

The movement has succeeded to create a strong front on the International level, representing countries of the third world in the International organisations on the top of which the United Nations.

CURRENT ACTIVITIES AND POSITIONS

- **Criticism of US policy:** In recent years the organisation has criticised certain aspects of US foreign policy. The US invasion of Iraq and the War on Terrorism, its attempts to stifle Iran and North Korea's nuclear plans, and its other actions have been denounced by some members of the Non-Aligned Movement as attempts to run roughshod over the sovereignty of smaller nations; at the most recent summit, Kim Yong-nam, the head of North Korea's parliament, stated that, "The United States is attempting to deprive other countries of even their legitimate right to peaceful nuclear activities."
- **Self-determination of Puerto Rico:** Since 1961, the organisation has supported the discussion of the case of Puerto Rico's self-determination before the United Nations. A resolution on the matter was to be proposed on the XV Summit by the Hostosian National Independence Movement.
- **Self-determination of Western Sahara:** Since 1973, the group has supported the discussion of the case of Western Sahara's self-determination before the United Nations. The movement re-affirmed in its last meeting (Sharm El Sheikh 2009) the support to the self-determination of the Sahrawi people by choosing between any valid option, welcomed the direct conversations between the parties, and remembered the responsibility of the United Nations on the Sahrawi issue.
- **Sustainable development:** The movement is publicly committed to the tenets of sustainable development and the attainment of the Millennium Development Goals, but it believes that the international community has not created conditions conducive to development and has

infringed upon the right to sovereign development by each member state. Issues such as globalisation, the debt burden, unfair trade practices, the decline in foreign aid, donor conditionality, and the lack of democracy in international financial decision-making are cited as factors inhibiting development.

- **Reforms of the UN:** The movement has been outspoken in its criticism of current UN structures and power dynamics, stating that the organisation has been utilised by powerful states in ways that violate the movement's principles. It has made a number of recommendations that it says would strengthen the representation and power of "non-aligned" states. The proposed UN reforms are also aimed at improving the transparency and democracy of UN decision-making. The UN Security Council is the element it considers the most distorted, undemocratic, and in need of reshaping.
- **South-South cooperation:** The movement has collaborated with other organisations of the developing world – primarily the Group of 77 – forming a number of joint committees and releasing statements and documents representing the shared interests of both groups. This dialogue and cooperation can be taken as an effort to increase the global awareness about the organisation and bolster its political clout.
- **Cultural diversity and human rights:** The movement accepts the universality of human rights and social justice, but fiercely resists cultural homogenisation. In line with its views on sovereignty, the organisation appeals for the protection of cultural diversity, and the tolerance of the religious, socio-cultural, and historical particularities that define human rights in a specific region.
- **Working groups, task forces, committees**
- Committee on Palestine
- High-Level Working Group for the Restructuring of the United Nations
- Joint Coordinating Committee (chaired by Chairman of G-77 and Chairman of NAM)
- Non-Aligned Security Caucus
- Standing Ministerial Committee for Economic Cooperation
- Task Force on Somalia
- Working Group on Disarmament
- Working Group on Human Rights
- Working Group on Peace-Keeping Operations

NAM CURRENT CHALLENGES

Current Challenges facing the NAM include the necessity of protecting the principles of International law, eliminating weapons of mass destruction , combating terrorism, defending human rights, working towards making the United Nations more effective in meeting the needs of all its member states in order to preserve International Peace , Security and Stability, as well as realising justice in the international economic system.

On the other hand, the long-standing goals of the Movement remain to be realised. Peace, development, economic cooperation and the democratisation of international relations, to mention just a few, are old goals of the non-aligned countries.

In conclusion, The Non-Aligned Movement, faced with the goals yet to be reached and the many new challenges that are arising, is called upon to maintain a prominent and leading role in the current International relations in defense of the interests and priorities of its member states and for achievement of peace and security for mankind.

QUESTIONS

1. Explain the ten basic principles of Non align movement , Bandung Conference?
2. Since its inception, the Movement of Non-Aligned Countries has waged a ceaseless battle to ensure that peoples being oppressed by foreign occupation and domination can exercise their inalienable right to self-determination and independence. In the light of above statement Justify the current activities and position of NAM ?
3. What is Non-alignment? Discuss its objectives and dynamic nature?
4. NAM is defined as an ideology concentration camp. Discuss the basic context of ideology of NAM with special reference to NAM summits?
5. Do you think the end of cold war or the conversion of world into unipolar declined the relevance of NAM?
6. Discuss the important purposes and principles of NAM in 14th Havana Summit of NAM?
7. Explain the historical evolution process of NAM?
8. Criticise the policy of NON- alignment adopted by developing nations?

CHAPTER 14

NAM Relavance in Contemporary World

NAM SIGNIFICANCE

NAM still holds high symbolic significance. Of course, NAM is also facing challenges while having its own weaknesses. NAM has its own strengths and their importance should not be downplayed. The movement puts the emphasis on the principle of cooperation among nations and continues its support for maintaining peace. It encourages disarmament, insists on the nations' right to self-determination, emphasises on the need for structural changes in the United Nations, especially the Security Council, in order to encourage optimal participation of the international community in international processes related to the fate of humanity, insists on the adoption and implementation of multilateral policies as well as focuses strongly on unanimity on issues such as human rights and cultural pluralism.

REASONS FOR NAM'S GROWTH

A Nationalism: Strong sense of nationalism amongst newly independent Asian, African and Latin American countries.

B Anti-Colonial Sentiments: Weary of colonial powers, newly independent countries sought means to counter their continuing influence.

C Economic Underdevelopment: Newly emerged countries wanted to develop themselves rather than waste resources by getting embodied in Cold War tensions.

D Visionary Leadership: the ability of towering personalities of developing nations to join hands with other nationalists.

E Presence of UN system: the presence of a collective forum where newly emerged countries could meet and voice their collective concerns.

NAM ANDCONTEMPERORY WORLD

The Non-Aligned Movement has covered a long distance since its inception in 1961 at Belgrade, the venue of the First NAM Summit. India's first Prime Minister Pt. Nehru, one of the founding father of NAM, described the non-aligned as the policy of friendship amongst nations. From its very inception the Non-Aligned Movement has successfully worked for promotion of friendship and cooperation amongst member states, end of domination and establishment of peace in the world at large.

1. Inculcate the spirit of Self esteem: India has played a significant role in shaping and guiding the Non-aligned Movement which began as a collective and constructive response of the newly liberated masses of Asia, Africa, Caribbean and Latin America. The Movement is responsible for inculcating self-esteem to these newly liberated countries and to a great extent responsible for the creation of more just and equitable world order.

2. Product of Cold War: There is a widespread scepticism about the relevance of non-alignment itself. Infact this scepticism is not new. So it was even during the Cold War era. The change is that now it is quite prevalent among Non-Aligned Countries themselves. Apart from the erroneous view held by many that Non-alignment was simply a product of Cold War and, therefore, with the claimed end of cold war it has lost its relevance there are other criticisms of the movement also. Its amorphous character has led critics to scoff at its marginality. The original criteria for membership have been diluted and the dividing line between non-alignment and alignment has been somewhat coloured. The regional quarrels and ambitions have tended to displace the larger objectives and demands. The movement's capacity to meet the rigourous of a new and more intensified cold war has been further eroded. The economic power of the rich nations combined with grave economic difficulties and challenges has placed new constraints on the activity, initiative and bounce of the non-aligned.

3. NAM is an ideological camp: These criticisms are correct to an extent. But what they miss is the evaluation and role of the movement in the context of its emergence and functioning. The most important aspect in that regard is need to realise that NAM did not originate as an ideological camp. It was, if anything, a revolt against bloc divisions and dominance of the international system by a few powers. A non-aligned country wanted a measure of freedom for itself and, at the same time, to acquire some leverage through this bigger association in the international system. In that sence NAM provided the emerging and struggling countries a certain psychological security, not fool-proof not even demonstrable, but nevertheless permitting some sense of belonging. In a harsh and cruel world it offered them some kind of an anchorage without entangling alliances and with their independence intact, making it possible for their voice to be heard with a little greater seriousness. The chief thrust of the movement, accordingly, had been towards independence, against colonialism, neo-colonialism, racialism and for the maintenance of world peace, democratisation of the international political structure and the establishment of a more equitable economic order.

4. NAM will not be Irrelevant : The end of the Cold War has not made the essence of non-alignment irrelevant. The essence is the right to consider every issue on merit and the right to take whatever action is considered feasible against what is regarded as a wrong irrespective of whether that wrong is perpetuated by one power bloc in a bipolar world or by one or both the superpowers in a bipolar world. As Nehru stated in his address to the United Nations, "where freedom is menaced or justice threatened or where aggression takes place, we cannot and shall not be neutral". To say it in another way, taking the essence of non-alignment as the assertion of independence in foreign affairs, non-alignment does not become irrelevant at any time.

NAM has achieved much in these tasks but a lot is left. The end of Cold War notwithstanding the developing countries, which also happen to be NAM countries remain developing and so their interests for development with dignity. Therefore, the last three non-aligned Summit Conferences in the Post-Cold War era Indonesia (1992), Colombia (1995) and South Africa (1998) expressly and categorically reaffirmed the continuing relevance of non-alignment. The colombia Conference asserted; "The Movement today constitutes a forum which provides us with a basic framework to coordinate our interests and positions". However, the global situation today presents a picture of strange paradoxes.

5. NAM and Globalisation: The end of Cold War had raised various hopes as well as possibilities of creating a new world order. But while economy has started moving along the path of the new dynamics of globalisation, expectations of humanity to attain a new, just and equitable international system based on respect, justice and equity among nations do not seem to be realised. Though wealth and trade have grown in an accelerated fashion, life expectancy and access to primary education have increased and infant mortality has noticeably gone down in a number of countries, poverty, hunger, unemployment, environment degradation and threat to peace through unjustified stockpiling of nuclear weapons show no signs of abatement. Similarly, notwithstanding the fact that a number of conflicts have been settled through dialogue and agreement giving significant fillip to regional peace, there has also been excerbation of existing disputes, emergence of new conflicts and reappearance of ethnic, religious and socio-economic rivalries making world a place far from being peaceful and secure. Simmering disputes, violent conflicts, aggression and foreign occupation, interference in the internal affairs of states, policies of hegemony and domination, ethnic strife, religious intolerance, xenophobia, new forms of racism and narrowly conceived nationalism, national and transnational terrorism are, inter alia, major and dangerous obstacles to harmonious coexistence among states and peoples. They have even led to the disintegration of states and societies. The NAM will have to take account of all these development, particularly the way they are affecting developing countries.

6. NAM is ceasing to be either a cohesive political grouping or an effective economic pressure group :- ow to shape NAM's world view in the light of the political and economic changes all around is a crucial question today. The United Nations system created after 1945 is out of date as far as developing country's issues are concerned. This needs to be reformed carefully making it more responsible and representative. Vetos and permanent members have lost much of their relevance. But unfortunately NAM is ceasing to be either a cohesive political grouping or an effective economic pressure group. Though NAM has consistently sought to improve the bargaining position of its member nations in global economic forums and at the U.N., it has had to contend with the reality that in the Post-Cold War period several countries have struck their own separate deals with the U.S. ultimately leading to an acceptance of the idea of unipolar world and giving the only superpower a total hegemonic role. The end of cold war and the birth of unipolarism are aberrations in the 350 years old sovereign state system. Multi-polarism is the traditional norm in the functioning of the sovereign state system. And presently it is in the off-line and non-alignment does not become irrelevant even in a multipolar world also.

7. NAM and International Organisations: NAM, therefore has to set its priorities carefully. NAM can be the carrier of South-South collaboration. It has a role to play in WTO negotiations to advance and protect the trading rights and opportunities of developing countries and in muscling up their negotiating positions and skills. NAM can stand up to arbitrary economic sanctions against developing nations, to the unfair cutting down of trade quotas with a view to protect the economy of the developed North. Emergences of "fortresses" in Europe and North America is a warning to the developing world that they must unite for their own economic emancipation. The European community with a market of 300 million people and the North America Free Trade Zone area covering 500 million people pose a great challenge to the countries of Asia, Africa and Latin America. To compete with them in trade and business will be more difficult for the developing countries unless they form an organisation for collective economic development. NAM can be an initiator for that. NAM can make the protests of developing nations against arbitrary application of western concepts of human rights. NAM has now an potentially effective role to play in bringing about meaningful nuclear arms control and disarmament by the nuclear powers.

8. NAM and Third world countries: With the end of Cold War there might be visible domination of inter-state warfare. But with the rise of ethnic and religious nationalism, socio-economic inequalities, collapse of state structures, with drawl of super power support etcetra, the changes and frequency of intra-state and regional conflicts have increased. So far as U.N.s role in the achievement of peace is concerned, it is increasingly becoming a rubber stamping body, endorsing and legitimizing the decisions and actions of the adhocist oligarohic political executive authority. UN seems to be becoming a tool of intervention in the hands of the unipolar oligarchy leading to the erosion of the sovereignty of the Third World and developing states.

The NAM, therefore, has to think of its rejuvenation rather than taking of becoming rededent. However, it has to redefine its role in the changed international situation. The changed scenario necessitates a shift of emphasis in priorities so as it can force new challenges. On the occasion 50 anniversary of Bandung, it is important to have widespread discussions and debates about identifying the challenges the movement has to address in the wake of the dynamics of globalisation. NAMs role in promoting a just international order would depend largely on its inner strength unity and cohesion. It is, therefore, incumbent on all member states to work earnestly towards promoting solidarity and unity of the Movement. It is expected that in order to enhance its role at the international level, the next NAM Summit of the Head of States or Government will take necessary initiatives to continue to work on expanding and reinforcing its ability and capacity for initiative, representation and negotiation, as well as, its ethical, political and moral strength as a forum representing the interests and aspirations of the developing world.

The fact remains that non-aligned has not lost its validity, since most of the problems faced by the developing nations during the cold war continue to persist. If India has ambition to play a major role in the global economy and rapidly to develop its technology, it must necessarily think of taking the leadership of the non-aligned, while taking into account the norms of international relations.

The time is ripe to evaluate the past and formulate the future policies of the non-aligned countries to change the existing international order and establish a new international order based on friendship, cooperation, justice and fair play to improve the lot of third world and to restore human rights, democracy and world peace.

NAM SUMMITS

- *Belgrade Summit, Yugoslavia* - 1961—26 member nations attended the summit and supported the freedom struggles in Algeria, Tunisia, Angola and the Congo.
- *Cairo Summit, Egypt* - 1964—47 member nations attended the summit and stressed the need for disarmament and non-interference.
- *Lusaka Summit, Zambia* - 1970—54 member nations attended and decided to break off ties with Portugal and South Africa due to lack of compliance with UN decisions regarding decolonisation and end of racial discrimination. The summit also called on Israel to withdraw from Palestine.
- *Algiers Summit, Algeria* - 1973—76 member nations attended the summit and stressed the need for economic cooperation between developing countries and recognised that their fate rests primarily in their own hands.
- *Colombo Summit, Sri Lanka* - 1976—86 member nations recognised the need to create new trade flows to make prosperity more widespread and equitable.
- *Havana Summit, Cuba* - 1979—94 states attended the summit. Radical countries like Cuba and Vietnam urged NAM towards socialist bloc to fight anti-colonialism; westernised countries

such as Singapore and Zaire urged need to ally with the West to avail access to resources and technological input. The Arab bloc also pressured NAM to expel Egypt for its unilateral agreement with Israel at Camp David. NAM resisted these pressures by condemning Egypt and Israel (without expelling them) and denouncing hegemonic designs of both superpowers.

- *New Delhi Summit, India* - 1983— 99 member nations urged for nuclear restraint and depoliticizing food aid and aimed to address increasing global inequalities.
- *Harare Summit, Zimbabwe* - 1986—101 member nations participated and the Summit stressed the need to strengthen frontline states in Africa facing destabilisation by intervention of Pretoria and for the need to pressure Pretoria to end apartheid in South Africa
- *Belgrade Summit, Yugoslavia* - 1989—102 member nations participated and the Summit highlighted the need to hold free and fair elections in Namibia, the need to resolve the ongoing trouble in Palestine and Afghanistan.
- *Jakarta Summit, Indonesia* - 1992—108 member nations attended but again there were tensions. Egypt, Cyprus and Indonesia favored closer ties with the West; Algeria Zimbabwe, Palestine and India wanted to confront the US; and Iran, Iraq, Cuba, Yemen and Libya wanted NAM to take on western hegemony. There were also calls for NAM to be like a Trade Union of developing nations to gain global negotiating leverage.
- *Columbia Summit, Cartagena* - 1995—This Summit recognised the need for reorienting NAM objectives in the unilateral world order. The Kashmir insurgency was also focused on.
- *Havana, Cuba* (2000) – 135 member nations focused on improving South to South cooperation and improving trade terms with northern countries to eradicate poverty. India called for membership suspension of countries with military rule, but this proposal was unanimously rejected.
- *Kula Lumpur, Malaysia* (2003) – Attended by 114 member nations, the focus was on the revitalisation of the NAM, for addressing issues of global concern.

NAM'S ROLE IN INTERNATIONAL RELATIONS

NAM played a limited role in supporting the OPEC price rise, in the formation of the United Nations Conference on Trade and Development, the formation of the Group of 77 and articulating the New International Economic Order.

NAM has grown in size and can potentially be very influential but it has been unable to fulfill its lofty objectives and thus stands discredited. Most of the member states, which are a part of it, do not use the NAM platform to resolve disputes nor do they contribute much effort to making it more effective. Yet the need for peaceful coexistence and better North-South relations makes the need for NAM even more urgent with its visionary blend of idealism and realism.

CRITICISM OF NAM

NAM has failed to help promote peace and many of its members have been involved in bloody internal and external violence (for example the civil war in Cambodia, or the war between Iran and Iraq).

NAM has also been unable to bear on lingering disputes like the ME conflict and the problems in Kashmir causing tensions between Pakistan and India and in the Cyprus which is resulting in tensions between Turkey and Greece. There is a dichotomy between what NAM leaders preach and practice; often they have adopted stances in the UN at variance with consensus developed in NAM.

NAM AND INDIA

India's policy of not aligning with any of the power/military blocs after world war II led to the emergence of the Non aligned movement (NAM) . It does not mean isolationism or neutrality, instead it is a positive policy of taking an independent stand on international matters. The seeds of the movement were sown at Bandung in 1955, in which 29 nations including India participated . At present its member ship of the NAM is 116. Aims of NAM ARE:-

1) Assuring newly independent states of their rightful place in the world order.
2) Ending of colonialism and imperialism
3) Promotion of international peace and security
4) Ending of Racial Discrimination
5) Total disarmament and opposition to nuclear weapons
6) Creation of new international economic order.

QUESTIONS

1. How far non- alignment movement is successful in contemporary world? Discuss with special reference to its relevance
2. India is known as the pioneer in the development of NON- alignment movement? Discuss its role
3. Explain the significance and growth of NAM with special reference to no-alignment summits?
4. How is the policy of non-alignment relevant in the context of the changed nature of International Politics ?
5. Explain the Indian foreign Policy in the context of Peace and Security?

CHAPTER 15

FOREIGN POLICY

INTRODUCTION

Foreign Policy is one of the wheels with which the process of international politics operates. So it is very essential to learn the concepts of foreign policies before deducting any conclusion in international politics. Foreign policy is not separate from national policy, instead, it is a part of it. It consists of national interests that are to be furthered in relation to other furthering national interests in their foreign policies within the limits of their strength and the realities of the external environment. In recent years, the term foreign policy has become so wide that it covers almost all sorts of relations of one government with the other. Obviously, then political relations also fall in the scope of foreign policy.

DEFINATION OF FORIGN POLICY :

The term 'foreign policy' has been defined in a number of ways.

George Modelski defines it as, "The system of activities evolved by communities for changing the behaviour of other states and for adjusting their own activities to the international environment".

C.C Rodee defines foreign policy as a group of principles which are adopted by the states to protect the national interests and to change the behaviour of others.

In his own words, "Foreign policy involves the formulation and implementation of a group of principles which shape the behaviour pattern of a state while negotiating with (contacting) other states to protect or further its vital interests"

The above definition makes it clear that foreign policy is the group of principles determined by the states. These principles involve those interests which influence the behaviour of the states, intending to establish their relations to further and promote them. This includes not only the general principles but also those means necessary to implement them. Thus, these principles are those broader interests which states strive to achieve in international relations.

DETERMINANTS OF FOREIGN POLICY

Foreign policy is that part of national policy which the states adopt in relation to other sovereign states. All these states are the components of the international system. They are sovereign, independent and to a large extent cling to the idea of nationalism.

Thus 1) the sovereignty of the states, (2) their inter-dependence, and (3) their domestic and international circumstances are the three elements which generate and determine the foreign policy and its direction.

The first element is the sovereignty of the state which determines the principle of safeguarding the territorial integrity of the states. The element of inter dependence necessitates the principle of bargaining in foreign policy as the states endeavour to achieve the maximum possible advantage under all circumstances. The third element the domestic and intermediate circumstances add the factor of realism. The foreign policy of all states is based on these three principles.

1) Principles of Safeguarding the territorial integrity

This is the primary duty of a state to protect the property of its citizens and to safe-guard their interests wherever they are. This duty also involves the concept of security of national boundaries and if necessary to occupy other alien parts of the territory. The states, aiming at the protection of their own territory, pursue the policy of "status quo". The American policy of Isolation (Monroe Doctrine) and Stimson doctrine of 1932 , may be cited as the best examples of policy of status quo. The states, aiming at subjugating occupied or non-occupied territory, may be names as pursuing the revisionist policy. The policy of safeguarding the interests of the citizens inside or outside the state, is known as policy of "prestige";

2) Theory of Bargaining

Inter dependence of the states is an important phenomenon in international politics. All the states, big or small, are dependent on one another for one or the other reasons. This inter-dependence may result in conflict or cooperation. So the states under these stresses endeavour to create a situation under which international behaviour may not be broken completely. Foreign policy strives to create such a balance with bargaining.

3) Theory of the promotion of National interest

It is the pious duty of all sovereign states to promote and further their national interests through their foreign policies. There may be a little bit of difference between the interests on one state with that of another as they naturally vary according to time, place and location, but the interests as self preservation, security and well-being of its citizens are the common interests on the basis of which foreign policy is generally formulated .

4) Specific Determinants of Foreign Policy:

i) Historical and National value
ii) Geography.
iii) Public opinion, and
iv) National capacity

i) ***Historical and National Values:*** The foreign policy is shaped and conditioned by the history of a nation. From history alone the nation inherits a style and culture which in their turn influence and decide the course of actions the nation is to follow in relation to other sovereign states. History is the record of the doings of a community, of its failures and successes. These successes and failures guide the course of foreign policy.

ii) ***Geography:*** Geography is the factor that directly determines the national goals and aspirations and hence is one of the most potent factors in influencing the formulation of the foreign policy. An analysis of the foreign policy goals of different nations will reveal the strong influence of geography. The foreign policy of Britain in pre-Second World War period was centered on the principles of balance of power, superiority on the seas and expansion of empire. Thee aspects of the policy were the natural corollary of Geography.'

iii) ***Public opinion:*** The establishment of democratic institutions, the increase in the standard of living, the scourge of First World War and expansion of education have made the world public opinion a significant factor in the foreign policy. the states never dare to pursue the interest contrary to world public opinion. At least they will pursue only those interests which are not opposed to world public opinion. Public opinion shapes the foreign policy provided it is clear and well shaped. It could be significant factor only in developed states. In developing or under-developed states either it is not reflected in foreign policy issued or it is too native to play a significant role.

iv) ***National Capacity:*** National capacity means the military preparedness of a state, its technological advancement and modern means of communication. The economic development and enlightened political institutions are also associated with the national capacity. A policy is doomed if it does not strike a balance with the national capacity, the change in American foreign policy in post Second World War period explains this. From 1823 the U.S.A had been pursuing the policy of isolation but the tremendous rate of economic growth in twentieth century compelled it to follow the policy of involvement in place of isolation. The increase in national capacity of India after 1971 brought diversions in the traditional policy of non-alignment.

National capacity is the pivot of foreign policy. It determines as well as implements it. In fact the foreign policy is directly associated with the national capacity. If the state increases its national capacity, its foreign policy will need a big change. It will strive to achieve a status of distinction in international relations, if it decreases, the state will have to compromise with its poor status. For example, at the end of Second World War Britain became a less powerful state in Europe as well as in the world. This change in national capacity has brought overwhelming diversions in British foreign policy.

External Factors

External factors are of two types – flexible and rigid.

(a) In flexible factors we include international organisations and world public opinion. These are dynamic elements as the international organisations, international law and the treaties create international environment. This international environment influences world public opinion. These are dynamic elements as the international organisations, international law and the treaties create international environment. This international environment influences world public opinion.

(b) The states, while formulating foreign policy, have to keep in mind this dynamics of international politics. The reactions of state, on the other hand, is not dynamic. We may term it as rigid factor. The states have some area of agreement and disagreement. They have some allied, some neighbours and some foes. These factors are permanent. For a clear understanding of these elements let us elaborate them.

i) ***International Organisation:*** The international organisations have started playing important role in foreign policy formulation. The states have to take a not of international law, treaties and contracts so that their violation may not jeopardise the policies. The Communist China, for a login time, showed utter disregard to these factors and consequently could not secure its due position in the field of international relations. Only after 1971, she recognised their importance and that move on the part of Communist China have introduced new dimensions in international politics.

ii) ***World Public Opinion:*** World public opinion is very dynamic element. Like a flicker of light it influences the foreign policies only too occasionally. In other words, the element of consistency is totally absent in it. Only if the domestic public opinion supports the world public opinion it becomes an important determinant of foreign policy. The opinion is a factor which faces many obstacles in crystallisation. The first and foremost is the ideological division of the world in which the actions good or bad of one part become naturally adverse to other part. The role of propaganda, absence of free press and economic backwardness of a larger number of states towards the evolution of a real public opinion.

iii) ***Reactions of the States***: The states have to take notice of the interests of other states while formulating their policies. They will never endeavour to pursue those interests which are totally opposed to the fundamental interests of other states. If a policy fails to apprehend the reactions of other in this light, it will come to apprehend the reactions of other in this light, it will come tod a disastrous end.

Hitler in 1939 committed a blunder when he refused to be guided by the British reactions and went ahead with his Polish invasion. The result is well known. Japan's failure in assessing the American reactions in Pearl Harbour incident agains brought disaster to Japanese policy which had intelligently avoided offending the U.S.A upto that period.

Policy Making Factors: In the formulation of foreign policy, the statesmen including all other policy makers, play a decisive role. As the final shape of foreign policy is the handwork of these elites, the impact of their views and personality is but natural. The dictators generally try to change the public opinion in their favour through a controlled press. Leaders like Mussolini, Hitler, Mao Tse-Tung and Ayub Khan have done the same. Generally, the policy makers have many tasks. They have to consider internal problems, public opinion, external circumstances and reaction of other states. In these tasks they are assisted by a number of departmental experts.

i) ***Head of the Government and Foreign Minister:*** In a totalitarian state foreign policy depends upon the whims of a dictator. In a democracy the general public is not competent enough to participate in it effectively. This phenomenon centralises the powers of formulating the policy in the hands of a few, termed in modern parlance, as elites. The American President Truman used to say that the president is the maker of foreign policy. In a parliamentary democracy it is the Prime Minister who wields this authority.

   Personality equation plays a very significant part in politics and administration. This sometimes, makes the foreign minister more important than the President, or Prime Minister. During Attlee's Premiership Sir Earnest Bevin was the prime mover and so was John Foster Dulles under Eisenhower. Dr. Henry Kissinger virtually became the symbol of American foreign policy in Nixon and Ford period.

ii) ***Legislature:*** The legislature is generally a clumsy house. It is very strong word unfit to be wielded properly. Neverthless, it is the last authority in decision making and the strings of purse are under its control. These factors make it a strong determinant of foreign policy. The post Second World War period has seen anew aspect of foreign policy, ie. the economic aid and assistance to promote the national interests. For that matter, the executives of foreign policy depend upon the legislature of sanctions of huge amounts. The U.S.A is the chief donor of economic assistance. This has made the Senate a powerful concluded by the executives-Prime Minister or President by they must be ratified by the legislatures before they are applied. This against makes the legislature, important determinants.

iii) ***Foreign office and other services:*** In theory the ministers make the policy and the permanent officials merely execute it, but in practice the officials formulate the policy and the ministers only render advice. It is equally true that if the minister is bent upon carrying out his own impressions then the bureaucracy has no alternative but to give way. Nevile Chamberlain clashed with the foreign office over his policy of Appeasement. He removed Lord Vansittart from his policies are less firm and clashes less pronounced, the advice of the officials carries much weight?

Foreign policy is not conducted by diplomacy along; it relies heavily on the military forces and on the scientists who supply them with up-to date weapons, one economists and also, especially today, on intelligence and propaganda services. In the world of today the weapons are not in use, on the contrary they are produced only to deter. Here the scientists start playing an important role. In the same manner the governments have to rely upon the information rendered by the intelligence agencies. The role of Central Intelligence Agency of the U.S.A is now an open secret. We know from the newspaper revelations that this agency was responsible for the coup in Chile, invasion of Cuba in 1991, the U2 reconnaissance flight over Soviet Union and murder of many heads of the governments of hostile states. In Soviet Union the technical cabinet also processes the information of the K.G.B and only the a policy is formulated.

iv) **Ideologies:** Ideology is the basis as well as the goal of foreign policy. The states establish their political and economic institutions on the basis of ideology and endeavour to translate those very principles in the sphere of foreign policy. As is obvious, a particular ideology has a goal which the state strives to achieve in international relation. The ideological division of the world between the Soviet bloc and American bloc has focused tow types of foreign policies. One is communist oriented and the other non communist. A sort of affinity can be traced among the states of identical ideologies while there is a feeling of animosity among the states adhering to contradictory ideologies. This is the root cause of cold war and post war tensions.

v) **National Interests and Nation Values:** National interest is the key concept in foreign policy. These are the aspirations of the state to be achieved through foreign policy. The policy makers are governed by their respective national interests. If they agree on certain points it is because they view that the interests they are piously pursuing are not jeopardised. If they agree to concessions, they do only when they are convinced that this brings advantage if their states. national interests are the governing factors which loom large in diplomatic conferences-bilateral or multilateral. The success and failure of all these conferences depend upon the national interests involved. A conference cannot see the light of success of its conditions affect them and the area of cooperation stretches to the horizons of national interest. Lord Palmerston was too right to say that friendship or enmity is never permanent in foreign policy, it is the national interests that are permanent and it was the pious duty of the states to follow them.

FOREIGN POLICY OBJECTIVES

If all the objectives of foreign policy are to be explained by one single word, that word undoubtedly is the national interest, but this word is too ambiguous to lead us to any clear understanding. Paul

Seabury opined that the national interest can indicate such ideal objectives which the states pursue through their foreign policy or it can simply be the interpretation of the policy makers or its meaning may be different individuals and group."

K.J Holsti holds that the national interests are 'an image of a future state of affairs and future set of conditions which governments through individual policy makes aspire to bring about by wielding influence abroad and by changing or sustaining the behaviour of states.

In principle the foreign policy is always formulated on the basis of national interests but in practice the policy may drift far-ff from these goals under the pressure of International environment and power pattern. The policy of the Soviet Union aims at the world revolution for spreading communism. The U.S.A since 1930 had specifically declared the support for democracies in the world. Both the countries have drifted from these aspired goals of their policies. The Soviet Union has been supporting governments of Iraq and Iran where a campaign of witch hunting for communists is official policy. It gives many surprises when the Soviet Union fails to reach a compromise with the communist regimes of China and Albania. The U.S.A in post War period found itself in awkward position of supporting the totalitarian regimes and fascist governments, which was least convincing inview of the old policy of supporting the democracies.

The objectives of foreign policy are divided in three categories namely.

i) Core values and interests.
ii) Middle range objectives, and
iii) Universal long range objectives.

i) **Core values and interests:** Core values and interests determine the foreign policy of a nation. The basis of these objectives are those necessities and beliefs on which depends the existence of the state. These necessities and beliefs are as follows.

a) ***National security:*** National security is the primary goal of a foreign policy. This is the article of faith and society generally consents to without any dissent. The treaties, contracts and alliances which the states conclude with other states rest on this objective. In 1823, the then president of the U.S.A declared the famous Monroe doctrine which aimed at checking the interference of European powers in the affairs of America. The deep involvement of Soviet Union in East European affairs, its historic concern to find to find a route through Dardanelles and Bosphorous, and its efforts to defend its eastern borders from any possible aggression are the Soviet interests related with the question of national security. The complexion of the government in Moscow would not bring any significant change in the Soviet Union's stand on these highly sensitive issues. The policy of status quo; This may include the protection of rights and property of the nationals living in foreign lands. This policy is know as 'policy of prestige'; The concept of national security is not confined to territorial integrity or security of national boarder. It may include the security of cultural and political institutions and beliefs and values.

b) ***Economic development:*** The promotion of economic interests of a nation is the fundamental goal of foreign policy as this is directly associated with state's existence. The status of a state in international relations is always determined by the economic standard. So the state would always strive to adopt a course of action which brings economic prosperity thereby making its armed forces well equipped, citizens much relaxed and state a mention that the national interests are more economic than political and foreign policy more guided by economic factors than by political ones. War, imperialism and colonialism, treaties, alliances and contracts are totally based on the idea of economic property. In post Second World War period, European states adopted the American line as American economic aid was more than necessary of economic recovery of Europe. India, at the dawn of its independence, shrewdly opted or a policy of nonalignment to seek the help of both the blocs for its economic prosperity. The Sino – American détente is again the confirmation of economic interests dominating the politics than the vice versa.

ii) **Middle range objective:** The middle range objective include international co-operation, prestige and protection of the interests of the nationals. These objectives can be illustrated as follows:

a) ***The interests of Pressure Groups:*** The existence of pressure groups with global interests, is a new phenomenon in politics which has a significant influence in foreign policy also. The pressure groups wield a considerable influence on their respective governments which have to include the interests of these pressure groups in foreign policy to bring stability in national politics or to assure the support of these groups in dominating the domestic political scene. This makes it clear that no government can get a smooth sailing without the support or these interest groups. That is why, to placate them, the governments have to deviate from political norms. The pro-Israel policy the U.S.A in the past was due to the considerable influence of the American Jews in American politics. India's repeated assurance to the Arab world to support them against Israel is because of the pressure of Muslim factor in India politics.

b) ***Non-Political Cooperation:*** In the field of international relations mutual cooperation is more than necessary today. So the objectives of a foreign policy inevitably include economic cultural and social cooperation. The economic aid to the developing states and the facilities the states give to the foreign students to pursue higher and technical education well explains this.

c) ***Promotion of National Prestige:*** The objective of this type includes those policies of states which are meant to focus an impressive image of the states abroad. The states generally resort to propaganda through mass media to create the desired effect. The competition between two super powers to reach the planets is motivated by this desire. The success of any of them in its mission would certainly prove the scientific and technological superiority of one over the other.

d) ***Territorial expansion:*** The policy of territorial expansion includes imperialism, colonialism which the states adhere to meet their economic and political aspirations. From 18th to 20th century the European states had adopted the policy of imperialism to capture the markets. Raw materials and to claim superiority in European affairs. In modern times the traditional imperialistic policy has undergone a change and this can be explained by illustrating its two prevalent forms. The first is a policy which aims at the increase of areas of influence, while the other seeks to capture the economic resources reducing the other state to the status of dependency. The economic or dollar imperialism of the West European countries and of the U.S.A falls in this category, while the Russian policy of imperialism can be covered in the former types; expansion of areas of influence or Ideology.

iii) **Universal long range objective:** These are objectives aiming at restricting the international system. The plans and dreams which an ideology forms to establish the international system of its own liking is the distant goal of foreign policy. Hitler's idea of Thousand years Reich', the idea of world revolution in socialist countries, the plans of the U.S.A to make the world for democracy are undoubtedly the foreign policy goals but with some distinction. While the primary and middle range goals are the policies immediately to be pursued, foreign policy is always coloured by them but the long range foals are the ambitions which the states may achieve in distant future and for them the states never press too much in the present.

QUESTIONS

1. Explain the concept of Foreign Policy given by different scholars of Politics?
2. What are the basic and specific determinants of Foreign Policy?
3. Examine the major objectives of Foreign policy in respect of Universal and middle range objectives?
4. Discuss the external and internal factors of the foreign policy with special reference to the Reaction of the states?
5. In the formulation of foreign policy, the statesmen including all other policy makers, play a decisive role. Discuss the major role of department experts in the formulation of foreign Policy

CHAPTER 16

The Cold War ERA

After the Second World War, the USA and USSR became two Super Powers. One nation tried to reduce the power of other. Indirectly the competition between the Super Powers led to the Cold War. Then America took the leadership of all the Capitalist Countries. Soviet Russia took the leadership of all the Communist Countries. As a result of which both stood as rivals to each other.

HISTORICAL PRESPECTIVE

There is a difference of views regarding the origin of Cold War. One view is that its beginning can be traced back to the time of the Bolshevik Revolution of 1917 when the Communists openly declared their intention to control and dominate the world. Some writers find the genesis of the Cold War in the period of the Grand Alliance of World War II.

Although the Western Powers and the Soviet Union cooperated during the War, there were sharp differences among them particularly over the treatment of anti-Nazi resistance forces in Poland and Yugoslavia, the establishment of the Second Front, coordination of military strategy and post-War reconstruction.

Still another view is that the Cold War actually crystallised only in 1947 when the Soviet Union and the Western Powers intensified and formalised the differences in the interpretation of the provisions of the Yalta and Potsdam Agreements. The delay in opening the Second Front, the secrecy over the atom bomb and refusal to invite the Polish provisional Government to San-Francisco made Russia suspicious of Anglo-American designs.

Likewise, the Western Powers were agitated over the occupation of considerable portions of territory in the Far East by Russia by declaring war against Japan at the last moment. Prof Young Hum Kim writes, "At the war's end, the basic incompatibility between Soviet Communism and Western democracy in terms of ideology and security took a new turn towards higher intensity as Stalin reverted from the policy of war-time expediency (alliance with the West) to the policy of pre-War orthodoxy (hard lined dogmatism)".

The view of some scholars is that the first signal for the development of Cold War was given by Winston Churchill in his Fulton speech in which he observed, "If the Western democracies stand together in strict adherence to the principle of United Nations Charter, their influence for furthering those principles will be immense and no one is likely to molest them. If, however, they become divided or falter in their duty and if these all important years are allowed to slip away, then indeed catastrophe may overwhelm us all".

Reasons for Cold War

Many reasons have been given for the Cold War. Though the Soviet Union and the Western Powers cooperated with each other during the World War II, there did not develop a spirit of real cooperation among them. Towards the end of the war, tension increased tremendously. The opposite stands taken by the Soviet Union and the Western Powers on various matters failed to arouse a spirit of cooperation and friendship.

The actions of both the parties showed that mutual distrust existed among them. Another cause of the Cold War was the existence of ideological differences between the Soviet Union and Western democracies. The Western Powers considered the Soviet Union a greater enemy than Hitler and Mussolini. They followed a policy of appeasement towards Hitler and Mussolini because they felt that Communism was a greater danger than Fascism and Nazism.

Narrow national interests after the end of the World War II also contributed to the Cold War. In spite of protests from the Western Powers, the Soviet Union continued her plans to increase her influence in Eastern Europe. After consolidating her position there, she started penetrating into the Middle East which was resented by the Western Powers.

Its beginning

The view of Possony is that "the Cold War began while the hot war was still raging." Even before the end of the World War II, the Soviet Union imposed Communist regimes in the East European countries of Poland, Bulgaria, Rumania, Hungary and Yugoslavia.

After putting Eastern Europe behind the iron curtain, the Soviet Union turned her attention towards Western Europe. She also put pressure on Turkey and Iran to get concessions. She engineered a Communist revolution against Greece and expanded her influence in Italy.

These moves of the Soviet Union were viewed with great concern by the Western countries. When Britain expressed her inability to check Soviet expansion, the United States took up the responsibility of containing the onward march of Communism.

The Truman Doctrine and the Marshall Plan were the steps to save the European Continent from further Communist influence. The Soviet Union also initiated the Molotov Plan and established the Council of Mutual Economic Assistance. These moves and counter-moves constituted the beginning of the Cold War.

Truman Doctrine

On 12 March 1947, President Truman addressed a joint session of the American Congress and enunciated what came to be known as the Truman Doctrine. Truman asked the Congress to sanction 400 million Dollars by June 1948 to help Greece and Turkey. In May 1947, the American Congress authorised aid to Greece and Turkey.

It was found in 1950 that American policy had completely changed the state of affairs in Greece and Turkey. The guerillas were completely eliminated from the Greek soil and peace was restored. The same was the case in Turkey. The danger from Communism was successfully checked by American action.

The Marshall Plan (1947)

The Marshall Plan was an extension of the principle underlying the Truman Doctrine. It dealt with Europe in general and not with any particular state or states as was the case with the Truman Doctrine. It was essentially an economic plan. It represented an elaborate programme which was to last for four years. It showed an anxiety on the part of the United States to avert the economic crisis which was apprehended as a result of the World War II.

It also underlined American determination to fight against Communism. The situation in France and Italy was a source of great anxiety to the United States. The Communist parties of France and Italy were gaining in strength. It was felt that in order to put a check on Communist influence, the United States must come to their help.

The Marshall Plan was welcomed in the United States as it was directed against the Soviet Union. By the time the programme was completed, its object was achieved and the danger from Communism was successfully met.

The Soviet Union and the Communist and non-Communist countries of Eastern Europe were invited to accept the Marshall Plan but the offer was rejected. It was contended that under the cover of the Plan, the United States aimed at creating an economic empire by taking advantage of the conditions in Europe. The negative attitude of the Soviet Union towards the Plan led to the continuance of the struggle between Eastern and Western Europe.

Brussels Treaty (1948)

The Marshall Plan stiffened the Cold War between Eastern and Western Europe instead of bringing about a repprochement between the two. The Soviet Union had already branded the Truman Doctrine as imperialistic. In order to check Russian supremacy and influence, Britain, France, Belgium, The Netherlands, Luxemburg, etc. signed the Treaty of Brussels in March 1948. The signatories to the treaty expressed their complete reliance on the Charter of the United Nations and pledged mutual military, economic and political cooperation. This treaty played a vital role in strengthening the unity and security of the Western countries.

NATO (1949)

The North Atlantic Treaty was signed on 4th April 1949 by the United States, Canada, Belgium, Denmark, France, Iceland, Italy, Luxemburg, the Netherlands, Norway, Portugal and the United Kingdom. Greece and Turkey became its members in February 1952. West Germany joined it m May 1955. The NATO was a defensive organisation.

After the signing of the Brussels Treaty and particularly when the conflict between Eastern and Western Europe over the German problem assumed serious proportions, the United States decided to establish a Mutual Military Assistance Organisation with the Western countries and the NATO was the result.

The NATO was intended to strengthen the morale of Western Europe. The association of the United States with the other NATO Powers was bound to halt Soviet expansion Westwards. As the stand taken by the United States was definite and clear, the Soviet leaders were not prepared to take any risk in Western Europe. The result was that the Communists made no territorial gains in Europe or the Atlantic area after April 1949.

Germany

After the World War II, there was a conflict of interests between Eastern and Western blocs over Germany. The defeat of Germany and her occupation by the Soviet Union and the Western Powers gave rise to complications in the field of European and international politics. The United States, Russia, Britain and France partitioned Germany among themselves into four zones. In January 1947, British and American zones were unified.

The French zone was also merged into it in the same year. The three zones came to be known as West Germany. East Germany came into existence under Russian control. As a result of the Cold War, Germany became the centre of dispute between Eastern and Western blocs and that continued for years.

When the Soviet Union proceeded to collect reparations from Eastern Germany, disputes and tension began to develop between the Soviet Union and the Western Powers. In 1948, the Western Powers introduced currency reforms in West Germany. In reply to that, the Soviet Union blockaded the city of Berlin by closing down all her entrances. However, the Western Powers managed to supply the necessary foodstuffs to the citizens of Berlin by airlift from June 1948 to September 1949.

The representatives of the Western Powers met in Bonn and drafted the Bonn Constitution. The Federal Republic of West Germany was born and elections were held in 1949. The Soviet Union proclaimed the German Democratic Republic in East Germany under her control. West Germany joined the Anglo-American bloc and East Germany joined the Soviet bloc. Tension between the two blocs continued over the question of Germany.

China

The United States refused to recognise the new Communist Government of China set up in 1949, and continued to recognise the Nationalist Government of Formosa under Chiang Kai-shek. The result was that the Nationalist Government of Formosa continued to be a permanent member of the Security Council till October 1971 when there was reconciliation between Communist China and the United States. If the United States backed Formosa, the Soviet Union backed Communist China and the cold war continued.

Korea

By 1949, the territorial limits of the cold war in Europe were more or less established. By 1950, the theatre of the cold war shifted from Europe to East Asia. Under the impact of the cold war, Korea was divided into North Korea and South Korea. In North Korea, a Communist government supported by the Soviet Union was set up. In South Korea, an American-sponsored Government was set up. On 25 June 1950, North Korea attacked South Korea.

The Security Council declared North Korea as the aggressor and authorised the creation of command under the Flag of the United Nations to repel the aggressor. The Korean War was virtually a conflict between the Soviet bloc and the Western bloc. If North Korea was fighting with Soviet weapons and Chinese troops, the United States was fighting on behalf of South Korea under the Flag of the United Nations. The result was that the Cold War was turned into a hot war. After the death of Stalin in 1953, an armistice was signed on 27th July 1953.

Anzus Pact (1951)

When the Communist success in China and the Korea war creased an atmosphere of uneasiness in the Pacific region, the United States signed a treaty with Australia and New Zealand in 1951 known as the Anzus Pact. It was to remain in force for an indefinite period. This Pacific security system was an endeavour of the Western Powers to meet the Communist challenge.

Indo-China

After the fall of Japan in 1945, Britain and China occupied Southern and Northern parts of Indo-China respectively. France regained her lost hold over the whole of Indo-China in 1946. The Vietminh refused to acknowledge the authority of France. Supported by Communist China, the Vietminh attacked the Red River Valley in 1949. As Communist China helped the Vietminh, the United States helped France with money and arms. The Soviet Union also helped the Vietminh.

The result was that a clash between the Soviet Union and the United States became almost inevitable. The fall of Dien Bien Phu in 1954 brought the final collapse of France in Indo-China. At the Geneva Conference in July 1954, Vietnam was partitioned between North Vietnam and South Vietnam. In spite of the Geneva Settlement, there was no peace in Vietnam.

The United States did everything in her power to help South Vietnam against North Vietnam which was supported by Communist China and the Soviet Union. In spite of strong action by the United States, there was no end of the war. Negotiations started in Paris in 1968 but without any settlement. The forces of North Vietnam made headway against South Vietnam in the beginning of 1972 and the United States intensified the bombing of North Vietnam. Mines were spread in the harbours and rivers of South Vietnam.

On many occasions, negotiations were started for peace but without any result. North Vietnam backed by the Soviet Union continued to fight till the fall of South Vietnam in April 1975. Thus the Cold War was fought in Indo-China between the Soviet Union and the United States and the Soviet Union was the victor.

SEATO

Like the NATO, the SEATO (1954) was born out of Communist fear. Its object was to put a stop to the further spread of Communist influence in South-East Asia. The United States was not happy over the establishment of a Communist regime on the mainland of China in 1949. She was also not happy over the events in Indo-China where French power was being liquidated. The decisions taken in Geneva in 1954 were not to her liking.

Hence the SEATO was set up by the United States, in collaboration with Britain, France, Australia, Thailand, The Philippines and Pakistan, to stop the further infiltration of Communist influence in that area. The signatories to the treaty agreed to consider enemy attack upon any one of them as an attack upon all of them and to cooperate with one another against the enemy In the long run, the SEATO failed in its objectives and had to be wound up but it served its purpose for the time being.

The Baghdad Pact

Another centre of the Cold War between the Eastern and Western blocs was the Middle East. Some of the countries of that region were associated with the Soviet Union and some with the American bloc. The Baghdad Pact was an attempt by the Western Powers to form an anti-Soviet bloc in the Middle East. This Pact was signed in 1955 between Turkey and Iraq. Later on, Britain, Pakistan and Iran joined it.

The United States guaranteed the territorial integrity of the Baghdad Pact countries. She joined the Baghdad Pact in the economic sphere in May 1956 and in the military sphere in 1958 to combat international Communism. When Iraq withdrew from the Pact in March 1959, it was renamed Central Treaty Organisation.

The Warsaw Pact (1955)

The Soviet Union was alarmed at the aggressive attitude of the Western Powers when the NATO was formed, but for a few years she was not able to set up a rival organisation. She strongly protested against the entry of West Germany into NATO.

On 4 May 1955, the Soviet Union, Poland, Hungary, Czechoslovakia, Bulgaria, Albania and East Germany signed the Warsaw Pact. The signatory states agreed to resist the attacks of the imperialists and capitalist states upon any member state. The Warsaw Pact, in its essential features, was a carbon copy of the NATO. Its only object was to meet the challenge from the NATO Powers. Between 1955 and 1958, West Asia became the centre of the Cold War. This fact is proved by the signing of the Baghdad Pact with a view to exclude the Soviet Union from that region.

Austria (1955)

No treaty had been concluded with Austria in spite of the lapse of many years after the ending of the World War in 1945. That was due to the differences between the Soviet Union and the Western Powers over the terms of the peace treaty.

However, at the Summit Conference of July 1955, the Austrian Peace Treaty was signed and Presidents Eisenhower and Bulganin exchanged assurances that neither of them will start a nuclear war. Both of them undertook not to seek political or economic union of Austria with Germany, directly or indirectly Austria was not to join the NATO and remain neutral.

Friedman writes, "The Austrian Peace Treaty is the first major international treaty on which the four erstwhile allies have been able to agree after years of an unbroken record of dissension and tension, sometimes threatening to lead to the brink of war." On the Suez Canal crisis of 1956, both the Super Powers stood on the same side and thus a major crisis was averted.

Eisenhower Doctrine (1957)

The United States proclaimed the Eisenhower Doctrine on 5 March 1957 by which the Truman Doctrine was extended to the Middle East. Its object was to check the possibility of Communist aggression, direct or indirect, in that region. The United States was to give military assistance and protect any state whose territorial integrity and political independence was threatened.

Hungary

There was a revolt in Hungary in 1956 and the Soviet Union sent her troops to suppress it. The Soviet action was condemned by the countries belonging to the American bloc. A demand was made that the Soviet Union must withdraw her troops but she refused.

Germany

There was a tussle between the Soviet Union and the Western Powers in 1956 over the issue of elections in Berlin. As the Social Democratic party won the elections by defeating the Communist party, the Soviet Union abrogated that election by applying her veto power. That led to tension between the Soviet Union and the Western Powers.

In November 1958, Khrushchev stated that the imperialists wanted to make Germany a chronic problem and were disturbing the peace of East Germany, Poland and other socialist states. He warned that any march towards East Germany would lead to disastrous consequences.

He handed over notes to Western Powers asking them to withdraw from West Berlin within six months. The reply of West Germany was that if the Soviet Union renounced unilaterally her international treaties, political tension would increase and the Soviet Union would be held responsible for violating international law. The Western Powers showed their determination to defend their rights.

During 1959, there were negotiations between the Soviet Union and the Western Powers regarding the unification of Germany. In September 1959, Khrushchev met Eisenhower at Camp David and agreed to resume talks on the Berlin question at the proposed Summit Conference to be held in May 1960 in Paris.

On 25 April 1960, Khrushchev warned the Western Powers that if they did not sign a peace treaty with East Germany, their right of access to West Berlin would cease and the Soviet Union would conclude a separate peace treaty with East Germany. He also declared that as the city of Berlin was situated within East Germany, the latter would have complete control over the whole of Berlin.

The Western Powers protested and maintained that their right over West Berlin was not due to any concession from the Soviet Union but was based on their conquest of Germany. They also contended that the Soviet Union could not revoke unilaterally all the treaties regarding Germany and Berlin. When Khrushchev met President Kennedy in Vienna in June 1961, he declared that the Camp David formula was dead.

A serious situation was created in Germany as a result of the influx of refugees from East Germany to West Germany in large numbers. On 13 August 1961, East Germany sealed her border between East Berlin and West Berlin and 25-mile long Berlin Wall was erected between two Berlins. There was great tension. After lengthy negotiations, the pass system was introduced between the two cities in September 1963.

There was another crisis in 1969 when the West German government decided to hold Presidential elections on 5 March 1969 in West Berlin. East Germany protested and reimposed restrictions on land routes to prevent the members of the Electoral College from reaching West Berlin. The West German Government managed to send the members of the Electoral College and other officials to West Berlin by air. President Nixon threatened action if the Soviet Union resisted and the result was that the Soviet Union kept quiet.

In September 1971, the Soviet Union, the United States, France and Britain signed the Berlin Accord. In November 1972, the Basic Treaty was signed between East Germany and West Germany. In September 1973, both East and West Germany became members of the United Nations and thus the Cold War ended in Germany.

Cuban Crisis (1962)

The Cold War was at its height at the time of the Cuban crisis in 1962. The Soviet Union sent military equipment to Cuba along with a larger number of technicians and other military personnel. The United States opposed the Soviet move and declared her intention to use all possible means to end the Soviet presence in Cuba. There was every danger of a war between the Soviet Union and the United States.

However, U Thant, Secretary-General of the United Nations, prevailed upon the United States to suspend the blockade of Cuba and asked Khrushchev to halt shipments to Cuba and also withdraw the offensive weapons from Cuba. The Soviet Union agreed to dismantle the Cuban missile sites and transport the missiles back to the Soviet Union. It was in this way that a great catastrophe was avoided.

The Congo

In the Congo, Soviet activity was of the most Cold War kind. The sending of vehicles, aircrafts, transport aircrafts, provisions and equipment in the summer 1960 was an act of intervention. Khrushchev sent a telegram to Kasavubu and Lumumba in July 1960 in which he declared that "if the hand of the aggressor is raised against the Congo, then the Soviet Union declares that the necessity will arise of taking more effective measures". The Soviet Union continued to help the Congo in order to balance her influence against that of the Western Powers.

Détente

After the Berlin crisis and the Cuban crisis, the stage was set for a thaw in the Cold War. It was realised by both sides that any nuclear war between them would lead to mutual destruction. That realisation pointed to the necessity of peaceful coexistence.

The result was the signing of the Nuclear Test Ban Treaty on 5 August 1963 between the Soviet Union, the United States and Britain. It provided for a limited ban on nuclear tests in the atmosphere including outer space or under water. A Hot Line Agreement was signed between the Super Powers.

The Nuclear Non-Proliferation Treaty was signed in 1968 between the Soviet Union and the United States. On 25 May 1972, two agreements were signed in Moscow by President Nixon and Communist Party Chief Brezhnev. Those agreements were the Treaty on Limitation of Anti-Ballistic Missile System and the Interim Agreement on certain measures with respect to the Limitation of Strategic Offensive Arms. Brezhnev visited Washington in June 1973. He signed with President Nixon an agreement by which they committed their countries to negotiate before the end of the next year a treaty calling for the reduction of nuclear weapons.

In June-July 1974, President Nixon visited the Soviet Union and agreed with Brezhnev to limit underground testing for five years. In November 1974, President Ford (successor of President Nixon) and Brezhnev met at Vladivostok and a US-Soviet agreement on guidelines for 10-year "cap on the arms race" was reached. The 35-Nation Summit Conference on Security and Cooperation in Europe opened on 30 July 1975 at Helsinki and concluded on 1 August 1975. It was attended by President Ford, Brezhnev, Prime Minister Wilson and others.

The Treaty on the Limitation of Strategic Offensive Arms signed in 1972 between the United States and the Soviet Union lapsed in October 1977 but both sides tried to preserve its main provisions. The Ford administration made little efforts for negotiations on a new agreement. However, after prolonged negotiations, a treaty was signed between the United States and the Soviet Union in Vienna on 18 June 1979 on the limitation of strategic offensive arms. This treaty is popularly known as SALT-II.

It is true that President Carter signed the SALT-II treaty but he began to have doubts about it even before he returned to Washington. The United States discovered the presence of a Soviet brigade in Cuba and demanded its withdrawal but the Soviet Union refused to oblige.

In 1979, the Shah of Iran was overthrown and the United States made a bid to secure base facilities in Kenya, Somalia and Oman to protect American interests in the Indian Ocean and the Persian Gulf region. The NATO decided to deploy American-made cruise missiles and advance medium-range Pershing II missiles in Western Europe from 1983.

When such was the situation, Soviet armed intervention in Afghanistan in December 1979 aggravated the situation. The American Government arranged secret supply of arms to Afghan rebels to pressurise the Soviet Union to negotiate but that did not happen.

When the United States intervened in El Salvador, the Soviet Union and her allies supplied arms to insurgents and also gave them training. President Reagan projected the issue of El Salvador as an international confrontation between the West and the Soviet Union.

There are certain differences between the old and new cold wars. Unlike the cold war of 1950's, the alliance partners are not actively involved in the new cold war. China, Japan and even Western European countries are lukewarm in their support and the war persists mainly between the two Super Powers.

In the old cold war, nuclear armaments build-up was not an issue and the main stress was on quantitative build-up of conventional arms. In the new cold war, there is a nuclear arms race between the two Super Powers and they are trying to achieve greater sophistication in conventional, weaponry. The new cold war is more threatening than the old cold war.

However, efforts are being made to stop the nuclear arms race. Talks on the limitation of missiles began in Geneva on 1 December 1981. The Soviets walked out in 1982 but the talks were resumed in 1985. There was a two-day summit at Geneva on 19 and 20 November 1985 between President Reagan and Soviet leader Gorbachev.

In a joint statement issued after the end of negotiations, the two leaders acknowledged that there were differences between them on vital issues but they affirmed that any confrontation between the two countries would have catastrophic consequences.

They emphasised the importance of preventing any war between them. They agreed to accelerate nuclear arms control negotiations and to meet again "in the near future". Gorbachev accepted an invitation from President Reagan to visit the United States and President Reagan agreed to visit the Soviet Union.

A summit meeting was held at Reykjavik on 12 and 13 October 1986. However, the negotiations broke down over the US refusal to yield on its Star War research. On 8 December 1987 the Intermediate Range Nuclear Forces Treaty for the destruction of Europe- based missiles was signed between the United States and the Soviet Union. For the United States, the treaty meant scrapping of Pershing missiles stationed in West Germany and Tomahawk cruise missiles in Britain, West Germany, Italy and Belgium. The Soviet Union was to eliminate Silo-based SS-4 rockets, SS-20. SS-22 and SS-23 missiles. On 1 June 1988, that treaty was ratified in Moscow by President Reagan and Soviet leader Gorbachev.

On 14 April 1988, Pakistan and Afghanistan formally signed a US and Soviet Union guaranteed Accord at Geneva by which the Soviet Union agreed to pull out all Soviet troops from Afghanistan within a maximum period of nine months from 15 May 1988. Half of those troops were to be withdrawn by 15 August 1988. This Accord was the result of the pressure exercised by the Soviet Union on Afghanistan and the United States on Pakistan.

In August 1988, South Africa, Angola and Cuba announced a cease-fire as agreed upon during the negotiations in Geneva. This was the result of Moscow's pressure on Angola and Cuba and that of Washington on South Africa. In the same month, Iran and Iraq ended the war which was going on for many years.

Definition of the Cold War

The term "Cold War" had an American origin and was used for the first time by Bernard Baruch who observed thus on 16 April 1947. "Let us not be deceived today. We are in the midst of a Cold War." The term was picked up by Walter Lippmann who through his book on the Cold War popularised it. After that, the term Cold War was used to describe the relations between the Soviet Union and the Western Powers after the World War 11. Cold War has been defined by R.K. Garthoff as "the conflict between the Communist Powers and the rest of the world waged by means short of overt major war."

Prof Young Hum Kim writes, "Though the term Cold War defies precise definition, it may be described as the international environment characterised by persistent tensions and conflicts between the free world and the Communist camp in general and between the United States and the Soviet Union in particular.

This new war of cold realities in international politics has been waged in every conceivable field of international life, especially in national defence, economic growth, diplomacy and ideology."

Cold War was not a state of armed struggle but a state in which the rivals while maintaining their peace-time diplomatic relations continued their hostility. They used all means other than war to weaken each other. The Cold War was an ideological war or a propaganda war or a diplomatic war. It was neither a condition of war nor a condition of peace. It was a state of uneasy peace. R. Bamet calls it "hot peace." Kennedy describes it as "hard and bitter peace."

In the graphic language of Hartman, "Cold War is a state of tension between countries in which each side adopts policies designed to strengthen it and weaken the other by falling short by actual war".

Infact, Cold War is a kind of verbal war which is fought through newspapers, magazines, radio and other propaganda methods. It is a propaganda to which a great power resorts against the other power. It is a sort of diplomatic war.

Origin of Cold War

There is no unanimity amongst scholars regarding the origin of the Cold War In 1941 when Hitler invaded Russia, Roosevelt the President of USA sent armaments to Russia. It is only because the relationship between Roosevelt and Stalin was very good. But after the defeat of Germany, when Stalin wanted to implement Communist ideology in Poland, Hungery, Bulgaria and Rumania, at that time England and America suspected Stalin.

Winston Churchill, the Prime Minister of England in his 'Fulton Speech' on 5th March 1946 said that Soviet Russia was covered by an Iron Curtain. It led Stalin to think deeply. As a result of which suspicion became wider between Soviet Russia and western countries and thus the Cold War took birth.

Causes of the Cold War

Various causes are responsible for the outbreak of the Cold War.

1. **Differences in the Ideologies:-**At first, the difference between Soviet Russia and USA led to the Cold War. The United States of America could not tolerate the Communist ideology of Soviet Russia. On the other hand, Russia could not accept the dominance of United States of America upon the other European Countries.
2. **Armaments Race:-**Secondly, the Race of Armament between the two super powers served another cause for the Cold War. After the Second World War, Soviet Russia had increased its military strength which was a threat to the Western Countries. So America started to manufacture the Atom bomb, Hydrogen bomb and other deadly weapons. The other European Countries also participated in this race. So, the whole world was divided into two power blocs and paved the way for the Cold War.
4. **RUSSIAN Declaration:** Fourthly, Russian Declaration made another cause for the Cold War. Soviet Russia highlighted Communism in mass-media and encouraged the labour revolution. On the other hand, America helped the Capitalists against the Communism. So it helped to the growth of Cold War.
5. **Fifthly,** the Nuclear Programme of America was responsible for another cause for the Cold War. After the bombardment of America on Hiroshima and Nagasaki Soviet Russia got afraid for her existence. So, it also followed the same path to combat America. This led to the growth of Cold War.
6. **Lastly,** the Enforcement of Veto by Soviet Russia against the western countries made them to hate Russia. When the western countries put forth any view in the Security Council of the UNO, Soviet Russia immediately opposed it through veto. So western countries became annoyed in Soviet Russia which gave birth to the Cold War.

Various Phases of the Cold War

The Cold War did not occur in a day. It passed through several phases.

First Phase (1946-1949)

- In this phase America and Soviet Russia disbelieved each other. America always tried to control the Red Regime in Russia. Without any hesitation Soviet Russia established Communism by destroying democracy in the Poland, Bulgaria, Rumania, Hungery, Yugoslavia and other Eastern European Countries.
- In order to reduce Russia's hegemony, America helped Greece and Turkey by following Truman Doctrine which came into force on 12 March 1947. According to Marshall Plan which was declared on 5 June, 1947 America gave financial assistance to Western European Countries.
- In this phase, non withdrawal of army from Iran by Soviet Russia, Berlin blaockade etc. made the cold was more furious. After the formation of NATO in 1949, the Cold War took a halt.

Second Phase (1949-1953)

- In this phase a treaty was signed between Australia, New Zealand and America in September, 1957 which was known as ANZUS. America also signed a treaty with Japan on 8 September, 1951. At that time by taking armaments from Russia and army from China, North Korea declared war against South Korea.
- Then with the help of UNO, America sent military aid to South Korea. However, both North Korea and South Korea signed peace treaty in 1953 and ended the war. In order to reduce the impact of Soviet Communism, America spent a huge amount of dollar in propaganda against Communism. On the other hand, Soviet Russia tried to be equal with America by testing atom bomb.

Third Phase (1953-1957)

- Now United States of America formed SEATO in 1954 in order to reduce Soviet Russia's influence. In 1955 America formed MEDO in Middle East. Within a short span of time, America gave military assistance to 43 countries and formed 3300 military bases around Soviet Russia. At that time, the Vietnamese War started on 1955.
- To reduce the American Power, Russia signed WARSAW PACT in 1955. Russia also signed a defence pact with 12 Countries. Germany was divided into Federal Republic of Germany which was under the American control where as German Democratic Republic was under Soviet Russia. In 1957 Soviet Russia included Sphutnick in her defence programme.
- In 1953 Stalin died and Khrushchev became the President of Russia. In 1956 an agreement was signed between America and Russia regarding the Suez Crisis. America agreed not to help her allies like England and France. In fact West Asia was saved from a great danger.

Fourth Phase (1957-1962)

- In 1959 the Russian President Khrushchev went on a historical tour to America. Both the countries were annoyed for U-2 accident and for Berlin Crisis. In 13 August 1961, Soviet Russia made a Berlin Wall of 25 Kilometres in order to check the immigration from eastern Berlin to Western Berlin. In 1962, Cuba's Missile Crisis contributed a lot to the cold war.
- This incident created an atmosphere of conversation between American President Kenedy and Russian President Khrushchev. America assured Russia that she would not attack Cuba and Russia also withdrew missile station from Cuba.

Fifth Phase (1962-1969)

- The Fifth Phase which began from 1962 also marked a mutual suspicion between USA and USSR. There was a world-wide concern demanding ban on nuclear weapons. In this period Hot Line was established between the White House and Kremlin. This compelled both the parties to refrain from nuclear war. Inspite of that the Vietnam problem and the Problem in Germany kept Cold War between USA and USSR in fact.

Sixth Phase (1969-1978)

- This phase commencing from 1969 was marked by DETENTE between USA and USSR- the American President Nixon and Russian President Brezhnev played a vital role for putting an end to the Cold War. The SALT of 1972, the summit Conference on Security' of 1975 in Helsinki and Belgrade Conference of 1978 brought America and Russia closer.
- In 1971, American Foreign Secretary Henry Kissinger paid a secret visit to China to explore the possibilities of reapproachment with China. The American move to convert Diego Garcia into a military base was primarily designed to check the Soviet presence in the Indian Ocean. During the Bangladesh crisis of 1971 and the Egypt-Israel War of 1973 the two super powers extended support to the opposite sides.

Last Phase (1979-1987)

- In this phase certain changes were noticed in the Cold War. That is why historians call this phase as New Cold War. In 1979, the American President Carter and Russian President Brezhnev signed SALT II. But in 1979 the prospects of mitigating Cold War were marred by sudden development in Afghanistan.
- Vietnam (1975), Angola (1976), Ethiopia (1972) and Afghanistan (1979) issues brought success to Russia which was unbearable for America. American President Carter's Human Rights and Open Diplomacy were criticised by Russia. The SALT II was not ratified by the US Senate. In 1980 America boycotted the Olympic held at Moscow.
- In 1983, Russia withdrew from a talk on missile with America. In 1984 Russia boycotted the Olympic game held at Los-Angeles. The Star War of the American President Ronald Regan annoyed Russia. In this way the 'New Cold War' between America and Russia continued till 1987.

Result of the Cold War

The Cold War had far-reaching implications in the international affairs.

- At first, it gave rise to a fear psychosis which resulted in a mad race for the manufacture of more sophisticated armaments. Various alliances like NATO, SEATO, WARSAW PACT, CENTO, ANZUS etc. were formed only to increase world tension.
- Secondly, Cold War rendered the UNO ineffective because both super powers tried to oppose the actions proposed by the opponent. The Korean Crisis, Cuban Missile Crisis, Vietnam War etc. were the bright examples in this direction.
- Thirdly, due to the Cold War, a Third World was created. A large number of nations of Africa, Asia and Latin America decided to keep away from the military alliances of the two super powers. They liked to remain neutral. So, Non-Alignments Movement became the direct outcome of the Cold War.

- Fourthly, Cold War was designed against mankind. The unnecessary expenditure in the armament production created a barrier against the progress of the world and adversely affected a country and prevented improvement in the living standards of the people.
- Fifthly, the principle 'Whole World as a Family', was shattered on the rock of frustration due to the Cold War. It divided the world into two groups which was not a healthy sign for mankind.
- Sixthly, The Cold War created an atmosphere of disbelief among the countries. They questioned among themselves how unsafe were they under Russia or America.
- Finally, The Cold War disturbed the World Peace. The alliances and counter-alliances created a disturbing atmosphere. It was a curse for the world. Though Russia and America, being super powers, came forward to solve the international crisis, yet they could not be able to establish a perpetual peace in the world.

INDIA AND THE COLD WAR

- As a leader of NAM, India's response to the ongoing Cold War was two-fold: At one level, it took particular care in staying away from the two alliances. Second, it raised its voice against the newly decolonised countries becoming part of these alliances. India's policy was neither negative nor passive. As Nehru reminded the world, non-alignment was not a policy of 'fleeing away'. On the contrary, India was in favour of actively intervening in world affairs to soften Cold War rivalries. India tried to reduce the differences between the alliances and thereby prevent differences from escalating into a full-scale war. Indian diplomats and leaders were often used to communicate and mediate between Cold War rivals such as in the Korea War in the early 1950s.
- It is important to remember that India chose to involve other members of the non-aligned group in this mission. During the Cold War, India repeatedly tried to activate those regional and international organisations, which were not a part of the alliances led by the US and USSR. Nehru reposed great faith in 'a genuine commonwealth of free and cooperating nations' that would play a positive role in softening, if not ending, the Cold War. Non-alignment was not, as some suggest, a noble international cause which had little to do with India's real interests. A non-aligned posture also served India's interests very directly, in at least two ways: First, non-alignment allowed India to take international decisions and stances that served its interests rather than the interests of the super-powers and their allies. Second, India was often able to balance one superpower against the other. If India felt ignored or unduly pressurised by one superpower, it could tilt towards the other. Neither alliance system could take India for granted or bully it.

CRITICISM OF INDIA NAM

India's policy of non-alignment was criticised on a number of counts. Here we may refer to only two criticisms:

1. Unprincipled

- First, India's non-alignment was said to be 'unprincipled'. In the name of pursuing its national interest, India, it was said, often refused to take a firm stand on crucial international issues. Second, it is suggested that India was inconsistent and took contradictory postures. Having criticised others for joining alliances, India signed the Treaty of Friendship in August 1971 with the USSR for 20 years. This was regarded, particularly by outside observers, as virtually joining the Soviet alliance system. The Indian government's view was that India needed diplomatic and possibly military support during the Bangladesh crisis and that in any case the treaty did not stop India from having good relations with other countries including the US.

2. Non-relevance of Nam

- Non-alignment as a strategy evolved in the Cold War context. As, we know with the disintegration of the USSR and the end of the Cold War in 1991, non-alignment, both as an international movement and as the core of India's foreign policy, lost some of its earlier relevance and effectiveness. However, non-alignment contained some core values and enduring ideas. It was based on a recognition that decolonised states share a historical affiliation and can become a powerful force if they come together. It meant that the poor and often very small countries of the world need not become followers of any of the big powers, that they could pursue an independent foreign policy. It was also based on a resolve to democratise the international system by thinking about an alternative world order to redress existing inequities. These core ideas remain relevant even after the Cold War has ended

Relevance of Nam after cold war:

- **Limited test Ban Treaty (LTBT)**- Banned nuclear weapon tests in the atmosphere, in outer space and under water. Signed by the US, UK and USSR in Moscow on 5 August 1963. Entered into force on 10 October 1963.
- **Nuclear Non-Proliferation Treaty (NPT)**- Allows only the nuclear weapon states to have nuclear weapons and stops others from aquiring them. For the purposes of the NPT, a nuclear weapon state is one which has manufactured and exploded a nuclear weapon or other nuclear explosive device prior to 1 January 1967. So there are five nuclear weapon states: US, USSR (later Russia), Britain, France and China. Signed in Washington, London, and Moscow on 1 July 1968. Entered into force on 5 March 1970. Extended indefinitely in 1995.
- **Strategic arms Limitation Talks I (SALT-I)**- The first round of the Strategic Arms Limitation Talks began in November 1969. The Soviet leader Leonid Brezhnev and the US President Richard Nixon signed the following in Moscow on 26 May 1972 – a) Treaty on the limitation of Anti-Ballistic Missile Systems (ABM Treaty); and b) Interim Agreement on the limitation of strategic offensive arms. Entered into force on 3 October 1972.
- **Strategic arms Limitation Talks II (SALT-II)**- The second round started in November 1972. The US President Jimmy Carter and the Soviet leader Leonid Brezhnev signed the Treaty on the limitation of strategic offensive arms in Vienna on 18 June 1979.
- **Strategic arms Reduction Treaty I (START-I)**- Treaty signed by the USSR President Mikhail Gorbachev and the US President George Bush (Senior) on the reduction and limitation of strategic offensive arms in Moscow on 31 July 1991.
- **Strategic arms Reduction Treaty II (START-II)**- Treaty signed by the Russian President Boris Yeltsin and the US President George Bush (Senior) on the reduction and limitation of strategic offensive arms in Moscow on 3 January 1993.

QUESTIONS

1. What is Cold War? Discuss the main causes and its implications in detail
2. For what reasons and to what extent did the Yalta Conference of July 1945 contribute to the development of the Cold War?
3. Evaluate the role of the policies of the United States in the origins of the Cold War between 1945 and 1949.
4. Compare and contrast the role of two leaders, each chosen from a different region in the development of the Cold War between 1953 and 1964.
5. Why did détente develop between 1969 and 1979?
6. Analyse the impact of Afghanistan (1979-1988) on the development of the Cold War.
7. "The Cold War came to an end primarily because of Gorbachev's changes in Soviet policies." To what extent do you agree with this statement.
8. Why did Truman believe Greece needed American aid in 1947?
9. How did George Kennan's containment doctrine change during the Truman, Eisenhower and Kennedy administrations? Which president was the most successful in containing Communism?
10. What were the causes of the American economic boom in the 1950s? How did prosperity affect the nation socially, politically, and economically?
11. Why were Americans so terrified of Communist infiltration after World War II? What impact did the Red hunts of the late 1940s and early 1950s have on American politics and society?
12. What impact did the Korean War have on American foreign policy?
13. Why was the launch of Sputnik I in 1957 so significant? What did its launch mean for Americans?
14. Was the United States, the USSR, or Cuba more to blame for the Cuban missile crisis? What impact did the crisis have on U.S.-Soviet relations?
15. Why has the Korean War often been called America's "forgotten war"? What purpose did the war serve, and what impact did it have?
16. In your opinion, was the Cold War inevitable? If not, was the United States or the USSR more to blame?

CHAPTER 17

BIPOLAR TO MULTIPOLAR WORLD

INTRODUCTION

THE EMERGENCE OF TWO POWER BLOCS

The two superpowers were keen on expanding their spheres of influence in different parts of the world. In a world sharply divided between the two alliance systems, a state was supposed to remain tied to its protective superpower to limit the influence of the other superpower and its allies.

The smaller states in the alliances used the link to the superpowers for their own purposes. They got the promise of protection, weapons, and economic aid against their local rivals, mostly regional neighbours with whom they had rivalries. The alliance systems led by the two superpowers, therefore, threatened to divide the entire world into two camps. This division happened first in Europe. Most countries of western Europe sided with the US and those of eastern Europe joined the Soviet camp. That is why these were also called the 'western' and the 'eastern' alliances.

The western alliance was formalised into an organisation, the North Atlantic T reaty Organisation (NATO), which came into existence in April 1949. It was an association of twelve states which declared that armed attack on any one of them in Europe or North America would be regarded as an attack on all of them. Each of these states would be obliged to help the other. The eastern alliance, known as the Warsaw Pact, was led by the Soviet Union. It was created in 1955 and its principal function was to counter NATO's forces in Europe.

International alliances during the Cold War era were determined by the requirements of the superpowers and the calculations of the smaller states. As noted above, Europe became the main arena of conflict between the superpowers. In some cases, the superpowers used their military power to bring countries into their respective alliances. Soviet intervention in east Europe provides an example. The Soviet Union used its influence in eastern Europe, backed by the very large presence of its armies in the countries of the region, to ensure that the eastern half of Europe remained within its sphere of influence. In East and Southeast Asia and in West Asia (Middle East), the United States built an alliance system called — the Southeast Asian T reaty Organisation (SEATO) and the Central T reaty Organisation (CENTO). The Soviet Union and communist China responded by having close relations with regional countries such as North Vietnam, North Korea and Iraq. The Cold War threatened to divide the world into two alliances. Under these circumstances, many of the newly independent countries, after gaining their independence from the colonial powers such as Britain and France, were worried that they would lose their freedom as soon as they gained formal independence. Cracks and splits within the alliances were quick to appear. Communist China quarrelled with the USSR towards the late 1950s, and, in 1969, they fought a brief war over a territorial dispute. The other important development was the Non-Aligned Movement (NAM), which gave the newly independent countries a way of staying out of the alliances.

You may ask why the superpowers needed any allies at all. After all, with their nuclear weapons and regular armies, they were so powerful that the combined power of most of the smaller states in Asia and Africa, and even in Europe, was no match to that of the superpowers. Yet, the smaller states were helpful for the superpowers in gaining access to (i) vital resources, such as oil and minerals, (ii) territory, from where the superpowers could launch their weapons and troops, (iii) locations from where they could spy on each other, and (iv) economic support, in that many small allies together could help pay for military expenses.

They were also important for ideological reasons. The loyalty of allies suggested that the superpowers were winning the war of ideas as well, that liberal democracy and capitalism were better than socialism and communism, or vice versa.

NATO: FORMATION, PRINCIPLES, OBJECTIVES AND ANALYSIS OF NATO

The Cold War widened the gap between America and Soviet Russia. One country tried to exert fear in the mind of other. In order to make Europe free from the clutches of Communism, the United States of America created an organisation. This was known as North Atlantic Treaty Organisation or NATO.

Formation

North Atlantic Treaty Organisation was formed in 1949. At first 12 countries like the United States of America, Canada, England, France,

Belgium, Netherland etc. participated in it. In 1952, Greece and Turkey joined NATO. In 1955 West Germany became its member. NATO was really meant to check the Russian influence over the European Countries.

Principles of the NATO

This treaty includes one Preamble including 14 articles.

The principles of the NATO were:

1. The members of NATO will solve themselves the disputes which arise among them.
2. They will make their relations strong through friendly co-operation.
3. They will help each other for individual as well as Common Security.
4. As far as the Sovereignty was concerned, they will help each other.
5. Any attack on a country of Europe or North America will be treated as attack an whole of Europe and North America.

Objectives

The objectives of NATO were:

(*a*) The NATO was meant to create fear psychosis for Soviet Russia.
(*b*) It warned Russia that if it attacks on any country of Europe or America, then the USA would help that affected country.
(*c*) This organisation also tried to unite all the countries of Europe and America under one umbrella. It also aimed at economic stability of these countries and advancement in military front.
(*d*) This organisation also mentally stabilised the European nations.
(*e*) The real objective of NATO was to save the country of Europe and America which was to be attacked by Russia.

Analysis of NATO

NATO was internationally criticised. Various historians opine that NATO had encouraged the Cold War.

Secondly, as it did not obey the principles of the UNO, others pointed out fingers at it. Russia said that NATO was established only to terrorise Russia.

Thirdly, NATO was a barrier for world peace. It inspired the countries to bring progress in armaments. (However, the formation of NATO inspired the countries for a race in armament.

Really, NATO was a part of the Cold War. It not only accelerated the Cold War but also encouraged the enmity between America and Russia.)

CENTRAL TREATY ORGANISATION (CENTO): STRUCTURE, PRINCIPLES AND OTHER DETAILS

The CENTO was another black chapter of the cold war. The sole motive behind CENTO was to separate the Middle East from the Communist influence of Soviet Russia. It was another changed image of Baghdad Pact.

Structure

Central Treaty Organisation was the other name of Bagdad Pact. In 1955 Iraq and Turkey signed Baghdad Pact whose aim was to prevent Middle East from the influence of Russian Communism. Later on, England and Pakistan joined it. The USA gave financial help to this Pact. But in 1959 Iraq resigned from Baghdad Pact. Then this organisation was named as 'Central Treaty Organisation' or CENTO,

Principles of CENTO

The CENTO had the following principles:

1. The members of this organisation were to pay attention for their own security and to make the defense of other countries strong.
2. A member country would not interfere in the affairs of other country.
3. The member countries would not keep relation with other countries of the world.
4. This organisation would remain in force for five years.
5. This organisation would be given new shape after the expiry of five years.

Aims and Objectives

The CENTO had the following objectives:

(*a*) It was determined to keep Soviet Russia away from the Middle East.
(*b*) This was also a warning to Soviet Russia and other Arab Countries.
(*c*) The member countries aspired for help from the United States of America.
(*d*) It was expected that peace would be established in the Middle East, it would help the growth of trade and commerce among the member countries.
(*e*) This organisation became successful in projecting the defence system of America and England.

Analysis of CENTO

In true sense of the term, the CENTO was not successful in achieving its goal. At first, there was no need of such type of organisation in the Middle East.

Secondly, it doubled the anger of Soviet Russia. When Pakistan joined in CENTO, Soviet Russia came closer to India.

Thirdly, the interference of Turkey and England became unbearable by the member states. So, they became annoyed.

Fourthly, America wanted to play an active role in CENTO which neither was nor accepted by the member states.

At last due to the lack of adequate FINANCE, the importance of CENTO in the international affairs was reduced.

End of the Cold War

The Cold War which went on between the USA and USSR was really very furious. The two Super Powers characterised by subtle military and political strategies marched towards a ruinous race for destructive armaments. These circumstances led to Korean Crisis, Congo Crisis, Cyprus Crisis etc. participating in the disarmament process, they tried to reduce their armaments.

In 1985, Soviet Russia's President Mikhail Gorbachev's Perestroika and Glassnost helped a lot in keeping peace in the world. As a result of which in 1991 Soviet Union was divided and Warsaw Pact, also broken into pieces in 1997. The Super Powers refrained from any production of mass destructive arms.

By accepting the invitation of America's President Ronald Regan, the President of Russia, Gorbachev gave a heart touching speech at White House in America which surprised the whole world. This contributed a lot to the easing of Cold War.

However Cold War wrote a black chapter in the history of the world. It not only divided the whole world into two groups but also pushed the people into constant fear and confusion. After the end of the Cold War the Peace Process is going on to achieve the decided goal for- mankind.

THE END OF BIPOLARITY

The Berlin Wall, which had been built at the height of the Cold War and was its greatest symbol, was toppled by the people in 1989. This dramatic event was followed by an equally dramatic and historic chain of events that led to the collapse of the 'second world' and the end of the Cold War. Germany, divided after the Second World War, was unified. One after another, the eight East European countries that were part of the Soviet bloc replaced their communist governments in response to mass demonstrations. The Soviet Union stood by as the Cold War began to end, not by military means but as a result of mass actions by ordinary men and women. Eventually the Soviet Union itself disintegrated. In this chapter, we discuss the meaning, the causes and the consequences of the disintegration of the 'second world'. We also discuss what happened to that part of the world after the collapse of communist regimes and how India relates to these countries now

WHAT WAS THE SOVIET SYSTEM?

The Union of Soviet Socialist Republics (USSR) came into being after the socialist revolution in Russia in 1917. The revolution was inspired by the ideals of socialism, as opposed to capitalism, and the need for an egalitarian society. This was perhaps the biggest attempt in human history to abolish the institution of private property and consciously design a society based on principles of equality. In doing so, the makers of the Soviet system gave primacy to the state and the institution of the party. The Soviet political system centred around the communist party, and no other political party or opposition was allowed. The economy was planned and controlled by the state.

After the Second World War, the east European countries that the Soviet army had liberated from the fascist forces came under the control of the USSR. The political and the economic systems of all these countries were modelled after the USSR. This group of countries was called the Second World or the 'socialist bloc'. The Warsaw Pact, a military alliance, held them together. The USSR was the leader of the bloc.

The Soviet Union became a great power after the Second World War. The Soviet economy was then more developed than the rest of the world except for the US. It had a complex communications network, vast energy resources including oil, iron and steel machinery production, and a transport sector that connected its remotest areas with efficiency. It had a domestic consumer industry that produced everything from pins to cars, though their quality did not match that of the Western capitalist countries. The Soviet state ensured a minimum standard of living for all citizens, and the government subsidised basic necessities including health, education, childcare and other welfare schemes. There was no unemployment. State ownership was the dominant form of ownership: land and productive assets were owned and controlled by the Soviet state.

The Soviet system, however, became very bureaucratic and authoritarian, making life very difficult for its citizens. Lack of democracy and the absence of freedom of speech stifled people who often expressed their dissent in jokes and cartoons. Most of the institutions of the Soviet state needed reform: the one-party system represented by the Communist Party of the Soviet Union had tight control over all institutions and was unaccountable to the people. The party refused to recognise the urge of people in the fifteen different republics that formed the Soviet Union to manage their own affairs including their cultural affairs. Although, on paper, Russia was only one of the fifteen republics that together constituted the USSR, in reality Russia dominated everything, and people from other regions felt neglected and often suppressed.

In the arms race, the Soviet Union managed to match the US from time to time, but at great cost. The Soviet Union lagged behind the West in technology, infrastructure (e.g. transport, power), and most importantly, in fulfilling the political or economic aspirations of citizens. The Soviet invasion of Afghanistan in 1979 weakened the system even further. Though wages continued to grow, productivity and technology fell considerably behind that of the West. This led to shortages in all consumer goods. Food imports increased every year. The Soviet economy was faltering in the late 1970s and became stagnant .

GORBACHEV AND THE DISINTEGRATION

Mikhail Gorbachev, who had become General Secretary of the Communist Party of the Soviet Union in 1985, sought to reform this system. Reforms were necessary to keep the USSR abreast of the information and technological revolutions taking place in the West. However, Gorbachev's decision to normalise relations with the West and democratise and reform the Soviet Union had some other effects that neither he nor anyone else intended or anticipated. The people in the East European countries which were part of the Soviet bloc started to protest against their own governments and Soviet control. Unlike in the past, the Soviet Union, under Gorbachev, did not intervene when the disturbances occurred, and the communist regimes collapsed one after another. These developments were accompanied by a rapidly escalating crisis within the USSR that hastened its disintegration. Gorbachev initiated the policies of economic and political reform and democratisation within the country. The refor ms were opposed by leaders within the Communist Party.

A coup took place in 1991 that was encouraged by Communist Party hardliners. The people had tasted freedom by then and did not want the old-style rule of the Communist Party. Boris Yeltsin emerged as a national hero in opposing this coup. The Russian Republic, where Yeltsin won a popular election, began to shake off centralised control. Power began to shift from the Soviet centre to the republics, especially in the more Europeanised part of the Soviet Union, which saw themselves as sovereign states. The Central Asian republics did not ask for independence and wanted to remain with the Soviet Federation. In December 1991, under the leadership of Yeltsin, Russia, Ukraine and Belarus, three major republics of the USSR, declared that the Soviet Union was disbanded. The Communist Party of the Soviet Union was banned. Capitalism and democracy were adopted as the bases for the post-Soviet republics.

The declaration on the disintegration of the USSR and the formation of the Commonwealth of Independent States (CIS) came as a surprise to the other republics, especially to the Central Asian ones. The exclusion of these republics was an issue that was quickly solved by making them founding members of the CIS. Russia was now accepted as the successor state of the Soviet Union. It inherited the Soviet seat in the UN Security Council. Russia accepted all the international treaties and commitments of the Soviet Union. It took over as the only nuclear state of the post-Soviet space and carried out some nuclear disarmament measures with the US. The old Soviet Union was thus dead and buried.

WHY DID THE SOVIET UNION DISINTEGRATE?

How did the second most powerful country in the world suddenly disintegrate? This is a question worth asking not just to understand the Soviet Union and the end of communism but also because it is not the first and may not be the last political system to collapse. While there are unique features of the Soviet collapse, there may be more general lessons to be drawn from this very important case.

There is no doubt that the internal weaknesses of Soviet political and economic institutions, which failed to meet the aspirations of the people, were responsible for the collapse of the system. Economic stagnation for many years led to severe consumer shortages and a large section of Soviet society began to doubt and question the system and to do so openly.

Why did the system become so weak and why did the economy stagnate? The answer is partially clear. The Soviet economy used much of its resources in maintaining a nuclear and military arsenal and the development of its satellite states in Eastern Europe and within the Soviet system (the five Central Asian Republics in particular). This led to a huge economic burden that the system could not cope with. At the same time, ordinary citizens became more knowledgeable about the economic advance of the West. They could see the disparities between their system and the systems of the West. After years of being told that the Soviet system was better than Western capitalism, the reality of its backwardness came as a political and psychological shock.

The Soviet Union had become stagnant in an administrative and political sense as well. The Communist Party that had ruled the Soviet Union for over 70 years was not accountable to the people. Ordinary people were alienated by slow and stifling administration, rampant corruption, the inability of the system to correct mistakes it had made, the unwillingness to allow more openness in government, and the centralisation of authority in a vast land. Worse still, the party bureaucrats gained more privileges than ordinary citizens. People did not identify with the system and with the rulers, and the government increasingly lost popular backing. Gorbachev's reforms promised to deal with these problems.

Gorbachev promised to reform the economy, catch up with the West, and loosen the administrative system. You may wonder why the Soviet Union collapsed in spite of Gorbachev's accurate diagnosis of the problem and his attempt to implement reforms. Here is where the answers become more controversial, and we have to depend on future historians to guide us better.

The most basic answer seems to be that when Gorbachev carried out his reforms and loosened the system, he set in motion forces and expectations that few could have predicted and became virtually impossible to control. There were sections of Soviet society which felt that Gorbachev should have moved much faster and were disappointed and impatient with his methods. They did not benefit in the way they had hoped, or they benefited too slowly. Others, especially members of the Communist Party and those who were served by the system, took exactly the opposite view. They felt that their power and privileges were eroding and Gorbachev was moving too quickly. In this 'tug of war', Gorbachev lost support on all sides and divided public opinion. Even those who were with him became disillusioned as they felt that he did not adequately defend his own policies.

All this might not have led to the collapse of the Soviet Union but for another development that surprised most observers and indeed many insiders. The rise of nationalism and the desire for sovereignty within various republics including Russia and the Baltic Republics (Estonia, Latvia and Lithuania), Ukraine, Georgia, and others proved to be the final and most immediate cause for the disintegration of the USSR. Here again there are differing views. One view is that nationalist urges and feelings were very much at work throughout the history of the Soviet Union and that whether or not the reforms had occurred there would have been an internal struggle within the Soviet Union. This is a 'what-if' of history, but surely it is not an unreasonable view given the size and diversity of the Soviet Union and its growing internal problems. Others think that Gorbachev's reforms speeded up and increased nationalist dissatisfaction to the point that the government and rulers could not control it.

Ironically, during the Cold War many thought that nationalist unrest would be strongest in the Central Asian republics given their ethnic and religious differences with the rest of the Soviet Union and their economic backwardness. However, as things turned out, nationalist dissatisfaction with the Soviet Union was strongest in the more "European" and prosperous part – in Russia and the Baltic areas as well as Ukraine and Georgia. Ordinary people here felt alienated from the Central Asians and from each other and concluded also that they were paying too high an economic price to keep the more backward areas within the Soviet Union.

CONSEQUENCES OF DISINTEGRATION

The collapse of the second world of the Soviet Union and the socialist systems in eastern Europe had profound consequences for world politics. Let us note here three broad kinds of enduring changes that resulted from it. Each of these had a number of effects that we cannot list here. First of all, it meant the end of Cold War confrontations. The ideological dispute over whether the socialist system would beat the capitalist system was not an issue any more. Since this dispute had engaged the military of the two blocs, had triggered a massive arms race and accumulation of nuclear weapons, and had led to the existence of military blocs, the end of the confrontation demanded an end to this arms race and a possible new peace.

Second, power relations in world politics changed and, therefore, the relative influence of ideas and institutions also changed. The end of the Cold War left open only two possibilities: either the remaining superpower would dominate and create a unipolar system, or different countries or groups of countries could become important players in the international system, thereby bringing in a multipolar system where no one power could dominate. As it turned out, the US became the sole superpower. Backed by the power and prestige of the US, the capitalist economy was now the dominant economic system internationally. Institutions like the World Bank and International Monetary Fund became powerful advisors to all these countries since they gave them loans for their transitions to capitalism. Politically, the notion of liberal democracy emerged as the best way to organise political life.

Third, the end of the Soviet bloc meant the emergence of many new countries. All these countries had their own independent aspirations and choices. Some of them, especially the Baltic and east European states, wanted to join the European Union and become part of the North Atlantic Treaty Organisation (NATO). The Central Asian countries wanted to take advantage of their geographical location and continue their close ties with Russia and also to establish ties with the West, the US, China and others. Thus, the international system saw many new players emerge, each with its own identity, interests, and economic and political difficulties. It is to these issues that we now turn

CHALLENGE TO BIPOLARITY

We have already seen how the Cold War tended to divide the world into two rival alliances. It was in this context that non-alignment offered the newly decolonised countries of Asia, Africa and Latin America a third option—not to join either alliance. The roots of NAM went back to the friendship between three leaders — Yugoslavia's Josip Broz Tito, India's Jawaharlal Nehru, and Egypt's leader Gamal Abdel Nasser — who held a meeting in 1956. Indonesia's Sukarno and Ghana's Kwame Nkrumah strongly supported them. These five leaders came to be known as the five founders of NAM. The first non-aligned summit was held in Belgrade in 1961. This was the culmination of at least three factors: (i) cooperation among these five countries, (ii) growing Cold War tensions and its widening arenas, and (iii) the dramatic entry of many newly decolonised African countries into the inter -national arena. By 1960, there were 16 new African members in the UN.

The first summit was attended by 25 member states. Over the years, the membership of NAM has expanded. The latest meeting, the 14th summit, was held in Havana in 2006. It included 116 member states and 15 observer countries.

As non-alignment grew into a popular international movement, countries of various different political systems and interests joined it. This made the movement less homogeneous and also made it more difficult to define in very neat and precise terms: what did it really stand for?

Increasingly, NAM was easier to define in terms of what it was not. It was not about being a member of an alliance. The policy of staying away from alliances should not be considered isolationism or neutrality. Non-alignment is not isolationism since isolationism means remaining aloof from world affairs. Isolationism sums up the foreign policy of the US from the American War of Independence in 1787 up to the beginning of the First World War. In comparison, the non-aligned countries, including India, played an active role in mediating between the two rival alliances in the cause of peace and stability. Their strength was based on their unity and their resolve to remain non-aligned despite the attempt by the two superpowers to bring them into their alliances.

Non-alignment is also not neutrality. Neutrality refers principally to a policy of staying out of war. States practising neutrality are not required to help end a war. They do not get involved in wars and do not take any position on the appropriateness or morality of a war. Non-aligned states, including India, were actually involved in wars for various reasons. They also worked to prevent war between others and tried to end wars that had broken out.

NEW INTERNATIONAL ECONOMIC ORDER

The non-aligned countries were more than merely mediators during the Cold War. The challenge for most of the non-aligned countries — a majority of them were categorised as the Least Developed Countries (LDCs) — was to be more developed economically and to lift their people out of poverty. Economic development was also vital for the independence of the new countries. Without sustained development, a country could not be truly free. It would remain dependent on the richer countries including the colonial powers from which political freedom had been achieved.

The idea of a New Inter -national Economic Order (NIEO) originated with this realisation. The United Nations Conference on T rade and Development (UNCTAD) brought out a report in 1972 entitled Towards a New T rade Policy for Development.

The report proposed a reform of the global trading system so as to:

(i) give the LDCs control over their natural resources exploited by the developed Western countries,

(ii) obtain access to Western markets so that the LDCs could sell their products and, therefore, make trade more beneficial for the poorer countries,

(iii) reduce the cost of technology from the Western countries, and (iv) provide the LDCs with a greater role in international economic institutions.

Gradually, the nature of non-alignment changed to give greater importance to economic issues. In 1961, at the first summit in Belgrade, economic issues had not been very important. By the mid-1970s, they had become the most important issues. As a result, NAM became an economic pressure group. By the late 1980s, however, the NIEO initiative had faded, mainly because of the stiff opposition from the developed countries who acted as a united group while the non-aligned countries struggled to maintain their unity in the face of this opposition.

Emergence of Multi-polar System:

With the disintegration of USSR, the end of the cold war left open only two of possibilities like either the remaining superpower would dominate and create a 'Uni-polar System' or different countries or groups of countries could become important players in the international system, there by bringing in a 'Multi-polar system, where nobody's power could dominate.

As it turned out, the US became the sole super power. Backed by the power and prestige of the US, the 'capitalistic economy' was now the dominant economic system internationally. Institutions like the World Bank and International Monetary Fund [IMF] became powerful advisors to all these countries since they gave them loans for their transitions to capitalism. Politically, the nation of liberal democracy emerged as the best way to organise political life.

SHOCK THERAPY IN POST-COMMUNIST REGIMES

The collapse of communism was followed in most of these countries by a painful process of transition from an authoritarian socialist system to a democratic capitalist system. The model of transition in Russia, Central Asia and east Europe that was influenced by the World Bank and the IMF came to be known as 'shock therapy'. Shock therapy varied in intensity and speed amongst the former second world countries, but its direction and features were quite similar. Each of these countries was required to make a total shift to a capitalist economy, which meant rooting out completely any structures evolved during the Soviet period. Above all, it meant that private ownership was to be the dominant pattern of ownership of property.

Privatisation of state assets and corporate ownership patterns were to be immediately brought in. Collective farms were to be replaced by private farming and capitalism in agriculture. This transition ruled out any alternate or 'third way', other than state-controlled socialism or capitalism Shock therapy also involved a drastic change in the external orientation of these economies. Development was now envisaged through more trade, and thus a sudden and complete switch to free trade was considered essential. The free trade regime and foreign direct investment (FDI) were to be the main engines of change. This also involved openness to foreign investment, financial opening up or deregulation, and currency convertibility.

Finally, the transition also involved a break up of the existing trade alliances among the countries of the Soviet bloc. Each state from this bloc was now linked directly to the West and not to each other in the region. These states were thus to be gradually absorbed into the Western economic system. The Western capitalist states now became the leaders and thus guided and controlled the development of the region through various agencies and organisations.

CONSEQUENCES OF SHOCK THERAPY

The shock therapy administered in the 1990s did not lead the people into the promised utopia of mass consumption. Generally, it brought ruin to the economies and disaster upon the people of the entire region. In Russia, the large state-controlled industrial complex almost collapsed, as about 90 per cent of its industries were put up for sale to private individuals and companies. Since the restructuring was carried out through market forces and not by government-directed industrial policies, it led to the virtual disappearance of entire industries. This was called 'the largest garage sale in history', as valuable industries were undervalued and sold at throwaway prices. Though all citizens were given vouchers to participate in the sales, most citizens sold their vouchers in the black market because they needed the money.

The value of the ruble, the Russian currency, declined dramatically. The rate of inflation was so high that people lost all their savings. The collective farm system disintegrated leaving people without food security, and Russia started to import food. The real GDP of Russia in 1999 was below what it was in 1989. The old trading structure broke down with no alternative in its place. The old system of social welfare was systematically destroyed. The withdrawal of government subsidies pushed large sections of the people into poverty. The middle classes were pushed to the periphery of society, and the academic and intellectual manpower disintegrated or migrated. A mafia emerged in most of these countries and started controlling many economic activities. Privatisation led to new disparities. Post-Soviet states, especially Russia, were divided between rich and poor regions. Unlike the earlier system, there was now great economic inequality between people.

The construction of democratic institutions was not given the same attention and priority as the demands of economic transformation. The constitutions of all these countries were drafted in a hurry and most, including Russia, had a strong executive president with the widest possible powers that rendered elected parliaments relatively weak. In Central Asia, the presidents had great powers, and several of them became very authoritarian. For example, the presidents of Turkmenistan and Uzbekistan appointed themselves to power first for ten years and then extended it for another ten years. They allowed no dissent or opposition. A judicial culture and independence of the judiciary was yet to be established in most of these countries.

Most of these economies, especially Russia, started reviving in 2000, ten years after their independence. The reason for the revival for most of their economies was the export of natural resources like oil, natural gas and minerals. Azerbaijan, Kazakhstan, Russia, Turkmenistan and Uzbekistan are major oil and gas producers. Other countries have gained because of the oil pipelines that cross their territories for which they get rent. Some amount of manufacturing has restarted.

TENSIONS AND CONFLICTS

Most of the former Soviet Republics are prone to conflicts, and many have had civil wars and insurgencies. Complicating the picture is the growing involvement of outside powers.

In Russia, two republics, Chechnya and Dagestan, have had violent secessionist movements. Moscow's method of dealing with the Chechen rebels and indiscriminate military bombings have led to many human rights violations but failed to deter the aspirations for independence.

In Central Asia, Tajikistan witnessed a civil war that went on for ten years till 2001. The region as a whole has many sectarian conflicts. In Azerbaijan's province of Nagorno-Karabakh, some local Armenians want to secede and join Armenia. In Georgia, the demand for independence has come from two provinces, resulting in a civil war. There are movements against the existing regimes in Ukraine, Kyrgyzstan and Georgia. Countries and provinces are fighting over river waters. All this has led to instability, making life difficult for the ordinary citizen.

The Central Asian Republics are areas with vast hydrocarbon resources, which have brought them economic benefit. Central Asia has also become a zone of competition between outside powers and oil companies. The region is next to Russia, China, Afghanistan, and Pakistan, and close to West Asia. After 11 September 2001, the US wanted military bases in the region and paid the governments of all Central Asian states to hire bases and to allow airplanes to fly over their territory during the wars in Afghanistan and Iraq. However, Russia perceives these states as its 'Near Abroad' and believes that they should be under Russian influence. China has interests here because of the oil resources, and the Chinese have begun to settle around the borders and conduct trade. In easter n Europe, Czechoslovakia split peacefully into two, with the Czechs and the Slovaks forming independent countries. But the most severe conflict took place in the Balkan republics of Yugoslavia. After 1991, it broke apart with several provinces like Croatia, Slovenia and Bosnia and Herzegovina declaring independence. Ethnic Serbs opposed this, and a massacre of non-Serb Bosnians followed. The NATO intervention and the bombing of Yugoslavia followed the inter-ethnic civil war.

INDIA AND POST-COMMUNIST COUNTRIES

India has maintained good relations with all the post-communist countries. But the strongest relations are still those between Russia and India. India's relations with Russia are an important aspect of India's foreign policy. Indo-Russian relations are embedded in a history of trust and common interests and are matched by popular perceptions. Indian heroes from Raj Kapoor to Amitabh Bachhan are household names in Russia and many post-Soviet countries. One can hear Hindi film songs all over the region, and India is part of the popular memory.

Russia and India share a vision of a multipolar world order. What they mean by a multipolar world order is the co-existence of several powers in the international system, collective security (in which an attack on any country is regarded as a threat to all countries and requires a collective response), greater regionalism, negotiated settlements of international conflicts, an independent foreign policy for all countries, and decision making through bodies like the UN that should be strengthened, democratised, and empowered. More than 80 bilateral agreements have been signed between India and Russia as part of the Indo-Russian Strategic Agreement of 2001.

India stands to benefit from its relationship with Russia on issues like Kashmir, energy supplies, sharing information on international terrorism access to Central Asia, and balancing its relations with China. Russia stands to benefit from this relationship because India is the second largest arms market for Russia. The Indian military gets most of its hardware from Russia. Since India is an oil-importing nation, Russia is important to India and has repeatedly come to the assistance of India during its oil crises. India is seeking to increase its energy imports from Russia and the republics of Kazakhstan and Turkmenistan. Cooperation with these republics includes partnership and investment in oilfields. Russia is important for India's nuclear energy plans and assisted India's space industry by giving, for example, the cryogenic rocket when India needed it. Russia and India have collaborated on various scientific projects.

QUESTIONS

1. Emergence of two power blocs was actually superpower rivalry. Discuss?
2. What do you mean by Bipolarity? Assess the new world order which emerged after the collapse of Soviet Union.
3. With the end of Cold War, NAM has lost its relevance.' Do you agree with this statement? Give reasons in support of your answer.
4. What are the main causes and consequences of Disintegration of Soviet Union?
5. What are the factors that lead to establish Multi Polar World?
6. What do you mean by Shock Therapy and what are its consequences?
7. Examine India nd Russian Relationship after the disintegration of Soviet Union?
8. Examine the structure , Principles and objectives of Military alliances of the Super Power of the world?
9. Examine the challenges faced by Bi-Polarity?

CHAPTER 18

US Hegemony in World Politics

OVERVIEW

We have seen that the end of Cold War left the US without any serious rival in the world. The era since then has been described as a period of US dominance or a unipolar world. In this chapter, we try to understand the nature, extent and limits of this dominance. We begin by narrating the story of the rise of the new world order from the First Gulf War to the US-led invasion of Iraq. We then pause to understand the nature of US domination with the help of the concept of 'hegemony'. After exploring the political, economic and cultural aspects of US hegemony, we assess India's policy options in dealing with the US. Finally, we turn to see if there are challenges to this hegemony and whether it can be overcome.

BEGINNING OF THE 'NEW WORLD ORDER'

The sudden collapse of the Soviet Union took everyone by surprise. While one of the two superpowers ceased to exist, the other remained with all its powers intact, even enhanced. Thus, it would appear that the US hegemony began in 1991 after Soviet power disappeared from the international scene. This is largely correct, but we need to keep in mind two riders to this. First, as we shall see in this chapter, some aspects of US hegemony did not emerge in 1991 but in fact go back to the end of the Second World War in 1945.

Second, the US did not start behaving like a hegemonic power right from 1991; it became clear much later that the world was in fact living in a period of hegemony. Let us therefore look at this process by which US hegemony got established more closely. In August 1990, Iraq invaded Kuwait, rapidly occupying and subsequently annexing it. After a series of diplomatic attempts failed at convincing Iraq to quit its aggression, the United Nations mandated the liberation of Kuwait by force. For the UN, this was a dramatic decision after years of deadlock during the Cold War. The US President George H.W. Bush hailed the emergence of a 'new world order'.

A massive coalition force of 660,000 troops from 34 countries fought against Iraq and defeated it in what came to be known as the First Gulf War. However, the UN operation, which was called 'Operation Desert Storm', was overwhelmingly American. An American general, Nor man Schwarzkopf, led the UN coalition and nearly 75 per cent of the coalition forces were from the US. Although the Iraqi

President, Saddam Hussein, had promised "the mother of all battles", the Iraqi forces were quickly defeated and forced to withdraw from Kuwait.

The First Gulf War revealed the vast technological gap that had opened up between the US military capability and that of other states. The highly publicised use of so-called 'smart bombs' by the US led some observers to call this a 'computer war'. Widespread television coverage also made it a 'video game war', with viewers around the world watching the destruction of Iraqi forces live on TV in the comfort of their living rooms.

Incredibly, the US may actually have made a profit from the war. According to many reports, the US received more money from countries like Germany, Japan and Saudi Arabia than it had spent on the war.

THE CLINTON YEARS

Despite winning the First Gulf War, George H.W. Bush lost the US presidential elections of 1992 to William Jefferson (Bill) Clinton of the Democratic Party, who had campaigned on domestic rather than foreign policy issues. Bill Clinton won again in 1996 and thus remained the president of the US for eight years. During the Clinton years, it often seemed that the US had withdrawn into its internal affairs and was not fully engaged in world politics. In foreign policy, the Clinton government tended to focus on 'soft issues' like democracy promotion, climate change and world trade rather than on the 'hard politics' of military power and security.

Nevertheless, the US on occasion did show its readiness to use military power even during the Clinton years. The most important episode occurred in 1999, in response to Yugoslavian actions against the predominantly Albanian population in the province of Kosovo. The air forces of the NATO countries, led by the US, bombarded targets around Yugoslavia for well over two months, forcing the downfall of the government of Slobodan Milosevic and the stationing of a NATO force in Kosovo.

Another significant US military action during the Clinton years was in response to the bombing of the US embassies in Nairobi, Kenya and Dar-es-Salaam, Tanzania in 1998. These bombings were attributed to Al-Qaeda, a terrorist organisation strongly influenced by extremist Islamist ideas. Within a few days of this bombing, President Clinton ordered Operation Infinite

Reach, a series of cruise missile strikes on Al-Qaeda terrorist targets in Sudan and Afghanistan. The US did not bother about the UN sanction or provisions of international law in this regard. It was alleged that some of the targets were civilian facilities unconnected to terrorism. In retrospect, this was merely the beginning.

9/11 AND THE 'GLOBAL WAR ON TERROR'

On 11 September 2001, nineteen hijackers hailing from a number of Arab countries took control of four American commercial aircraft shortly after takeoff and flew them into important buildings in the US. One airliner each crashed into the North and South Towers of the World Trade Centre in New York. A third aircraft crashed into the Pentagon building in Arlington, Virginia, where the US Defence Department is headquartered. The fourth aircraft, presumably bound for the Capitol building of the US Congress, came down in a field in Pennsylvania. The attacks have come to be known as "9/11". (In America the convention is to write the month first, followed by the date; hence the short form '9/ 11' instead of '11/9' as we would write in India).

The attacks killed nearly three thousand persons. In terms of their shocking effect on Americans, they have been compared to the British burning of Washington, DC in 1814 and the Japanese attack on

Pearl Harbour in 1941. However, in terms of loss of life, 9/11 was the most severe attack on US soil since the founding of the country in 1776. The US response to 9/11 was swift and ferocious. Clinton had been succeeded in the US presidency by George W. Bush of the Republican Party, son of the earlier President George H. W. Bush. Unlike Clinton, Bush had a much harder view of US interests and of the means by which to advance them. As a part of its 'Global War on Terror', the US launched 'Operation Enduring Freedom' against all those suspected to be behind this attack, mainly Al-Qaeda and the T aliban regime in Afghanistan. The Taliban regime was easily overthrown, but remnants of the Taliban and Al-Qaeda have remained potent, as is clear from the number of terrorist attacks launched by them against Western targets since.

The US forces made arrests all over the world, often without the knowledge of the government of the persons being arrested, transported these persons across countries and detained them in secret prisons. Some of them were brought to Guantanamo Bay, a US Naval base in Cuba, wher e the prisoners did not enjoy the protection of international law or the law of their own country or that of the US. Even the UN representatives were not allowed to meet these prisoners.

THE IRAQ INVASION

On 19 March 2003, the US launched its invasion of Iraq under the codename 'Operation Iraqi Freedom'. More than forty other countries joined in the US-led 'coalition of the willing' after the UN refused to give its mandate to the invasion. The ostensible purpose of the invasion was to prevent Iraq from developing weapons of mass destruction (WMD). Since no evidence of WMD has been unearthed in Iraq, it is speculated that the invasion was motivated by other objectives, such as controlling Iraqi oilfields and installing a regime friendly to the US.

Although the government of Saddam Hussein fell swiftly, the US has not been able to 'pacify' Iraq. Instead, a full-fledged insurgency against US occupation was ignited in Iraq. While the US has lost over 3,000 military personnel in the war, Iraqi casualties are very much higher. It is conservatively estimated that 50,000 Iraqi civilians have been killed since the US-led invasion. It is now widely recognised that the US invasion of Iraq was, in some crucial respects, both a military and political failure. [Map of Post-Soviet Countries]

WHAT DOES HEGEMONY MEAN?

Politics is about power. Just as individuals want to gain and retain power, groups too want to gain and retain power. We routinely talk of someone becoming powerful or someone doing something for power. In the case of world politics too, countries and groups of countries are engaged in constantly trying to gain and retain power. This power is in the form of military domination, economic power, political clout and cultural superiority.

Therefore, if we wanted to understand world politics, it is necessary that we understand the distribution of power among the countries of the world. For instance, during the years of the Cold War (1945-91) power was divided between the two groups of countries, and the US and the Soviet Union represented the two 'camps' or centres of power in international politics during that period. The collapse of the Soviet Union left the world with only a single power, the United States of America. Sometimes, the international system dominated by a sole superpower, or hyper-power, is called a 'unipolar' system. This appears to be a misapplication of the idea of 'pole' derived from physics. It may be more appropriate to describe an international system with only one centre of power by the term 'hegemony'.

We can identify three very different understandings of what hegemony is. Let us examine each of these meanings of hegemony and relate them to contemporary international politics.

HEGEMONY AS HARD POWER

The roots of the word hegemony lie in classical Greek. The word implies the leadership or predominance of one state, and was originally used to denote the preponderant position of Athens vis-à-visthe other city-states of ancient Greece. Thus, the first meaning of hegemony relates to the relations, patterns and balances of military capability between states. It is this notion of hegemony as military preponderance that is especially germane to the current position and role of the US in world politics.

The bedrock of contemporary US power lies in the overwhelming superiority of its military power. American military dominance today is both absolute and relative. In absolute terms, the US today has military capabilities that can reach any point on the planet accurately, lethally and in real time, thereby crippling the adversary while its own forces are sheltered to the maximum extent possible from the dangers of war. But even more awesome than the absolute capabilities of the US is the fact that no other power today can remotely match them. The US today spends more on its military capability than the next 12 powers combined. Furthermore, a large chunk of the Pentagon's budget goes into military research and development, or, in other words, technology. Thus, the military dominance of the US is not just based on higher military spending, but on a qualitative gap, a technological chasm that no other power can at present conceivably span. Undoubtedly, the US invasion of Iraq reveals several American vulnerabilities. The US has not been able to force the Iraqi people into submitting to the occupation forces of the US-led coalition. To fully understand the nature of American weakness, however, we need to have a historical perspective. Imperial powers through history have used military forces to accomplish only four tasks: to conquer, deter, punish and police. As the Iraq invasion shows, the American capacity to conquer is formidable. Similarly, the US capability to deter and to punish is self-evident. Where US military capability has thus far been shown to have serious weaknesses is in policing an occupied territory.

HEGEMONY AS STRUCTURAL POWER

The second notion of hegemony is very different from the first. It emerges from a particular understanding of the world economy. The basic idea is that an open world economy requires a hegemony or dominant power to support its creation and existence. The hegemony must possess both the ability and the desire to establish certain norms for order and must sustain the global structure. The hegemony usually does this to its own advantage but often to its relative detriment, as its competitors take advantage of the openness of the world economy without paying the costs of maintaining its openness. Hegemony in this second sense is reflected in the role played by the US in providing global public goods. By public goods we mean those goods that can be consumed by one person without reducing the amount of the good available for someone else. Fresh air and roads are examples of public goods. In the context of the world economy, the best examples of a global public good are sea-lanes of communication (SLOCs), the sea routes commonly used by merchant ships. Free trade in an open world economy would not be possible without open SLOCs. It is the naval power of the hegemony that underwrites the law of the sea and ensures freedom of navigation in international waters. Since the decline of British naval power after the Second World War, the multi-oceanic US Navy has played this role.

Another example of a global public good is the Inter net. Although it is seen today as making the virtual world of the World Wide Web possible, we should not forget that the Internet is the direct outcome of a US military research project that began in 1950. Even today, the Internet relies on a global network of satellites, most of which are owned by the US government. As we know, the US is present in all parts of the world, in all sectors of the world economy and in all areas of technology. The US share of the world economy remains an enormous 28 per cent. The US also accounts for 15 per cent of world trade, if intra-European Union trade is included in world trade data. There is not a single sector of the world economy in which an American firm does not feature in the "top three" list.

It is important to remember that the economic preponderance of the US is inseparable from its structural power, which is the power to shape the global economy in a particular way. After all, the Bretton Woods system, set up by the US after the Second World War, still constitutes the basic structure of the world economy. Thus, we can regard the World Bank, Inter national Monetary Fund (IMF) and World Trade Organisation (WTO) as the products of American hegemony.

HEGEMONY AS SOFT POWER

It would however be a mistake to see US hegemony in purely military and economic terms without considering the ideological or the cultural dimension of US hegemony. This third sense of hegemony is about the capacity to 'manufacture consent'. Here, hegemony implies class ascendancy in the social, political and particularly ideological spheres. Hegemony arises when the dominant class or country can win the consent of dominated classes, by persuading the dominated classes to view the world in a manner favourable to the ascendancy of the dominant class. Adapted to the field of world politics, this notion of hegemony suggests that a dominant power deploys not only military power but also ideological resources to shape the behaviour of competing and lesser powers. The behaviour of the weaker countries is influenced in ways that favour the interests of the most powerful country, in particular its desire to remain pre-eminent. Consent, in other words, goes hand-in-hand with, and is often more effective than, coercion. The predominance of the US in the world today is based not only on its military power and economic prowess, but also on its cultural presence. Whether we choose to recognise the fact or not, all ideas of the good life and personal success, most of the dreams of individuals and societies across the globe, are dreams churned out by practices prevailing in twentieth-century America.

America is the most seductive, and in this sense the most powerful, culture on earth. This attribute is called 'soft power': the ability to persuade rather than coearave. Over time we get so used to hegemony that we hardly notice it, any more than we notice the rivers, birds, and trees around us.

You couldn't have forgotten Andrei and his 'cool' pair of blue jeans. When his parents were youngsters in the Soviet Union, blue jeans were the ultimate symbol of 'liberation' for their generation. Young men and women often spent over a year's salary to buy blue jeans from foreign tourists on the black market. Somehow, for an entire Soviet generation blue jeans came to represent aspirations of the 'good life' that were not available in their own country.

During the Cold War, the US found it difficult to score victories against the Soviet Union in the realm of hard power. It was in the area of structural power and soft power that the US scored notable victories. Although the Soviet centrally-planned economy provided an alternate model of internal economic organisation, the world economy throughout the Cold War years remained a world capitalisteconomy. But it was in the area of soft power that the US was ultimately triumphant. As the example of blue jeans in the Soviet Union clearly shows, the US was able to engineer a generational divide in Soviet society on the basis of a cultural product.

CONSTRAINTS ON AMERICAN POWER

History tells us that empires decline because they decay from within. Similarly, the biggest constraints to American hegemony lie within the heart of hegemony itself. We can identify three constraints on American power. None of these constraints seemed to operate in the years following 9/11. However, it now appears that all three of these constraints are slowly beginning to operate again.

The first constraint is the institutional architecture of the American state itself. A system of division of powers between the three branches of government places significant brakes upon the unrestrained and immoderate exercise of America's military power by the executive branch. The second constraint on American power is also domestic in nature, and stems from the open nature of American society. Although the American mass media may from time to time impose or promote a particular perspective on domestic public opinion in the US, there is nevertheless a deep scepticism regarding the purposes and methods of gover nment in American political culture. This factor, in the long run, is a huge constraint on US military action overseas.

However, it is the third constraint on the US that is perhaps the most important. There is only one organisation in the international system that could possibly moderate the exercise of American power today, and that is the North Atlantic Treaty Organisation (NATO). The US obviously has an enormous interest in keeping the alliance of democracies that follow the market economies alive and therefore it is possible that its allies in the NATO will be able to moderate the exercise of US hegemony.

INDIA'S RELATIONSHIP WITH THE US

During the Cold War years, India found itself on the opposite side of the divide from the US. India's closest friendship during those years was with the Soviet Union. After the collapse of the Soviet Union, India suddenly found itself friendless in an increasingly hostile international environment. However, these were also the years when India decided to liberalise its economy and integrate it with the global economy. This policy and India's impressive economic growth rates in recent years have made the country an attractive economic partner for a number of countries including the US. It is important that we do not lose sight of the fact that two new factors have emerged in Indo-US relations in recent years. These factors relate to the technological dimension and the role of the Indian-American diaspora. Indeed, these two factors are interrelated. Consider the following facts:

The US absorbs about 65 per cent of India's total exports in the software sector. 35 per cent of the technical staff of Boeing is estimated to be of Indian origin. 300,000 Indians work in Silicon Valley.

15 percent of all high-tech start-ups are by Indian-Americans. Like all other countries, India too has to decide exactly what type of relationship it wants with the US in this phase of global hegemony. The choices are not exactly easy. Within India, the debate seems to be around three possible strategies. Those Indian analysts who see international politics largely in terms of military power are fearful of the growing closeness between India and the US. They would prefer that India maintains its aloofness from Washington and focuses upon increasing its own comprehensive national power. Other analysts see the growing convergence of interests between the US and India as a historic opportunity for India. They advocate a strategy that would allow India to take advantage of US hegemony and the mutual convergences to establish the best possible options for itself. Opposing the US, they argue, is a futile strategy that will only hurt India in the long run.

A third group of analysts would advocate that India should take the lead in establishing a coalition of countries from the developing world. Over time, this coalition would become more powerful and may succeed in weaning the hegemony away from its dominating ways. India-US relations are perhaps too complex to be managed by a single strategy. India needs to develop an appropriate mix of foreign policy strategies to deal with the US.

HOW CAN HEGEMONY BE OVERCOME?

How long will hegemony last? How do we get beyond hegemony? These become, for obvious reasons, some of the burning questions of our time. History provides us with some fascinating clues to answer these questions. But what about the present and the future? In international politics, very few factors formally curtail the exercise of military power by any country. There is no world gover nment like the government of a country. International organisation is not world government. Thus, international politics is 'politics without government'. There are some rules and norms called the laws of war that restrict, but do not prohibit, war. But few states will entrust their security to international law alone. Does this mean that there is no escape from war and hegemony?

In the short term, we must recognise that no single power is anywhere near balancing the US militarily. A military coalition against the US is even less likely given the differences that exist among big countries like China, India, and Russia that have the potential to challenge US hegemony. Some people argue that it is strategically more prudent to take advantage of the opportunities that hegemony creates. For instance, raising economic growth rates requires increased trade, technology transfers, and investment, which are best acquired by working with rather than against the hegemony. Thus, it is suggested that instead of engaging in activities opposed to the hegemonic power, it may be advisable to extract benefits by operating within the hegemonic system. This is called the 'bandwagon' strategy.

Another strategy open to states is to 'hide'. This implies staying as far removed from the dominant power as possible. There are many examples of this behaviour. China, Russia, the European Union—all of them, in different ways, are seeking to stay below the radar, as it were, and not overly and unduly antagonise the US. However, this would not seem to be viable for the big, second-rank powers for very long. While it may be an attractive, viable policy for small states, it is hard to imagine mega-states like China, India, and Russia or huge agglomerations such as the EU being able to hide for any substantial length of time. Some people believe that resistance to American hegemony may not come from other states, which as we have seen are powerless to confront the US today, but rather from non-state actors. These challenges to American hegemony will emerge in the economic and cultural realms, and will come from a combination of non-governmental organisations (NGOs), social movements, and public opinion; it may arise from sections of the media and intellectuals, artists, and writers. These various actors may well form links across national boundaries, including with Americans, to criticise and resist US policies.

You might have heard the saying that we now live in a 'global village'. In this global village, we are all neighbours of the village headman. If the behaviour of the headman becomes intolerable, we will not have the option of leaving the global village, because this is the only world we know and the only village we have. Resistance will then be the only option available.

QUESTIONS

1. What are the constraints on American Hegemony Today? Which one of these do you expect to get more important in the future?
2. If the big and resourceful state cannot resist the US Hegemony , it is unrealistic to expect much smaller and weaker non- state actors to offer any reitance Examine this proposition and give your opinion.

3. What was the foreign policy of U.S during Clinton Years? How was it different from Gorge H. W. Bush's time?
4. When did U.S show its military power during Clinton Years? Why did President Clinton order Operation Infinite Reach?
5. Why did U.S launch Global War Terror? What happened on 11th September 2001?
6. When did U.S launch Operation Enduring Freedom?
7. Why did U.S invade Iraq on 19th March, 2003? Why is this invasion termed as military and political failure on the part of U.S?
8. What does Hegemony mean? Explain three kinds of U.S Hegemony with the help of examples.
9. Evaluate India's changing relationship with the U.S.
10. What are the three possible strategies of Indo-U.S relations suggested by the three schools of thought?
11. What are the three possible ways of overcoming U.S Hegemony?
12. What is 'Band Wagon Strategy'?
13. What do you mean by 'Hide Strategy' to overcome U.S Hegemony?
14. How can non-state actors help in overcoming U.S Hegemony?
15. How is U.S dominance since the Cold War different from its position as a Super Power

CHAPTER 19

International Organisations in a Uni-Polar World

INTRODUCTION:- WHAT ARE INTERNATIONAL ORGANISATIONS?

International organisations include Inter-governmental Organisations (IGOs) and Non-Governmental Organisations (NGOs). IGOs have official delegates appointed by member nations. NGOs, on the other hand, are comprised of private individuals or institutions.

Why there is Need for IGOs

IGOs provide a less binding sense of regulation in comparison to national governments, yet their presence is significant in an increasingly integrated world. While some contend that international organisations ensure compliance to wishes of powerful nations, others view them as deterrents to hegemonic designs.

Different Categories :-Categorizing IGOs

IGOs can be placed into four distinct categories:

i. IGOs can have a *general membership* and a *general purpose* (UN system)
ii. IGOs can have a *general membership* and a *limited purpose* (World Bank)
iii. IGOs can have a *limited membership* and a *general purpose* (OIC, EU)
iv. IGOs can have a *limited membership* and a *limited purpose* (NATO)

History of International Organisations

The Greek city states like Sparta and Athens developed military and defence organisations like NATO and the Warsaw Pact. Twelve city states also formed the Amphictyonic League to protect the Temple at Delphi.

The Romans developed administrative, legal and military structures which aided international organisation at a later stage in history. In 1305, Pierre Dubories, a French lawyer proposed alliances between Christian powers, which led to several such formations, the Hanseatic League most prominent amongst them.

Subsequently, the 'Grand Design' of 1603 comprised of 15 Christian republics, it aimed to end violence and settle disputes peacefully, yet it too was an overtly Christian organisation confined to Europe. Establishment of a world government and enduring peace did begin to preoccupy prominent thinkers though, like the Italian poet Dante (13 century) and the philosophers, Rousseau and Kant (18 century).

The European Congress in Westphalia in 1648, which ended 30 years of a bloody war, was not able to establish a formal organisation but it did promote diplomatic ties amongst many prominent states. The French Revolution of 1789 similarly brought wide recognition of the right of self determination. Then the Congress of Vienna in 1815 provided principles for navigation of international rivers and identified provisions for abolishing slavery.

The US Monroe Doctrine of 1825 also set the stage for international cooperation by issuing a strong proclamation against external interventions. The Brussels Congress of 1874 provided a code of land warfare approved by 15 nations. The Hague Commissions of 1899 &1907 stressed on arbitration to avoid violence and on the equality of all independent states.

Also public international unions like the International Telegraphic Union (1865), the Universal Postal Union (1847) and the Rhine River Commission (1804) became prototypes for international organisations formed in the 20 century, like the League of Nations and the UN system.

The League of Nations

The League of Nations was a general membership, general purpose IGO. The League was formed in 1919 to prevent war through collective security and settling disputes through negotiations and diplomacy; and to improve global welfare.

Despite these bold aims, it could not prevent aggression by the fascist powers in late 1930s.The UN replaced the League after WWII.

United Nations

The UN is a general membership and general purpose IGO. The UN was established in 1954 and is now made up of 191 states. UN membership is open to all "peace-loving states". The General Assembly determines admission upon recommendation of the Security Council.

The term UN was coined by Roosevelt during WWII, to refer to the Allies. The name was transferred to the UN as it was founded by the victorious powers in the war as a condition of the Atlantic Charter and other wartime agreements.

The UN system is financed in two ways: assessed and voluntary contributions from member states. The General Assembly is a principal organ of the UN and it includes representatives from all member states.

The UN Security Council is the most powerful UN organ, which passes resolutions, determines the need for sanctions and is comprised of China, Russia, US, UK and France, all of whom have veto powers. There are also non-veto non-permanent members appointed to the Security Council, which are brought onto the Council from the General Assembly.

The world witnessed two devastating wars in the 20th century. The First World War broke out in 1914 and continued till 1918. Millions of people were killed, wounded, maimed, crippled and rendered homeless. The horror and tragedy of the First World War led to a universal desire for peace.

It was felt that some international organisation should be created to prevent future wars. Out of this desire was born the League of Nations. The primary aim of the League of Nations was to preserve peace and promote international cooperation.

The League of Nations failed to maintain peace and the Second World War broke out in 1939. The outbreak of the Second World War revealed to the world the weaknesses of the League of Nations. It was felt that a much stronger international organisation should be created, if the world was to have peace. The Second World War which broke out in 1939 came to an end in 1945.

The Atlantic charter

Even before the end of the war, in August 1941, the U.S. President, Franklin Roosevelt, and the British Prime Minister, Winston Churchill, met on a battleship, 'the Cruiser', in the mid-Altantic and drew up the Atlantic Charter which was released on 14th August, 1941.

The Charter had the following objectives:

(1) To maintain international peace and security;
(2) To encourage international cooperation in the spheres of social, economic and cultural developments;
(3) To develop friendly relations among nations on the principles of equal rights and self-determination;
(4) To recognise the fundamental rights of all people.

United Nations declaration or the Washington declaration:

On 1st January, 1942, representatives of 26 Allied countries met in Washington and signed a Declaration of United Nations. The signatories endorsed the principles of the Atlantic Charter. This was the first time that the term 'United Nations' was used.

The UN Charter finally emerged after three major conferences—the Dumbarton Oaks Conference (1944), the Yalta Conference (1945) and the San Francisco Conference (1945). At the Dumbarton Oaks Conference the representatives of four major powers (Britain, the United States, the Soviet Union and China) agreed on proposals for the aims, structure and functioning of the United Nations. They voted for an Assembly, a Security Council, a Secretariat and an International Court. The Yalta Conference decided on the voting procedure to be followed by the Security Council.

Membership of the United Nations was to be opened to all peace- loving states. Representatives of fifty nations met at San Francisco to sign the Atlantic Charter. Poland signed it later and became one of the original 51 member states.

The United Nations officially came into existence on 24th October, 1945. The Charter had been ratified by the five big powers Britain, China, France, the Soviet Union, and the United States and by a majority of the other signatories.

The 24th October is celebrated as United Nations Day. Today, the organisation has 192 members.

The headquarters of the United Nations is located in New York, USA. The organisation has six official languages- English, French, Spanish, Russian, Chinese and Arabic. Its flag bears its emblem, a map of the world encircled by two bent olive branches.

Aims of the United Nations

The objectives of the United Nations, according to its Charter, are:

(1) To maintain international peace and security
(2) To develop friendly relations among nations on the basis of equality and the principle of self determination.
(3) To foster worldwide cooperation in solving economic, social, cultural and humanitarian problems.

(4) To promote human rights and fundamental freedom for the people of the world.
(5) To serve as a centre where various nations can coordinate their activities towards the attainment of the objectives of the United Nations.
(6) To save succeeding generations from the scourge of war.

The organs of the United Nations

The UN has six principal organs to carry out its functions:

1. The General Assembly,
2. The Security Council,
3. The Economic and Social Council,
4. The Trusteeship Council,
5. The International Court of Justice and
6. The Secretariat.

1.The General Assembly: The General Assembly is the largest organ of the UN. All members of the UN are members of the General Assembly. Each state can send up to five representatives but is entitled to one vote in the Assembly. This ensures that all the member states have equal status.

The General Assembly meets once a year for three months. But special sessions may be held during times of crisis. At the beginning of every session, the Assembly elects a new President.

The functions of the General Assembly are as follows:

1. It can discuss any matter affecting international peace and security.
2. It makes recommendations for peaceful settlements of disputes.
3. It passes the budget of the UN.
4. It elects the non-permanent members of the Security Council.
5. It also elects the members of the Economic and Social Council and the Trusteeship Council.
6. It admits new members to the UN on the recommendation of the Security Council.
7. The Security Council and the General Assembly elect the members of the International Court of Justice.
8. In recent years the General Assembly has increased its power through a resolution called Uniting for Peace Resolution. The General Assembly can make recommendations for "collective measures, including the use of armed forces", in case the Security Council is unable to take a decision during a crisis.

Decisions are taken in the General Assembly by a simple majority vote. In some important cases a two-thirds majority vote is required for taking a decision.

2.The Security Council: The Security Council is the most important and effective organ of the UN. It is the executive wing of the UN. The Security Council consists of 15 members. Five of them are permanent members, namely Britain, China, France, Russia and the USA. The ten non-permanent members are elected by the General Assembly for a term of two years.

Each member has one vote. Decisions are taken by a majority vote of at least nine members including the five permanent members. Each permanent member has the power to reject or veto a decision. This means a negative vote by any one of the permanent members would lead to a cancellation of the resolution. The Council is powerless to act if there is such a veto by any permanent member although it may be supported by all other permanent members.

The Security Council has the basic responsibility of maintaining peace and security in the world. The Security Council meets once a month but in the event of an emergency, a meeting may be held whenever required.

Functions of the Security Council:

1. To maintain international peace and security in the world.
2. To investigate international disputes and recommend appropriate methods of settling them.
3. To call on member states to apply economic sanctions against the aggressor and thus to put pressure on the guilty state to stop aggression.
4. The Security Council may take military action against the aggressor, if required.

3. The International Court of Justice:

The International Court of Justice, located in The Hague, Netherlands, is the principal judicial organ of the United Nations.

The Court consists of 15 Judges from different countries elected by the General Assembly and the Security Council. They are elected for a nine-year term. No two judges can be citizens of the same country.

Functions of the International Court of Justice:

1. To settle disputes brought to it by member nations.
2. To provide legal advice to any organ of the UN on request.

4. The Trusteeship Council: The Trusteeship Council was set up immediately after the Second World War. It was set up to ensure the proper administration and development of those areas of the world that were under foreign rule. The Council was also to take steps to help them attain self-government. By 1994, all Trust Territories had attained self-government. The Council will now meet only if required to do so.

5.The Economic and Social Council: The Economic and Social Council consists of 54 members elected by the General Assembly for a three-year term.

The ECOSOC discusses major economic and social issues. It is mainly concerned with the management of the UN's social, economic, cultural and humanitarian activities.

Its main functions are as follows:

1. To promote economic and social progress.
2. To solve problems relating to health, illiteracy, unemployment, etc.
3. To coordinate the functions of the agencies of the UN like the International Monetary Fund (IMF), the International Labour Organisation (ILO), the Food and Agricultural Organisation (FAO), the World Health Organisation (WHO), the United Nations Educational Scientific and Cultural Organisation (UNESCO), the United Nations International Children's Fund (UNICEF), etc.

6.The Secretariat: The Secretariat is the principal administrative department of the UN. It is headed by the Secretary-General appointed by the General Assembly on the recommendation of the Security Council for a term of five years. He can be re-elected.

The staff of the Secretariat is appointed by the Secretary-General. They are chosen from among the 192 member countries. The Secretary- General holds a key position in the administration of the affairs of the UN. He organises conferences, oversees peacekeeping operations, drafts reports on economic and social trends, prepares studies on human rights, mediates in international disputes and prepares budget estimates.

It is to be noted that the United Nations can achieve success only if the member states cooperate with it. All member countries must abide by the policies and programmes of the United Nations, if the latter is to succeed as a peace-keeping organisation.

IMPORTANT AGENCIES OF THE UNITED NATIONS!

The UN has two major functions to perform:

- *(i)* To maintain international peace and security by solving disputes between nations and by developing friendly relations among them;
- *(ii)* To foster worldwide cooperation and understanding to solve international economic, social, cultural and humanitarian problems.

To maintain international peace and security, the UN functions through its General Assembly, the Security Council, the International Court of Justice, and the Secretariat. To solve economic, social, cultural and humanitarian problems and to develop international cooperation, a number of specialised agencies have been established. They work under the supervision of the UN's Economic and Social Council.

1.The United Nations Educational, Scientific and Cultural Organisation (UNESCO): The UNESCO was created in 1946 with its headquarters in Paris. It encourages the spread of universal education. It believes that a better understanding among the different nations could be achieved through collaboration in education, science and culture.

The UNESCO devotes a large portion of its funds to projects for educational and scientific development in Third World countries. It also encourages an exchange of technology between countries and international cooperation between artists, scientists and scholars.

2.The United Nations international children's fund (UNICEF): The UNICEF has its headquarters in New York. The organisation was established in 1946 with the aim of providing aid to children and their mothers in countries devastated by the Second World War.The UNICEF looks into the issues of child health, nutrition and education. It provides medical aid and medicines to fight disease, especially in the underdeveloped countries of the world. It also assists in the running of childcare centres. It tries to solve the problem of child labour.

A large portion of its funds comes through the sale of greetings cards.

3.The International Labour Organisation (ILO): The ILO was set up in 1918 after the end of the First World War. It has its headquarters in Geneva, Switzerland. It was later on turned into a specialized agency of the United Nations entrusted with the task of improving the conditions of labour throughout the world.Through various schemes, the ILO helps the member countries in vocational training and small-scale handicrafts. It attempts to improve the conditions of work and the standard of living of workers. It sets international standards for basic human rights child labour and social well-being. It pays special attention to the problems of women and children.It also endeavors to popularise workers' cooperatives. The ILO's decisions are not binding but they exert moral pressure on Governments.

4.The World Health Organisation (WHO): The WHO was established on 7th April, 1948, which is observed as the World Health Day. The headquarter of the WHO is in Geneva.The main purpose of the WHO is to improve the standard of health all over the world. It believes that good health is a fundamental right of every human being. The WHO helps countries to strengthen their health systems. It helps them by giving important medicines and other supplies for medical care. It also undertakes programmes for immunisation against major infectious diseases.

The WHO is concerned about proper food supply and nutrition. It helps to provide safe drinking water and adequate sanitation to everybody. It had organised the International Drinking Water Supply and Sanitation Decade (1981-1990).

5.The Food and Agriculture Organisation (FAO): The FAO was founded in 1945 with its headquarters in Rome.The FAO undertakes programmes for developing agriculture, forestry and fisheries. Its aim is to eliminate hunger. It has developed a programme called 'Food for All'.

6.The United Nations Development Programme (UNDP): The UNDP was formed in 1950 with its headquarters in Paris.The projects initiated by the UNDP aim at helping developing nations to make better use of their natural and human resources, to expand productivity and improve the living standards of the people. It attempts to strengthen and expand educational systems at the university level and support research methods for new discoveries.

The UNDP also provides loans and grants to encourage self-help activities in the poor countries. It is also one of the agencies which work to support global programmes on HIV and AIDS. India has benefited greatly through these agencies

SIGNIFICANCE OF UNITED NATIONS

The United Nations is an international organisation of self-governed states founded after the second world war. It was created to maintain international peace and security. It's goals were to develop friendly relations among nations and promote social progress to improve standards of life globally.

One reason why the United Nations was created was to be a central location where nations could come to discuss long and short term problems in our world. The United Nations is a neutral area where representatives from each nation come to meet and resolve conflicts. The United Nations was set up to try to prevent wars between nations. The secondary generals partial views are a strong asset of the United Nations.

The United Nations made the world a better place. The United Nations has not just worked on peace, but it has done a great deal more in the past four decades. It has helped set major settings for the norms of world trade. The United Nations has affected the following: the economy, loans of countries, air traffic control, international laws, and the development of programs. These are just a few of other issues attended to by the United Nations.

The United Nations today addresses issues of the: AIDS virus, Kosovo, NATO, and other health issues. The United Nations works towards preventing another World War and is against nuclear bombs.

The United Nations today deals with many world conflicts that have occurred over the last four decades. The United Nations plays an important role in international conflicts.

CRITICISM OF THE UN

- The UN provides a platform to discuss global security concerns and highlights development and environmental needs. There are charges that the UN is increasingly attempting to usurp or conversely not doing enough to override national sovereignty. In general, the UN has shown a reluctance to act upon its resolutions.
- Others say the UN gives precedence to government authority over individual liberty. They point to the inclusion on the UNCHR of Sudan, Cuba and Libya, which have poor records on human rights.These above countries however, argue that Western countries, with their history of colonialist aggression, have no right to point fingers.
- There are also internal institutional failures of the UN such as allegations of mis-management and corruption regarding the Oil for Food Program.Some point to the UN failure to act (or succeed) in security issues such as the ethnic cleansing campaign in Rwanda or its failure to successfully deliver food to starving citizens of Somalia, which was usually seized by local warlords instead of reaching those who needed it.

- It is said that being in majority Arab states have an unfairly large influence which has enabled a large number of UN resolutions condemning Israel. Alternatively, some argue that the UN is ruled by a "tyranny of the rich". Critics point out to the repeated use of the veto to protect Israel, and the failure of the UN to enforce its resolutions on powerful countries like the US while enforcing them on weaker states like Iraq or Syria.
- Given the above criticism there is often talk of abandoning or of reforming the UN (including the expansion of the Security Council, since it does not include many of the prominent powers of the world like Germany and Japan. Since the UN was formulated after WWII and it is therefore criticised as no longer reflecting realities of the current world order).

OTHER INTERNATIONAL ORGANISATIONS

Some international agreements create **international organisations,** which are institutions that set rules for nations and provide venues for diplomacy. There are two types of international organisations: **international governmental organisations** (IGOs) and **international nongovernmental organisations**(INGOs or, more commonly, NGOs). In recent years, **multinational corporations** (MNCs) have also had a significant impact on the international system.

IGOs and NGOs exist for a variety of reasons, such as controlling the proliferation of conventional and nuclear weapons, supervising trade, maintaining military alliances, ending world hunger, and fostering the spread of democracy and peace.

IMPORTANT INTERNATIONAL ORGANISATIONS

Name	*Type*	*Date Founded*	*Members as of 2006*
Amnesty International	NGO	1961	1.8 million members in 150 countries
European Union (EU)	IGO	1992	25 states, including the United Kingdom, Sweden, and Estonia
International Olympic Committee	(IOC)	NGO	1894 115 individuals, who represent the IOC in their home countries
Organisation of Petroleum Exporting Countries (OPEC)	IGO	1960	11 states, including Venezuela, Qatar, and Indonesia
Salvation Army	NGO	1878	Runs programs in more than 100 countries; has 3.5 million volunteers
Save the Children	NGO	1932	Helps children in poverty around the world, including the United States and Nepal
United Nations (UN)	IGO	1946	191 states, including Burkina Faso, Denmark, the United States, and Jamaica
World Bank	IGO	1945	Offers loans to more than 100 states, including Cameroon and Senegal

International Governmental Organisations

IGOs form when governments make an agreement or band together. Only governments belong to IGOs, which are sometimes also known by the acronym IO (for *international organisation*). The United Nations (UN), the North Atlantic Treaty Organisation (NATO), the World Trade Organisation (WTO), and the European Union (EU) are all examples of IGOs.

Nongovernmental Organisations

Unlike governmental organisations, NGOs are made up of individuals, not businesses or governments. NGOs serve a variety of functions and represent numerous interests. Organisations that are not affiliated with governments but that nevertheless play an important role in international politics are called **non-governmental actors.** Not all NGOs have a positive impact on global politics. Although Amnesty International has helped defend human rights, for example, the international terrorist organisation al Qaeda has killed civilians in an effort to cripple economies and topple governments. Since the end of World War II, nongovernmental actors have become more important in the global arena.

Know the NGO Lingo

People have devised a variety of acronyms to define specific types of NGOs, including:

INGO: international nongovernmental organisation

BINGO: business-oriented nongovernmental organisation

RINGO: religious-oriented nongovernmental organisation

ENGO: environmental nongovernmental organisation

GONGO: government-operated nongovernmental organisation

QUANGO: quasi-autonomous nongovernmental organisation

Multinational Corporations

MNCs, or businesses that operate in more than one country, are another type of nongovernmental actor in the international system. Although MNCs are nongovernmental actors, they are not NGOs: As businesses, MNCs cannot be considered NGOs. Their primary aim is TO MAKE MONEY. In the twenty-first century, MNCs dominate the global economy: According to the Coca-Cola corporation, for example, more than 70 million Coke products are consumed daily in Africa.

Example: Some MNCs—such as Coca-Cola, Microsoft, and IBM, to name a few—are worth more than many small countries, which means that they have the power to be major players in international politics. In 2000, for instance, the Central Intelligence Agency declassified several documents that incriminated ITT, the International Telephone and Telegraph Company, of having funded rebels to topple the government of Chile and establish a new, more business-friendly government in the early 1970s.

a)WTO

The World Trade Organisation (WTO) is the only international organisation dealing with the global rules of trade between nations. Its main function is to ensure that trade flows as smoothly, predictably and freely as possible.

The result is assurance. Consumers and producers know that they can enjoy secure supplies and greater choice of the finished products, components, raw materials and services that they use. Producers and exporters know that foreign markets will remain open to them.

The result is also a more prosperous, peaceful and accountable economic world. Virtually all decisions in the WTO are taken by consensus among all member countries and they are ratified by members' parliaments. Trade friction is channelled into the WTO's dispute settlement process where the focus is on interpreting agreements and commitments, and how to ensure that countries' trade policies conform with them. That way, the risk of disputes spilling over into political or military conflict is reduced.

By lowering trade barriers, the WTO's system also breaks down other barriers between peoples and nations.

At the heart of the system — known as the multilateral trading system — are the WTO's agreements, negotiated and signed by a large majority of the world's trading nations, and ratified in their parliaments. These agreements are the legal ground-rules for international commerce. Essentially, they are contracts, guaranteeing member countries important trade rights. They also bind governments to keep their trade policies within agreed limits to everybody's benefit.

The agreements were negotiated and signed by governments. But their purpose is to help producers of goods and services, exporters, and importers conduct their business.

The goal is to improve the welfare of the peoples of the member countries.

b) International Labor Organisation

A United Nations agency that strives to serve as a uniting force between governments, businesses and workers to "promote decent work throughout the world." The organisation was founded on the belief that peace in the workplace is essential to prosperity; it emphasises the need for workers to enjoy "conditions of freedom, equity, security and human dignity" through their employment.

For nearly 100 years, the ILO has promoted international labour standards through its field offices in Africa, Latin America and the Caribbean, the Arab States, Asia and the Pacific, and Europe and Central Asia. The organisation provides training on fair employment standards, provides technical cooperation for projects in partner countries, analyses labour statistics and publishes related research, and regularly holds events and conferences to examine critical social and labor issues. The ILO was awarded the Nobel Peace Prize in 1969.

Amnesty International or AI is a worldwide, non-governmental organisation, which campaigns for internationally recognised human rights, as set forth in the Universal Declaration of Human Rights and other international human rights standards (Amnesty International 2005). In particular, AI campaigns to free all prisoners of conscience, ensure fair and prompt trials of political prisoners, abolish the death penalty, torture and other cruel treatment of prisons, end political killings and forced disappearances, oppose all kinds of human rights abuses and increase awareness of human rights abuses all over the world. In the pursuit of its goals, AI sends research teams to investigate claims of human rights abuses, publicises its findings and mobilises its members to lobby against the abuses by writing to the government officials concerned, protests, demonstrates, organises fund-raisers, educates the public about the offense and, often, all of these. Working primarily on the local level, Ai notifies each of its more than 7,000 local groups and more than 1 million members, including 300,000 in the US alone, in 150 countries. These members write protest letters to the concerned government officials. Ai observers a neutrality policy called the "country rule," which forbids members from becoming active in their own nation to protect mistreatment and prevent political disloyalties from affecting coverage.

AI members come from all shades of cultural, political and religious beliefs but are united by a common goal of working for the promotion of human rights in the world (Amnesty International 2005). It is a democratic, self-governing movement, whose major policy decisions are made by an

International Council, composed of representatives from all national sections. Funds come primarily from these national sections and local volunteers, not from governments. Since its founding, AI has defended more than 44,600 prisoners in hun...dreds of countries and for which it was awarded the Nobel Peace Prize in 1977 .

International Monetary Fund (IMF): The International Monetary Fund (IMF) was created to promote international monetary cooperation; to facilitate the expansion and balanced growth of international trade; to promote exchange stability; to assist in the establishment of a multilateral system of payments; to make its general resources temporarily available to its members experiencing balance of payments difficulties under adequate safeguards; and to shorten the duration and lessen the degree of lack of equilibrium in the international balances of payments of members.

On December 27, 1945, the IMF was established at the United Nations Monetary and Financial Conference, held at Bretton Woods, New Hampshire. At its birth, it was to oversee stability in international monetary affairs and to facilitate the expansion of world trade. Also created to aid these purposes was the International Bank for Reconstruction and Development (World Bank). Both were specialised agencies of the United Nations, and membership in the World Bank required countries to first be members of the IMF. The World Bank was given control over long-term financing for nations in need, while the IMF's responsibility was to monitor exchange rates, provide short-term financing for balance of payments adjustments, provide a forum for discussion about international monetary concerns, and give technical assistance to member countries.

The Fund's legal authority is based on an international treaty called the Articles of Agreement that came into force in December 1945. The first Article in the Agreement outlines the purposes of the Fund and, although the Articles have been amended three times in the course of the last 47 years prior to 1998, the first Article has never been altered.

QUESTIONS

1. The League was formed in 1919 to prevent war through collective security and settling disputes through negotiations and diplomacy; and to improve global welfare. Despite these bold aims, it could not prevent aggression by the fascist powers in late 1930s.The UN replaced the League after WWII. Discuss the factors that led to the establishment of United Nations?
2. What is an international Organisations ? Discuss its role according to present scenario
3. Describe in detail the various United Nations Agencies and its functions?
4. Examine the structure and the organisation of different organs of the United Nations?
5. Justify the role of United Nations In the present world?
6. What are the different types of International Organisations? Discuss the major role of Multinational Corporations with evidence
7. Write a short Note on
   (a) IMF
   (b) WTO
   (c) Amnesty International
   (d) International Labour Organisation.

CHAPTER 20

European Union – An International Organisation

INTRODUCTION

European Union (EU), international organisation comprising 28 European countries and governing common economic, social, and security policies. Originally confined to western Europe, the EU undertook a robust expansion into central and eastern Europe in the early 21st century. The EU's members are Austria, Belgium, Bulgaria,Croatia, Cyprus, the Czech Republic, Denmark, Estonia, Finland, France, Germany,Greece, Hungary, Ireland, Italy, Latvia, Lithuania, Luxembourg, Malta, the Netherlands, Poland, Portugal, Romania, Slovakia, Slovenia, Spain, Sweden, and theUnited Kingdom. The EU was created by the Maastricht Treaty, which entered into force on November 1, 1993. The treaty was designed to enhance European political and economic integration by creating a single currency (the euro), a unified foreign and security policy, and common citizenship rights and by advancing cooperation in the areas of immigration, asylum, and judicial affairs. The EU was awarded theNobel Prize for Peace in 2012, in recognition of the organisation's efforts to promote peace and democracy in Europe.

Origins

The EU represents one in a series of efforts to integrate Europe since World War II. At the end of the war, several western European countries sought closer economic, social, and political ties to achieve economic growth and military security and to promote a lasting reconciliation between France and Germany. To this end, in 1951 the leaders of six countries—Belgium, France, Italy, Luxembourg, the Netherlands, and West Germany—signed the Treaty of Paris, thereby, when it took effect in 1952, founding the European Coal and Steel Community (ECSC). (The United Kingdom had been invited to join the ECSC and in 1955 sent a representative to observe discussions about its ongoing development, but the Labour government of Clement Attlee declined membership, owing perhaps to a variety of factors, including the illness of key ministers, a desire to maintain economic independence, and a failure to grasp the community's impending significance.) The ECSC created a free-trade area for several key economic and military resources: coal, coke, steel, scrap, and iron ore. To manage the

ECSC, the treaty established several supranational institutions: a High Authority to administrate, a Council of Ministers to legislate, a Common Assembly to formulate policy, and a Court of Justice to interpret the treaty and to resolve related disputes. A series of further international treaties and treaty revisions based largely on this model led eventually to the creation of the EU.

Creation of the European Economic Community

On March 25, 1957, the six ECSC members signed the two Treaties of Rome that established the European Atomic Energy Community (Euratom)—which was designed to facilitate cooperation in atomic energy development, research, and utilisation—and the European Economic Community (EEC). The EEC created a common market that featured the elimination of most barriers to the movement of goods, services, capital, and labour, the prohibition of most public policies or private agreements that inhibit market competition, a common agricultural policy (CAP), and a common external trade policy.

The treaty establishing the EEC required members to eliminate or revise important national laws and regulations. In particular, it fundamentally reformed tariff and trade policy by abolishing all internal tariffs by July 1968. It also required that governments eliminate national regulations favouring domestic industries and cooperate in areas in which they traditionally had acted independently, such asinternational trade (i.e., trade with countries outside the EEC). The treaty called for common rules on anticompetitive and monopolistic behaviour and for common inland transportation and regulatory standards. Recognizing social policy as a fundamental component of economic integration, the treaty also created the European Social Fund, which was designed to enhance job opportunities by facilitating workers' geographic and occupational mobility.

Significantly, the treaty's common market reforms did not extend to agriculture. The CAP, which was implemented in 1962 and which became the costliest and most controversial element of the EEC and later the EU, relied on state intervention to protect the living standards of farmers, to promote agricultural self-sufficiency, and to ensure a reliable supply of products at reasonable prices.

Like the ECSC, the EEC established four major governing institutions: a commission, a ministerial council, an assembly, and a court. To advise the Commission and the Council of Ministers on a broad range of social and economic policies, the treaty created an Economic and Social Committee. In 1965 members of the EEC signed theBrussels Treaty, which merged the commissions of the EEC and Euratom and the High Authority of the ECSC into a single commission. It also combined the councils of the three organisations into a common Council of Ministers. The EEC, Euratom, and the ECSC—collectively referred to as the European Communities—later became the principal institutions of the EU.

The Commission (officially known as the European Commission) consists of a permanent civil service directed by commissioners. It has had three primary functions: to formulate community policies, to monitor compliance with community decisions, and to oversee the execution of community law. Initially, commissioners were appointed by members to renewable four-year terms, which were later extended to five years. The Commission is headed by a president, who is selected by the heads of state or heads of government of the organisation's members. In consultation with member governments, the president appoints the heads of the Directorate-Generals, which manage specific areas such as agriculture, competition, the environment, and regional policy. The Commission has shared its agenda-setting role with the European Council (not to be confused with the Council of Europe, an organisation that is not an EU body), which consists of the leaders of all member countries. Established in 1974, the European Council meets at least twice a year to define the long-term agenda for European political and economic integration. The European Council is led by a president, an office that originally rotated among the heads of state or heads of government of member countries every six months. Upon the adoption of the Lisbon Treaty in 2009, the presidency was made permanent, with the office holder being selected by European Council members. The president of the European Council serves a term of two and a half years—renewable once—and functions as the "face" of the EU in policy matters. The first "president of the EU," as the office came to be known, was former Belgian prime minister Herman Van Rompuy.

The main decision-making institution of the EEC and the European Community (as the EEC was renamed in 1993) and the EU has been the Council of the European Union (originally the Council of Ministers), which consists of ministerial representatives. The composition of the council changes frequently, as governments send different representatives depending on the policy area under discussion. All community legislation requires the approval of the council. The president of the council, whose office rotates among council members every six months, manages the legislative agenda. Council meetings are chaired by a minister from the country that currently holds the presidency. The exception to this rule is the Foreign Affairs Council, which, since the ratification of the Lisbon Treaty, is under the permanent supervision of the EU high representative for foreign affairs and security policy.

The Common Assembly, renamed the European Parliament in 1962, originally consisted of delegates from national parliaments. Beginning in 1979, members were elected directly to five-year terms. The size of members' delegations varies depending upon population. The Parliament is organised into transnational party groups based on political ideology—e.g., the Party of European Socialists, theEuropean People's Party, the European Federation of Green Parties, and theEuropean Liberal, Democrat and Reform Party. Until 1987 the legislature served only as a consultative body, though in 1970 it was given joint decision-making power (with the Council of Ministers) over community expenditures.

The European Court of Justice (ECJ) interprets community law, settles conflicts between the organisation's institutions, and determines whether members have fulfilled their treaty obligations. Each member selects one judge, who serves a renewable six-year term; to increase efficiency, after the accession of 10 additional countries in 2004 the ECJ was allowed to sit in a "grand chamber" of only 13 judges. Eight impartial advocates-general assist the ECJ by presenting opinions on cases before the court. In 1989 an additional court, the Court of First Instance, was established to assist with the community's increasing caseload. The ECJ has established two important legal doctrines. First, European law has "direct effect," which means that treaty provisions and legislation are directly binding on individual citizens, regardless of whether their governments have modified national laws accordingly. Second, community law has "supremacy" over national law in cases where the two conflict. The promulgation of the Lisbon Treaty signaled the acceptance of these legal doctrines by national courts, and the ECJ has acquired a supranational legal authority.

Throughout the 1970s and '80s the EEC gradually expanded both its membership and its scope. In 1973 the United Kingdom, Denmark, and Ireland were admitted, followed by Greece in 1981 and Portugal and Spain in 1986. (The United Kingdom had applied for membership in the EEC in 1963 and in 1966, but its application was vetoed by French Pres. Charles de Gaulle.) The community's common external trade policy generated pressure for common foreign and development policies, and in the early 1970s the European Political Cooperation (EPC; renamed the Common Foreign and Security Policy by the Maastricht Treaty), consisting of regular meetings of the foreign ministers of each country, was established to coordinate foreign policy. In 1975 the European Regional Development Fund was created to address regional economic disparities and to provide additional resources to Europe's most deprived areas. In the same year, members endorsed the Lomé Convention, a development-assistance package and preferential-trade agreement with numerous African, Caribbean, and Pacific countries. Members also made several attempts to manage their exchange rates collectively, resulting in the establishment of theEuropean Monetary System in 1979.

SINGLE EUROPEAN ACT

The Single European Act (SEA), which entered into force on July 1, 1987, significantly expanded the EEC's scope. It gave the meetings of the EPC a legal basis, and it called for more intensive coordination of foreign policy among members, though foreign policy decisions were made outside community institutions. The agreement brought the European Regional Development Fund formally into the community's treaties as part of a new section on economic and social cohesion that aimed to encourage the development of economically depressed areas. As a result of the act, there was a substantial increase in funding for social and regional programs. The SEA also required the community's economic policies to incorporate provisions for the protection of the environment, and it provided for a common research and technological-development policy, which was aimed primarily at funding transnational research efforts.

More generally, the SEA set out a timetable for the completion of a common market. A variety of legal, technical, fiscal, and physical barriers continued to limit the free movement of goods, labour, capital, and services. For example, differences in national health and safety standards for consumer goods were a potential impediment to trade. To facilitate the completion of the common market by 1992, the community's legislative process was modified. Originally, the Commission proposed legislation, the Parliament was consulted, and the Council of Ministers made a final decision. The council's decisions generally needed unanimity, a requirement that gave each member a veto over all legislation. The SEA introduced qualified majority voting for all legislation related to the completion of the common market. Under this system, each member was given multiple votes, the number of which depended on national population, and approval of legislation required roughly two-thirds of the votes of all members. The new procedure also increased the role of the European Parliament. Specifically, legislative proposals that were rejected by the Parliament could be adopted by the Council of Ministers only by a unanimous vote

THE MAASTRICHT TREATY

The Maastricht Treaty (formally known as the Treaty on European Union), which was signed on February 7, 1992, created the European Union. The treaty met with substantial resistance in some countries. In Denmark, for example, voters who were worried about infringements upon their country's sovereignty defeated a referendum on the original treaty in June 1992, though a revised treaty was approved the following May. Voters in France narrowly approved the treaty in September, and in July 1993 British Prime Minister John Major was forced to call a vote of confidence in order to secure its passage. An amended version of the treaty officially took effect on November 1, 1993.

The treaty consisted of three main pillars: the European Communities, a common foreign and security policy, and enhanced cooperation in home (domestic) affairs and justice. The treaty changed the name of the European Economic Community to the European Community (EC), which became the primary component of the new European Union. The agreement gave the EC broader authority, including formal control of community policies on development, education, public health, and consumer protection and an increased role in environmental protection, social and economic cohesion, and technological research. It also established EU citizenship, which entailed the right of EU citizens to vote and to run for office in local and European Parliament elections in their country of residence, regardless of national citizenship.

The Maastricht Treaty specified an agenda for incorporating monetary policy into the EC and formalised planning that had begun in the late 1980s to replace national currencies with a common currency managed by common monetary institutions. The treaty defined a set of "convergence criteria" that specified the conditions under which a member would qualify for participation in the common currency. Countries were required to have annual budget deficits not exceeding 3 percent of gross domestic product (GDP), public debt under 60 percent of GDP, inflation rates within 1.5 percent of the three lowest inflation rates in the EU, and exchange-rate stability. The members that qualified were to decide whether to proceed to the final stage—the adoption of a single currency. The decision required the establishment of permanent exchange rates and, after a transition period, the replacement of national currencies with the common currency, called the euro. Although several countries failed to meet the convergence criteria (e.g., in Italy and Belgium public debt exceeded 120 percent of GDP), the Commission qualified nearly all members for monetary union, and on January 1, 1999, 11 countries—Austria, Belgium, Finland, France, Germany, Ireland, Italy, Luxembourg, the Netherlands, Portugal, and Spain—adopted the currency and relinquished control over their exchange rates. Greece failed to qualify, and Denmark, Sweden, and the United Kingdom chose not to apply for membership. Greece was admitted to the euro beginning in 2001. Initially used only by financial markets and businesses, the euro was introduced for use by the general public on January 1, 2002.

MODIFICATIONS IN MAASTRICHT TREATY

The Maastricht Treaty significantly modified the EEC's institutions and decision-making processes. The Commission was reformed to increase its accountability to the Parliament. Beginning in 1995, the term of office for commissioners, who now had to be approved by the Parliament, was lengthened to five years to correspond to the terms served by members of the Parliament. The ECJ was granted the authority to impose fines on members for non-compliance. Several new institutions were created, including the European Central Bank, the European System of Central Banks, and the European Monetary Institute. The treaty also created a regional committee, which served as an advisory body for commissioners and the Council of Ministers on issues relevant to sub-national, regional, or local constituencies.

One of the most radical changes was the reform of the legislative process. The range of policies subject to qualified majority voting in the Council of Ministers was broadened. The treaty also endowed the Parliament with a limited right of rejection over legislation in most of the areas subject to qualified majority voting, and in a few areas, including citizenship, it was given veto power. The treaty formally incorporated the Court of Auditors, which was created in the 1970s to monitor revenue and expenditures, into the EC.

As part of the treaty's second pillar, members undertook to define and implement common foreign and security policies. Members agreed that, where possible, they would adopt common defense policies, which would be implemented through theWestern European Union, a security organisation that includes many EU members. Joint actions—which were not subject to monitoring or enforcement by the Commission or the ECJ—required unanimity.

The EU's third pillar included several areas of common concern related to the free movement of people within the EU's borders. The elimination of border controls conflicted with some national immigration, asylum, and residency policies and made it difficult to combat crime and to apply national civil codes uniformly, thus creating the need for new Europe-wide policies. For example, national asylum policies that treated third-country nationals differently could not, in practice, endure once people were allowed to move freely across national borders.

ENLARGEMENT AND POST-MAASTRICHT REFORMS

On January 1, 1995, Sweden, Austria, and Finland joined the EU, leaving Iceland, Norway, and Switzerland as the only major western European countries outside the organisation. Norway's government twice (1972 and 1994) attempted to join, but its voters rejected membership on each occasion. Switzerland tabled its application in the early 1990s. Norway, Iceland, and the members of the EU (along with Liechtenstein) are members of a free trade area called the European Economic Area, which allows freedom of movement for goods, services, capital, and people.

Treaty of Amsterdam

Two subsequent treaties revised the policies and institutions of the EU. The first, theTreaty of Amsterdam, was signed in 1997 and entered into force on May 1, 1999. Building on the social protocol of the Maastricht Treaty, it identified as EU objectives the promotion of employment, improved living and working conditions, and proper social protection; added sex-discrimination protections and transferred asylum, immigration, and civil judicial policy to the community's jurisdiction; granted the Council of Ministers the power to penalise members for serious violations of fundamental human rights; and gave the Parliament veto power over a broad range of EC policies as well as the power to reject the European Council's nominee for president of the Commission.

The Treaty of Nice

A second treaty, the Treaty of Nice, was signed in 2001 and entered into force on February 1, 2003. Negotiated in preparation for the admission of new members from eastern Europe, it contained major reforms. The maximum number of seats on the Commission was set at 27, the number of commissioners appointed by members was made the same at one each, and the president of the Commission was given greater independence from national governments. Qualified majority voting in the Council of Ministers was extended to several new areas. Approval of legislation by qualified voting required the support of members representing at least 62 percent of the EU population and either the support of a majority of members or a supermajority of votes cast. Although national vetoes remained in areas such as taxation and social policy, countries choosing to pursue further integration in limited areas were not precluded from doing so.

After the end of Cold War, many of the former communist countries of eastern and central Europe applied for EU membership. However, their relative lack of economic development threatened to hinder their full integration into EU institutions. To address this problem, the EU considered a stratified system under which subsets of countries would participate in some components of economic integration (e.g., a free trade area) but not in others (e.g., the single currency).Turkey, at the periphery of Europe, also applied for membership, though its application was controversial because it was a predominantly Islamic country, because it was widely accused of human rights violations, and because it had historically tense relations with Greece (especially over Cyprus). Despite opposition from those who feared that expansion of the EU would stifle consensus and inhibit the development of Europe-wide foreign and security policies, the EU in 2004 admitted 10 countries (Cyprus, the Czech Republic,

Estonia, Hungary, Latvia, Lithuania, Malta, Poland, Slovakia, and Slovenia), all but two of which (Cyprus and Malta) were former communist states; Bulgaria and Romania joined in 2007. Negotiations on Turkey's membership application began in 2005 but faced numerous difficulties.

Building on the limited economic and political goals of the ECSC, the countries of western Europe have achieved an unprecedented level of integration and cooperation. The degree of legal integration, supranational political authority, and economic integration in the EU greatly surpasses that of other international organisations. Indeed, although the EU has not replaced the nation-state, its institutions have increasingly resembled a parliamentary democratic political system at the supranational level.

In 2002 the Convention on the Future of Europe, chaired by former French presidentValéry Giscard d'Estaing, was established to draft a constitution for the enlarged EU. Among the most difficult problems confronting the framers of the document was how to distribute power within the EU between large and small members and how to adapt the organisation's institutions to accommodate a membership that would be more than four times larger than that of the original EEC. The framers also needed to balance the ideal of deeper integration against the goal of protecting members' national traditions. The drafting process evoked considerable controversy, particularly over the question of whether the constitution should mention God and the Christian heritage of much of European society (the final version did not). The proposed constitution was signed in 2004 but required ratification by all EU members to take effect; voters in France and the Netherlands rejected it in 2005, thereby scuttling the constitution at least in the short term. It would have created a full-time president, a European foreign minister, a public prosecutor, and a charter of fundamental rights. Under the constitution the powers of the European Parliament would have been greatly expanded and the EU given a "legal personality" that entailed the sole right to negotiate most treaties on its members' behalf.

Under the leadership of Germany, work began in early 2007 on a reform treaty intended to replace the failed constitution. The resulting Lisbon Treaty, signed in December 2007, required approval by all 27 EU member countries in order to take effect. The treaty, which retained portions of the draft constitution, would establish an EU presidency, consolidate foreign policy representation for the EU, and devolve additional powers to the European Commission, the European Court of Justice, and the European Parliament. Unlike the draft constitution, the Lisbon Treaty would amend rather than replace existing treaties. The treaty failed, at least in the short term, in June 2008 after it was rejected by voters in a national referendum in Ireland. However, in a second referendum, in October 2009, Irish voters—apparently concerned that another "no" vote would imperil Ireland's ailing economy—overwhelmingly approved the treaty. A week after the Irish vote, Poland completed its ratification of the treaty as well. At that time the treaty remained to be ratified by only one country, the Czech Republic. Although the Czech Parliament already had approved the treaty, Czech Pres. Václav Klaus expressed concern that it would threaten Czech sovereignty and refused to sign it. In early November, after the Czech Constitutional Court ruled that the treaty did not imperil the Czech constitution, Klaus reluctantly endorsed the document, completing the country's ratification process. Having been approved by all 27 member countries, the treaty entered into force on December 1, 2009.

THE EURO-ZONE DEBT CRISIS

The sovereign debt crisis that rocked the euro zone beginning in 2009 was the biggest challenge yet faced by the members of the EU and, in particular, its administrative structures. The economic downturn began in Greece and soon spread to include Portugal, Ireland, Italy, and Spain (collectively, the group came to be known informally as "PIIGS"), threatening the survival of the single currency and, some believed, the EU itself. As confidence in the afflicted economies continued to erode, rating agencies downgraded the countries' creditworthiness. Borrowing costs soared as government bond yields rose, and the PIIGS countries found it increasingly difficult to obtain financing. A series of stopgap measures were undertaken by the EU and the International Monetary Fund in an attempt to halt the spread of the crisis, but it soon became apparent that a larger, more-organised response would be required.

Representing the two largest economies in the euro zone, German ChancellorAngela Merkel and French Pres. Nicolas Sarkozy spearheaded the effort to stabilise the euro—which had plunged to a four-year low against the U.S. dollar—and preserve the solvency of at-risk euro-zone members. A bailout package was approved for Greece in May 2010, and, over the next two years, similar rescue funds were assembled for Ireland, Portugal, Spain, and Cyprus. The economic crisis, and the austerity measures associated with it, took a staggering political toll on ruling parties across the continent. Between March 2011 and May 2012, more than half of the euro zone's 17 members saw their governments collapse or change hands.

The debt crisis had revealed dangerous shortcomings within the regulatory measures that governed the euro zone's shared economy, most notably the lack of any enforcement mechanism for the fiscal rules that were outlined in the Maastricht Treaty. EU leaders attempted to correct this with a new fiscal pact, signed on March 2, 2012. The treaty bound signatories to limit government deficits to 3 percent of GDP or face automatic penalties. EU leaders also created the European Stability Mechanism, a permanent bailout fund that officially replaced the EU's temporary rescue measures in October 2012. The European Commission also proposed the integration of the euro zone's 6,000 financial institutions into a single banking union, with oversight provided by the European Central Bank. The system would allow for the centralised supervision of banks' capital reserves, as well as the restructuring or direct recapitalisation of imperiled banks without regard to national boundaries. As markets calmed and the imminent danger to the euro zone began to diminish, EU leaders focused on returning the region to a path of economic growth. The bailout of the Cypriot banking sector in March 2013 was dealt with almost as a matter of course, while lingering issues, such as endemic youth unemployment, remained a subject of concern. The EU welcomed its 28th member on July 1, 2013, when Croatia completed the accession process.

In early 2014 the EU faced what was perhaps its greatest foreign policy crisis since the collapse of Yugoslavia. In November 2013 the former Soviet republics ofGeorgia and Moldova signed an association agreement with the EU, pledging closer political and economic ties. Ukraine, which had been scheduled to sign the agreement, backed out at the last minute under pressure from Russia. The reversal by Ukrainian Pres. Viktor Yanukovych triggered a wave of popular protests that turned violent in February 2014. A bloody government crackdown left scores dead and hundreds wounded, and, with his political base disintegrating, Yanukovych fled to Russia. As an interim government assumed power in the Ukrainian capital of Kiev, unidentified troops fielding Russian equipment took control of key sites in Crimea, a Ukrainian autonomous republic that had a predominantly Russian population. Armed gunmen seized the regional parliament building, and a pro-Russian prime minister was installed. As the Russian troop buildup continued, the self-declared Crimean government announced its independence from Ukraine. A referendum was hastily scheduled, and 97 percent of Crimean voters stated their preference to join the Russian Federation. EU leaders called for dialogue and enacted economic sanctions against a number of high-ranking Kremlin officials, and Russian Pres.Vladimir Putin completed the formal annexation of Crimea on March 21, 2014. That same day

Ukrainian interim Prime Minister Arseniy Yatsenyuk signed a portion of the EU association agreement that had originally sparked the crisis.

The Ukraine crisis expanded as pro-Russian militants occupied government buildings in eastern Ukraine. An existing EU sanctions package against Russian individuals and businesses was expanded, and in April 2014 the EU, theInternational Monetary Fund, and the World Bank negotiated a $17 billion bailout deal to bolster the flagging Ukrainian economy.

Attention was soon focused closer to home, however, as Brussels struggled with the emergence of Euroskepticism as a popular movement. Elections for the European Parliament in May 2014 saw unprecedented wins by the U.K. Independence Party in Britain and the National Front in France, as voters across the continent turned to antiestablishment parties. While the main centre-right and centre-left coalitions retained a majority in the European Parliament, EU leaders were forced to address a strong electoral performance by parties whose stated goals were the radical restructuring or outright elimination of the defining characteristics of the EU.

QUESTIONS

1. Discuss the reforms introduced in Lisbon Treaty of European Union?
2. What is European Union? How it is governed
3. What is Euro and Euro Zone Crisis?
4. What do you mean by The Treaty of Masstricht of European Union? Discuss the various reforms introduced after the establishment of this treaty in the European Union.
5. What are the most important arguments in favour of the EU and the UN having constitutional qualities? Refer to constitutional theories and exemplify with relevant organisational qualities.
6. To what extent can the European Union and its different institutions be said to be democratic or undemocratic. Use references to liberal, republican and deliberative theories on democracies and to the specific EU institutions and their procedures.

CHAPTER 21

International Relation and Globalisation

INTRODUCTION

As more nations, people, and cultures adopt to the ever changing international community, diplomats, politicians, and representatives must meet and deal with accordingly to the needs and wants of nations. Diplomacy can be exerted in many forms; through peace talks, written constitutions, field experiences, etc. Culture is a familiar term and remains unchanged by definition. However, globalisation and international relations have constantly altered culture both positively and negatively.

Globalisation increases worldwide technology, and the readability of fast, effective communication and consumption of popular products. Globalisation links cultures and international relations on a variety of levels; economics, politically, socially, etc. International relations have used globalisation to reach its goal: of understanding cultures. International relations focus on how countries, people and organisations interact and globalisation is making a profound effect on International relations. Understanding culture, globalisation, and international relations is critical for the future of not only governments, people, and businesses, but for the survival of the human race.

In today's increasingly interdependent and turbulent world, many of the leading issues in the news concern international affairs.

Meaning of Globalisation

Globalisation – the process of continuing integration of the countries in the world – is strongly underway in all parts of the globe. It is a complex interconnection between capitalism and democracy, which involves positive and negative features, that both empowers and dis-empowers individuals and groups.

From the other hand Globalisation is a popular term used by governments, business, academic and a range of diverse non-governmental organisations. It also, however, signifies a new paradigm within world politics and economic relations. While national governments for many years dictated the international political and economic scene, international organisations such as the World Bank, International Monetary Fund and the World Trade Organisation have now become significant role players. In this "Global Village" national governments have lost some of their importance and perhaps their powers in favour of these major international organisations.

As a process of interaction and integration among people, companies and governments of different nations Globalisation is a process driven by the International Trade and Investment and aided by Information technology. This process on the environment on culture, on political system, on economic development and prosperity, and on human physical well-being in societies around the world.

In short we can say, Globalisation implies increased flow of information and interaction around the world. To say more things are flowing does not mean that they are flowing more equitably or that all the flows are beneficial. While flows among developed states may be increasing dramatically, increases are far less dramatic for developing states.

Advantages and Disadvantages of Globalisation

Globalisation has a range of advantages while it has also disadvantages.

The Advantages include GDP Increase; statistics shows that GDP in developing countries has increased twice as much as before, Unemployment is reduced, Education has increased. Competition on Even Platform, The Companies all around the world are competing on a single global platform which allows better options o consumers. It increased fee trade between nations; The Corporations have greater flexibility to operate across borders. Global mass media ties the world together. Increased flow of communications allows vital information to be shared between individuals and corporations around the world. It increases in environmental protection in developed nations. Spread of democratic ideas to developed nations. Reduced cultural barriers increases in the global village effect.

The Disadvantages are considered to be Uneven Distribution of Wealth, Income Gap Between Developed and Developing Countries, where the wealth of developed countries continues to grow twice as much as the developing world.

Different Wage Standards for Developing Countries, which is explained by the following fact that the technology worker may get more value for his work in a developed country than a worker in a developing country thus there are in the later many dynamic, industrious and enterprising people who are well educated and ready to work with rigour.

Te reveal of Globalisation is also considered as a disadvantage which is explaining by future factors such as war that can be demand the reveal of the globalisation and current process of globalisation may just be impossible to reverse.

There is also another aspect of disadvantage of globalisation in media sphere. The threat that control of world media by a handful of corporations will limit cultural expression.

And the final in my estimation is the chance of reactions for globalisation being violent in an attempt to preserve cultural heritage.

Nature of Globalisation

Globalisation is a process in which economic, political, and socio-cultural relations are established across a long geographic distance. Globalisation gains its strength from the possibilities opened up by technologies, strategies and policies. The reality takes effect when the fears, ideas, actions and reactions occur due to globalisation. In a fully globalised society, borders no longer protect people, goods, and symbols. The world becomes this worldwide network where the borders fade away. A factor within globalisation is consolidation. This is when globalisation is forcing companies that used to enjoy protected home markets to compete with foreign rivals. Globalisation is something that is acknowledged and then acted upon. When globalisation is properly acted upon, political policies begin to affect economic strategies, which then affect social reactions and so on. This process occurs at many different interconnected geographic levels. Globalisation is a journey, a process and it is on-going. Globalisation is a reality that touches our lives in ways most people never stop to think about.

Some would say that the world was as globalised 100yrs ago as it is today, with trade and migration. In the 1930's depression, the Nation drew back from their international markets. But the rise of the Western states to build and strengthen international ties in the aftermath of World War II laid the groundwork for today's globalisation. The fall of protectionist barriers has stimulated free movement of capital and paved the way for companies to set up several bases around the world. Today the rise of the Internet has boosted globalisation tremendously.

What has caused Globalisation?

Globalisation is not a new phenomena. The world economy has become increasingly interdependent for a long time. However, in recent decades the process of globalisation has accelerated; this is due to a variety of factors, but important ones include improved trade, increased labour and capital mobility and improved technology.

Main reasons that have caused globalisation

1. Improved transport, making global travel easier. For example, there has been a rapid growth in air-travel, enabling greater movement of people and goods across the globe.
2. Containerisation. From 1970, there was a rapid adoption of the steel transport container. This reduced the costs of inter-modal transport making trade cheaper and more efficient.
3. Improved technology which makes it easier to communicate and share information around the world. E.g. internet. For example, to work on improvements on this website, I will go to a global online community, like elance.com. There people from any country can bid for the right to provide a service. It means that I can often find people to do a job relatively cheaply because labour costs are relatively lower in the Indian sub-continent.
4. Growth of multinational companies with a global presence in many different economies.
5. Growth global trading blocks which have reduced national barriers. (e.g. European Union, NAFTA, ASEAN)
6. Reduced tariff barriers encouraging global trade. Often this has occurred through the support of the WTO.
7. Firms exploiting gains from economies of scale to gain increased specialisation. This is an important feature of new trade theory.
8. Growth of global media.
9. Global trade cycle. Economic growth is global in nature. This means countries are increasingly interconnected. (e.g. recession in one country affects global trade and invariably causes an economic downturn in major trading partners.)
10. Financial system increasingly global in nature. When US banks suffered losses due to sub-prime mortgage crisis, it affected all major banks in other countries who had bought financial derivatives from US banks and mortgage companies.
11. Improved mobility of capital. In past few decades there has been a general reduction in capital barriers, making it easier for capital to flow between different economies. This has increased the ability for firms to receive FINANCE. It has also increased the global interconnectedness of global financial markets.
12. Increased mobility of labour. People are more willing to move between different countries in search for work. Global trade remittances now play a large role in transfers from developed countries to developing countries.

In evaluation we would make the following points:

- It is hard to precisely define globalisation there are different interpretations about what we actually mean, therefore, there are differing factors that explain it.
- Improved technology is undoubtedly very influential in helping globalisation; without technologies such as the internet and global communication it would not have been possible to witness the increased interdependence of companies and countries.
- Increased free trade is important. However, there are various trade barriers still in existence and this has not stopped the growth of globalisation.
- Could there be a backlash against globalisation as people look for local alternatives to multinational products? I think this is unlikely as people prefer the security of buying established brand names.

Effects of Globalisation

With the roster of the mentioned disadvantages and advantages Globalisation culminates also effective facts. The following are considered the Effects of Globalisation;

- enhancement in the information flow between geographically remote locations
- the global common market has a freedom of exchange of goods and capital
- there is a broad access to a range of goods for consumers and companies
- worldwide production markets emerge
- free circulation of people of different nations leads to social benefits
- global environmental problems like cross-boundary pollution, over fishing on oceans, climate changes are solved by discussions
- more trans border data flow using communication satellites, the Internet, wireless telephones, etc.
- international criminal courts and international justice movements are launched
- the standards applied globally like patents, copyright laws and world trade agreements increase
- corporate, national and sub-national borrowers have a better access to external finance
- worldwide financial markets emerge
- multiculturalism spreads as there is individual access to cultural diversity. This diversity decreases due to hybridisation or assimilation
- international travel and tourism increases
- world-wide sporting events like the Olympic Games and the FIFA World Cup are held
- enhancement in worldwide fad diets and pop culture
- local consumer products are exported to other countries
- immigration between countries increases
- cross-cultural contacts grow and cultural diffusion takes place
- there is an increase in the desire to use foreign ideas and products, adopt new practices and technologies and be a part of world culture
- free trade zones are formed having less or no tariffs
- due to development of containerisation for ocean shipping, the transportation costs are reduced
- subsidies for local businesses decrease
- capital controls reduce or vanquish
- there is supranational recognition of intellectual property restrictions, i.e., patents authorised by one country are recognised in another

Advocates of Globalisation

Globalisation is promoted by governments of rich countries and major international organisations dominated by rich countries:

1. Organisation for Economic Cooperation and Development (OECD): Inter-governmental think tank from world's 29 richest countries. OECD states produce 2/3 of world's goods and services.

MAJOR FUNCTIONs of the Organisation for Economic Co-operation and Development (OECD) is to promote policies that will improve the economic and social well-being of people around the world.

The OECD provides a forum in which governments can work together to share experiences and seek solutions to common problems. OECD work with governments to understand what drives economic, social and environmental change. OECD measure productivity and global flows of trade and INVESTMENTs. OECD analyse and compare data to predict future trends. OECD set international standards on a wide range of things, from agriculture and tax to the safety of chemicals.

OECD also look at issues that directly affect everyone's daily life, like how much people pay in taxes and social security, and how much leisure time they can take. OECD compare how different countries' school systems are readying their young people for modern life, and how different countries' pension systems will look after their citizens in old age.

Drawing on facts and real-life experience, OECD recommend policies designed to improve the quality of people's lives. OECD work with business, through the Business and Industry Advisory Committee to the OECD, and with labour, through the Trade Union Advisory Committee. OECD have active contacts as OECDll with other civil society organisations. The common thread of our work is a shared commitment to market economies backed by democratic institutions and focused on the OECDllbeing of all citizens. Along the way, OECD also set out to make life harder for the terrorists, tax dodgers, crooked businessmen and others whose actions undermine a fair and open society.

2. International Monetary Fund (IMF): The International Monetary Fund (IMF) was created to promote international monetary cooperation; to facilitate the expansion and balanced growth of international trade; to promote exchange stability; to assist in the establishment of a multi-lateral system of payments; to make its general resources temporarily available to its members experiencing balance of payments difficulties under adequate safeguards; and to shorten the duration and lessen the degree of lack of equilibrium in the international balances of payments of members.

On December 27, 1945, the IMF was established at the United Nations Monetary and Financial Conference, held at Bretton Woods, New Hampshire. At its birth, it was to oversee stability in international monetary affairs and to facilitate the expansion of world trade. Also created to aid these purposes was the International Bank for Reconstruction and Development (World Bank). Both were specialised agencies of the United Nations, and membership in the World Bank required countries to first be members of the IMF. The World Bank was given control over long-term financing for nations in need, while the IMF's responsibility was to monitor exchange rates, provide short-term financing for balance of payments adjustments, provide a forum for discussion about international monetary concerns, and give technical assistance to member countries.

The Fund's legal authority is based on an international treaty called the Articles of Agreement that came into force in December 1945. The first Article in the Agreement outlines the purposes of the Fund and, although the Articles have been amended three times in the course of the last 47 years prior to 1998, the first Article has never been altered.

3. WTO: The World Trade Organisation (WTO) is the only international organisation dealing with the global rules of trade between nations. Its main function is to ensure that trade flows as smoothly, predictably and freely as possible.

The result is assurance. Consumers and producers know that they can enjoy secure supplies and greater choice of the finished products, components, raw materials and services that they use. Producers and exporters know that foreign markets will remain open to them.

The result is also a more prosperous, peaceful and accountable economic world. Virtually all decisions in the WTO are taken by consensus among all member countries and they are ratified by members' parliaments. Trade friction is channelled into the WTO's dispute settlement process where the focus is on interpreting agreements and commitments, and how to ensure that countries' trade policies conform with them. That way, the risk of disputes spilling over into political or military conflict is reduced.

By lowering trade barriers, the WTO's system also breaks down other barriers between peoples and nations.

At the heart of the system — known as the multilateral trading system — are the WTO's agreements, negotiated and signed by a large majority of the world's trading nations, and ratified in their parliaments. These agreements are the legal ground-rules for international commerce. Essentially, they are contracts, guaranteeing member countries important trade rights. They also bind governments to keep their trade policies within agreed limits to everybody's benefit.

The agreements were negotiated and signed by governments. But their purpose is to help producers of goods and services, exporters, and importers conduct their business.

The goal is to improve the welfare of the peoples of the member countries

CONCLUSION

In conclusion we would like to state an estimation that despite all the formidable obstacles and stumbling blocks the effectiveness of the Globalisation and cohesive efforts of people and the government will help to stand a positive stead prevail over the disadvantages. It will fortify to prevent migration which is inherent in third-world and back water countries and reduce social inequality which in its turn will benefit the advantages of the Globalisation. All these mentioned facts are time-consuming and labour-intensive process but it will distinctly fortify and develop the Globalisation.

QUESTIONS

1. Analyse the impact of various international organisation on the Globalised Economy of the World?
2. What is Globalisation? Discuss its major advantages and disadvantages?
3. Examine the relationship between International relations and Globalisation?
4. What are the main causes of Globalisation? Critically examine it

CHAPTER 22

GLOBALISATION AND ITS IMPACT ON THIRD WORLD COUNTRIES

INTRODUCTION

A significant transformation of the post cold war global economy has occurred. There is pressing need to integrate the politics of international relations with the current wave of globalisation to which the third world is part of.

Profound changes underlies this current phase of globalisation. Since the sixteenth century, the primacy of the nation–state has been the organizing principle of the international political order. The nation-state has largely displaced such pre-modern forms of political organisation as city-states, tribes, and empires, while simultaneously the market has become the primary means of organizing economic relations, displacing other means of exchange; reciprocity, redistribution, and imperial command economies. These two opposed forms of social organisation, the modern state and the market, have evolved together through recent centuries, and their mutual interaction have become increasingly crucial to the character and dynamics of international relations in this twenty first century era of globalisation to which the third world as mentioned earlier is a player.

Changes in the world economy as a result of the globalisation process have indeed elevated politico-social and economic issues as they affect relations among actors in the international system to the highest level of international relations.

This study, then proceeds on two levels. At one level, it is a practical inquiry into the reality of the contemporary international relations and how relations interactions among actors is transforming international; relations in the twenty first century. At another level, this work is theoretical; it attempts to integrate the principal ways in which scholars have conceived of globalisation and international relations. An attempt will be made, throughout the discussion that follows, to draw out implications of the duo as they affect the third world in the contemporary global economy.

GLOBALISATION: TOWARDS A CONCEPTUAL CLARIFICATION

Globalisation has become the biggest buzz word in contemporary academic discourse and the popularity of the term is not accidental. It is a broad process permeating the whole world, with far reaching impacts covering economic, political and cultural dimensions of contemporary life.

Globalisation is derived from the word 'global', which refers to things affecting the world (Oxford Dictionary, 2000:503). Globalisation heralds the emergence of a global cultural system. A global culture that is, more or less a kaleidoscope of trans-national socio-cultural characterisation. This includes the existence of global consumption pattern; the existence of a world satellite information system; the cultivation of cosmopolitan lifestyles, the standardisation of strategies of address critical world problems for instance famine, terrorism or the scourges of HIV/AIDS.

It might seem that globalisation is the unitarisation of the world as a 'single space'. It has been viewed as the compression of the world and the intensification of consciousness of the world as one whole entity (Robertson, 1992:46). It has been perceived as a process (or a set of processes) which embody a transformation in the spatial organisation or social relations and transactions, expressed in transcontinental or interregional flows and networks of activity, interaction and power. In a nutshell, globalisation describes the growing interdependence of peoples and countries (Held and Mc Graw, 1996:24).

Globalisation is also defined as increasing integration of the nation economies with the rest of the world. Its features are economic integration through:

...trade and capital flows (investment) increasing adoption of common relations between sovereign nations, creation and nurturing of institutions that supports the process of integration in addition to integration in other areas such as national value, cultural beliefs as well as religious beliefs.

Globalisation is essentially the geographical dimension of the phenomenon of imperialism, a transition to geo-finance system. Eskor Toyo saw it as:

A phase in the anti-stagflation, counter-revolutionary, tripartite competition, and neo-monopolistic propaganda offensive of imperialism.

Along side the notion of globalisation is the three fold domination of the world by the transnational capital, the hegemony of neo-liberalism and the emergence of a global 'historic bloc'. The latter segment in the contemporary world is led by transnational capitalist class. It is important to note that this is not a monolithic bloc advancing a unified and uncontested agenda.

According to the World Bank perspective:

Globalisation is about an increasingly interconnected and interdependent world, it is all about international trade, investment and finances that have been growing faster than national incomes.

THE SITUATING THIRD WORLD IN A GLOBALISING WORLD.

Indeed, globalisation represents the triumph of a capitalist world economy tied together by a global division of labour (Wallestine, 1979:46).This capitalist world economy is driven by the logic of capital accumulation. However though, globalisation has brought about the integration of the third world as well as its progress in an uneven and unbalanced manner.

This has meant that the third world has continued to be on the margins of the globalised world economy. Of course, someone was bound to be marginalised for it is in the nature of capitalism that capitalist accumulation can only take place on the basis of some countries loosing put those which gain and control the entire system of production and reproduction (Naburere,2000:32). Third world position in this globalised world economy is no different despite her famed human and material endowment.

Different types of globalisation has been identified .These include mercantilist (1450-1800); free –trade globalisation (1830-70); and the monopolist and colonialist globalisation of late 19th century and early 20th century. The fourth type of globalisation is that of the development of underdevelopment countries (1960-70); while the fifth is the globalisation of the SAP era, the 1970 to date (Toyo, 2000:16).Globalisation is also the third phase of scientific technological revolution, the promotion by transport and communication revolution of a greater linking up of economies and cultures of the world and continues expansion of world trade (Toyo, 2000:12).

Globalisation in the contemporary world is characterised by objects in motion- they include ideas and ideologies, people and goods, images and messages, technologies and techniques. It is a world of flows (Appadurai, 2001:5). It is also a world of structures and organisation.

Globalisation is not a single unified phenomenon but a syndrome of processes and activities, which embody a set of ideas and policy framework organised around the global division of labour and power (Mittelman, 2000:4). It is usually apprehended at two levels. The first level is the increase in interactions. The second level is the intensification of worldwide social relations, which link distant localities in such a way that local happenings are shaped by events from distant points on the globe and vice versa. It is within this context that third world international relations can indeed, be situated and appreciated.

It is also useful to describe globalisation from a particularistic standpoint that explicates one's position in the global hierarchy as has been presented by Mittelman:

It is worth noting also that the dominant form of globalisation means a historical transformation in the economy of livelihoods and modes of existence; in politics, a loss the degree of control exercised, for some, however little to begin with –such that the locus of power gradually shifts in varying proportions above and below the territorial state; and in culture, a devaluation of a collectivity's achievements or perceptions of them. This structure in turn may engender either accommodation or resistance (Mittelman, 2000:6).

The economic essentials of globalisation are evident in the acclaim of multilateral agencies with respect to the third world. According to the World Bank, globalisation is good for economic growth and growth is good for the poor. This is a simple yet forceful fact-based conclusion and cannot be dismissed by specific examples to the contrary and such examples could be countered by more examples where globalisation works for the benefit of the poor (World Bank; 2000:14). In this regard it has been argued that globalisation would attract Direct Foreign Investment (FDI) and international aid to the Third World. It was also promoted that globalisation would enhance competition which would encourage rationality and efficiency in capitalism (Toyo, 2000:22). But there is inequality in this type of capitalist competition, because there is no level playing field.

The Impact of Globalisation on the International Relations of Third World Countries

There has been a lot of debate among scholars and policy makers both within the developed world and the third world with respect to the impact of globalisation on third world international relations. While it has been praised for being an opportunity for the third world countries to make it in the twenty first century, it has also being criticised for its anti third world posture. This implies first that it is another way of projecting European values on the rest of the world. Hence it is termed cultural imperialism (Philips, 1985:113). To the critical minded third world, globalisation has been seen as a replacement of imperialism or modernity. It displaces a focus on domination of third world countries by the so-called developed world, or of local and national economies by transnational corporations. It is a method to preserve the continuing exploitation of much of the world by few 'super powers'.

It is important in the light of the above to clearly state that there is increasing fear of marginlisation and possible re-colonisation of the third world with reference to global relations. This is accentuated by the fact that almost all the structures, upon which the foundation of the global village is to be built, are controlled by the so-called developed countries.

Furthermore, globalisation of trade and liberalisation of economies have been described as inequitable and inimical to the third world in general. Economic structure is yet another important structure which is wholly controlled by the developed world. Besides, the fact that most, if not all the third world countries are largely indebted to the developed nations, leaves them with very little or no control over their national economies how much more that of the global economy. It is glaring that relations between the debt ridden third world nations and the other part of the world is that of a slave-master or master-slave relations.

Politically speaking, globalisation is changing the context in which governments operate. The challenge to policy makers is made more acute by a lot of other 'internationalisations' under way. International actors and events that nationally affect even so called domestic issues in third world countries. Thus the national sovereignty and national policy autonomy of third world countries are undermined as a result of the world begin seen and referred to as a 'global village'. The principle of erstwhile freedom of internal affairs of state is no longer held sacrosanct as events such as human rights and democracy are now internationalised.

In addition, there is the crisis of loyalty between the national government of third world nations and the international government. This is because for the Staff of these globalised governments even when their policies are contrary to the national government, these people/group of people, still dance to the tune of the globalised government.

The security structure too is not left out in this regard. This is because the developed nations through science and sophisticated technology have been able to hijack the global security through which it can exercise relational and structural powers. That is causing the third world nations to do what ordinarily it would no consider doing, or determining the rules to which the third world countries have to behave within the global structure. For instance, the insistence by America that Nigeria should hand over Charles Taylor for prosecution by the International Criminal Court is a case that readily comes to bare.

Another impact that globalisation has on the third world is the destruction of traditional cultures among those who are drawn into that economy and its practices. People have a right to cultural diversity but this is no longer the case following the tenets of globalisation. The possibility of having universally accepted paradigms in the assessment of the cultures is very remote.

From the foregoing, we have been trying to examine the impact of globalisation on the international relations of third world countries. However, some analyst have it that globalisation has a possible prospect for the third world countries. This is because of the possibility of trying to become economically competitive in the global economy that values high technological goods. Although, one way of achieving this economic relevance is for the indebtedness of the third world to get the International Monetary Fund (IMF) and the World Bank write off write off their multilateral debts so that they can start afresh.

Another means through which the third world can reap from the benefits of globalisation is for them to develop strong regional groupings. It is through such regional groupings that they can jointly secure fairer deal for themselves in the security, economic, political and all other relevant structures of the global economy. Infact, Samir Amin captured it succinctly when he argued thus;

What we need is a concept of regionalisation in which we will fit into global re-organisation of the world, which I will call a polycentric world. That is starting from the regions are very unequally developed and therefore need to negotiate- there is need to reshape the global system with a view to opening avenues to develop the least developed of these areas (Uroh, 1998:172).

CONCLUDING REMARKS

In this work, we have been able to examine the concept as well as impact of globalisation on the international relations of third world countries. It is revealing to note that the impact of globalisation is not one sided. That is, it has positive and negative impact for example in the words of Kofi Annan, (The United Nations Secretary General);

If globalisation is to succeed it must succeed for the poor and rich alike. It must deliver rights no less than riches. It must provide social justice and equity no less than economic prosperity and enhanced communication (Annan, 2002:11).It is truism that the choice to make it in this twenty first era of globalisation lies principally on how the third world wants to accept the challenges of globalisation. As well as make choices. It is time to reflect more now on how these choices could either develop or under-develop the third world.

QUESTIONS

1. What is Globalisation ? Discuss the various challenges of Globalisation in the third world?
2. Discuss the impact of Third World countries due to Globalisation?

CHAPTER 23

SAARC AND RECENT DEVELOPMENTS

"*An international organisation dedicated to mutual assistance and* ***economic*** cooperation among nations in South Asia. Heads of state of member nations meet once in a year and foreign secretaries twice a year. It was established in 1985 and maintains its headquarters in Kathmandu" – SAARC PROFILE

The **SAARC logo** shows two hands joining together. There are seven doves in between the two hands. The two hands symbolise friendship and goodwill among all the eight countries.

INTRODUCTION

The idea of regional cooperation among the South Asian countries first came about in the year 1980 and SAARC was first established on Dec 8, 1985 after the Head of States of Maldives, India, Sri Lanka, Pakistan, Bangladesh, Bhutan, Nepal approved of the Charter. Afghanistan joined the SAARC at the 14th SAARC Summit which was held in Delhi in 2007.Countries like China, Japan, Republic of Korea, USA, Iran, Mauritius, Australia, Myanmar and the European Union joined the SAARC as observers.

SAARC FOUNDATIONS AND ITS MEMBER STATES

South Asian Association for Regional Co-operation (SAARC), organisation of South Asian nations, founded in 1985 and dedicated to economic, technological, social, and cultural development emphasizing collective self-reliance. Its seven founding members are Bangladesh, Bhutan, India, the Maldives, Nepal, Pakistan, and Sri Lanka. Afghanistan joined the organisation in 2007. Meetings of heads of state are usually scheduled annually; meetings of foreign secretaries, twice annually. Headquarters are in Kathmandu, Nepal.

AREAS OF REGIONAL COOPERATION

The 11 stated areas of cooperation are agriculture; education, culture, and sports; health, population, and child welfare; the environment and meteorology; rural development (including the SAARC Youth Volunteers Program); tourism; transport; science and technology; communications; women in development; and the prevention of drug trafficking and drug abuse. The charter stipulates that decisions are to be unanimous and that "bilateral and contentious issues" are to be avoided.

CHARTER AND ARTICLES OF SAARC

We, the Heads of State or Government of BANGLADESH, BHUTAN, INDIA, MALDIVES, NEPAL, PAKISTAN and SRI LANKA;

1. **Desirous** of promoting peace, stability, amity and progress in the region through strict adherence to the principles of the UNITED NATIONS CHARTER and NON-ALIGNMENT, particularly respect for the principles of sovereign equality, territorial integrity, national independence, non-use of force and non-interference in the internal affairs of other States and peaceful settlement of all disputes;

2. **Conscious** that in an increasingly interdependent world, the objectives of peace, freedom, social justice and economic prosperity are best achieved in the SOUTH ASIAN region by fostering mutual understanding, good neighbourly relations and meaningful cooperation among the Member States which are bound by ties of history and culture;

3. **Aware** of the common problems, interests and aspirations of the peoples of SOUTH ASIA and the need for joint action and enhanced cooperation within their respective political and economic systems and cultural traditions;

4. **Convinced** that regional cooperation among the countries of SOUTH ASIA is mutually beneficial,desirable and necessary for promoting the welfare and improving the quality of life of the peoples of the region;

5. **Convinced** further that economic, social and technical cooperation among the countries of SOUTH ASIAwould contribute significantly to national and collective self-reliance;

6. **Recognising** that increased cooperation, contacts and exchanges among the countries of the region will contribute to the promotion of friendship and understanding among their peoples;

7. **Recalling** the DECLARATION signed by their Foreign Ministers in NEW DELHI on August 2, 1983 and noting the progress achieved in regional cooperation;

8. **Reaffirming** their determination to promote such cooperation within an institutional framework;

DO HEREBY AGREE to establish an organisation to be known as **SOUTH ASIAN ASSOCIATION FOR REGIONAL COOPERATION** hereinafter referred to as the ASSOCIATION, with the following objectives, principles, institutional and financial arrangements:

Article I

OBJECTIVES

The objectives of the ASSOCIATION shall be:

a) to promote the welfare of the peoples of SOUTH ASIA and to improve their quality of life;
b) to accelerate economic growth, social progress and cultural development in the region and to provide all individuals the opportunity to live in dignity and to realise their full potentials;
c) to promote and strengthen collective self-reliance among the countries of SOUTH ASIA;
d) to contribute to mutual trust, understanding and appreciation of one another's problems;
e) to promote active collaboration and mutual assistance in the economic, social, cultural, technical and scientific fields;
f) to strengthen cooperation with other developing countries;
g) to strengthen cooperation among themselves in international forums on matters of common interests; and
h) to cooperate with international and regional organisations with similar aims and purposes.

Article II

PRINCIPLES

1. Cooperation within the framework of the ASSOCIATION shall be based on respect for the principles of sovereign equality, territorial integrity, political independence, non - interference in the internal affairs of other States and mutual benefit.
2. Such cooperation shall not be a substitute for bilateral and multilateral cooperation but shall complement them.
3. Such cooperation shall not be inconsistent with bilateral and multilateral obligations.

Article III

MEETINGS OF THE HEADS OF STATE OR GOVERNMENT

The Heads of State or Government shall meet once a year or more often as and when considered necessary by the Member States.

Article IV

COUNCIL OF MINISTERS

1. A Council of Ministers consisting of the Foreign Ministers of the Member States shall be established with the following functions:
   a) formulation of the policies of the ASSOCIATION;
   b) review of the progress of cooperation under the ASSOCIATION;
   c) decision on new areas of cooperation;

   d) establishment of additional mechanism under the ASSOCIATION as deemed necessary;
   e) decision on other matters of general interest to the ASSOCIATION.

2. The Council of Ministers shall meet twice a year. Extraordinary session of the Council may be held by agreement among the Member States.

Article V

STANDING COMMITTEE

1. The Standing Committee comprising the Foreign Secretaries shall have the following functions:
   a) overall monitoring and coordination of programme of cooperation;
   b) approval of projects and programmes, and the modalities of their financing;
   c) determination of inter-sectoral priorities;
   d) mobilisation of regional and external resources;
   e) identification of new areas of cooperation based on appropriate studies.
2. The Standing Committee shall meet as often as deemed necessary.
3. The Standing Committee shall submit periodic reports to the Council of Ministers and make reference to it as and when necessary for decisions on policy matters.

Article VI

TECHNICAL COMMITTEES

1. Technical Committees comprising representatives of Member States shall be responsible for the implementation, coordination and monitoring of the programmes in their respective areas of cooperation.
2. They shall have the following terms of reference:
   a) determination of the potential and the scope of regional cooperation in agreed areas;
   b) formulation of programmes and preparation of projects;
   c) determination of financial implications of sectoral programmes;
   d) formulation of recommendations regarding apportionment of costs;
   e) implementation and coordination of sectoral programmes;
   f) monitoring of progress in implementation.
3. The Technical Committees shall submit periodic reports to the Standing Committee.
4. The Chairmanship of the Technical Committees shall normally rotate among Member States in alphabetical order every two years.
5. The Technical Committees may, inter-alia, use the following mechanisms and modalities, if and when considered necessary:
   a) meetings of heads of national technical agencies;
   b) meetings of experts in specific fields;
   c) contact amongst recognised centres of excellence in the region.

Article VII

ACTION COMMITTEES

The Standing Committee may set up Action Committees comprising Member States concerned with implementation of projects involving more than two but not all Member States.

Article VIII

SECRETARIAT

There shall be a Secretariat of the ASSOCIATION.

Article IX

FINANCIAL ARRANGEMENTS

1. The contribution of each Member State towards financing of the activities of the ASSOCIATION shall be voluntary.
2. Each Technical Committee shall make recommendations for the apportionment of costs of implementing the programmes proposed by it.
3. In case sufficient financial resources cannot be mobilised within the region for funding activities of the ASSOCIATION, external financing from appropriate sources may be mobilised with the approval of or by the Standing Committee.

Article X

GENERAL PROVISIONS

1. Decisions at all levels shall be taken on the basis of unanimity.
2. Bilateral and contentious issues shall be excluded from the deliberations.

IN FAITH WHEREOF We Have Set Our Hands And Seals Hereunto. **DONE** In **DHAKA, BANGLADESH,** On This The Eighth Day Of December Of The Year One Thousand Nine Hundred Eighty Five.

Hussain Muhammad Ershad
PRESIDENT OF THE PEOPLE'S REPUBLIC OF BANGLADESH
Jigme Singye Wangchuk
KING OF BHUTAN
Rajiv Gandhi
PRIME MINISTER OF THE REPUBLIC OF INDIA
Maumoon Abdul Gayoom
PRESIDENT OF THE REBUPLIC OF MALDIVES
Birendra Bir Bikram Shah Dev
KING OF NEPAL
Muhammad Zia-ul-Haq
PRESIDENT OF THE ISLAMIC REPUBLIC OF PAKISTAN
Junius Richard Jayewardene
PRESIDENT OF DEMOCRATIC SOCIALIST REPUBLIC OF SRI LANKA

MEANING OF THE CHARTER:- The South Asian Association for Regional Cooperation (SAARC) comprising Bangladesh, Bhutan, India, the Maldives, Nepal, Pakistan and Sri Lanka is a dynamic institutionalised regional cooperation in South Asia, basically perceived as an economic grouping to work together for accelerating the pace of socio-economic and cultural development. Cooperation in the SAARC is based on respect for the principles of sovereign equality, territorial integrity, political independence, non-interference in the internal affairs of the member states and mutual benefit. Regional cooperation is seen as a complement to the bilateral and multilateral relations of SAARC members. Decisions are taken on the basis of unanimity. Bilateral and contentious issues are excluded from the deliberations of SAARC.Though economic cooperation among South Asian nations was not a new phenomenon yet the quest for economic integration remained inhibited by the colonial heritage of these countries

The SAARC Secretariat

The SAARC Secretariat is based in Kathmandu. It coordinates and monitors implementation of activities, prepares for and services meetings, and serves as a channel of communication between the Association and its member states as well as other regional organisations.The Secretary General, who is appointed by the Council of Ministers from member countries in alphabetical order for a three-year term, heads the Secretariat. The previous Secretaries Generals were from Bangladesh, India, Maldives, Nepal, Pakistan and Sri Lanka. The next Secretary General is to be from Bhutan. Seven Directors on deputation from member states assist the Secretary General. The SAARC Secretariat and member states observe 8 December as the SAARC Charter Day.

SAARC Regional Centres

Regional Centres covering Agriculture, Tuberculosis, Documentation, Meteorological Research, and Human Resource Development have been established in different SAARC capitals: SAIC (Dhaka, 1998) STC (Katmandu, 1992) SDC (New Delhi, 1994) SMRC (Dhaka, 1995) SHRDC (Islamabad, 1999) SCC (Kandy, 2004) SCZMC (Malé, 2004) and SIC (Katmandu, 2004). In addition, three new regional centres coveringCulture, Coastal Zones Management, and Information are being established.

SAARC Recognised Bodies

As an organisation, SAARC mainly operates through six apex bodies which ensure regional cooperation on multiple levels:

- **SAARC Chamber of Commerce and Industry (SCCI):** The entity encourages intra-regional trade by creating business linkages among the entrepreneurs. Its primary focus is on the holistic growth of service sector and small & medium enterprises.
- **SAARCLAW (South Asian Association for Regional Cooperation in Law):** The desire to establish an association within the SAARC region "to disseminate information" and "promote an understanding of the concerns and developments" prompted the birth of SAARC LAW in 1991. This association of legal communities of SAARC nations was established in Colombo.
- **South Asian Federation of Accountants (SAFA):** In 1984, this organisation came into existence with an objective of strengthening and serving the accountancy profession in the South Asian Region.
- **South Asia Foundation (SAF):** A non-profit and non-political organisation founded by UNESCO Goodwill Ambassador Madanjeet Singh in 2000, SAF encourages regional cooperation through UNESCO Madanjeet Singh Institutions of Excellence. The institutions offer courses on varied subjects ranging from Climate and Green Energy to Human Rights and Visual Arts.

- **South Asia Initiative to End Violence Against Children (SAIEVAC):** Founded in 2005, this regional forum aims at "ending all forms of violence against children in South Asia."
- **Foundation of SAARC Writers and Literature (FOSWAL):** It's the first non-government organisation working towards nurturing and strengthening cultural connectivity through interactions among SAARC nations.

SAFTA

In a landmark move, SAARC nations unanimously decided to form South Asian Free Trade Area (SAFTA). Although the agreement was reached at the 12th SAARC summit in 2004, it came into force on 1 January 2006. The agreement not only created a free trade area of 1.8 billion people in SAARC nations (except Afghanistan), but also removed trade barriers to increase the level of economic cooperation.

Achievements and Criticism of SAARC

According to the declaration of the 16thSAARC Summit (April 2010), SAARC's "scope and substance of cooperation had expanded to diverse fields." The SAARC Summits have indeed created a platform for closed-door bilateral talks exclusive to the participating nations. These meetings have somewhat led to the progress in regional cooperation.

The scope of regional cooperation in SAARC has proliferated, and it has started to engage political, economic, social, cultural and other aspects in its dialogue. Even the member nations' interactions with the Chambers of Commerce and Industry and the corporate sectors seem to be developing gradually.

However, SAARC is seen as a failure by many analysts. According to observers, it has "achieved very little" over the last three decades. Besides deteriorating regional security environment and growth of terrorism in Pakistan and Afghanistan, inter-state disputes are also a nagging concern for the grouping. Social and economic sectors have registered a dismal growth, and so is the intra-regional trade.

There's a need for India and other member states to collectively tackle challenges such as poverty, energy crisis, and terrorism among others. India should take the centre stage and remove the perceived mistrust and a sense of insecurity among the member nations. But first, India and Pakistan should focus on improving bilateral ties.

CONCLUSION

Though the formation of SAARC is a landmark step taken by the leaders of the region, the main rational behind its establishments to develop a congenial environment through summit diplomacywhere all nations may interact peacefully with each other, cultivate sustainable peace and promote mutual economic well being by harnessing available resources in the region through the peaceful process of economic integration. Nevertheless, after 21 years of establishment, neither South Asian nations have been able to push the process of integration into full swing nor the organisation itself has become viable enough to promote peace, harmony and economic integration or prevent conflicts in the region. The political tensions and conflicts surrounding the countries of a South Asia pose a question of uncertainty and challenge to the formation of South Asian Union at par with European Union that would allow free movement of people; common currency and common foreign and economic policies which ultimately will sow the seeds of peace. In order to achieve the objectives the SAARC would have to evolve into a full-fledged 'regional entity' that can cultivate peace in the region. The realisation of durable peace and the future of economic integration through SAARC depend upon the ability and interest of South Asian leaders to resolve domestic as well as long-standing differences through peaceful deliberations.

QUESTIONS

1. Explain the charter of SAARC? How many countries have signed it and why?
2. What are the functions of Standing Committee of SAARC mentioned under article V? Explain in brief
3. Explain the major aims, objectives, principles and working of SAARC as mentioned in article I to X in the charter of SAARC?
4. What is the major function of SAARC?
5. What are the aims and objectives of SAARC?
6. Who founded SAARC? Name its permanent members?
7. What are the functions of Technical Committee of SAARC?
8. What do you know about The SAARC SECRETARIAT?
9. Name the different regional centres of SAARC?
10. Examine the main areas of regional cooperation under SAARC?

CHAPTER 24

SAARC Summit overview with Recent Developments

INTRODUCTION

The world today is at a turning point. The changes that we are undergoing are global in scope, revolutionary, fundamental and structural in content. As we have entered the 21stcentury a sense of optimism prevails for attaining peace and prosperity through effective role-play of regional as well as global organisations.

Many view Asia as having a variety of characteristics in common with Europe of the nineteenth century: underdeveloped international institutions, mixed domestic orders, rising nationalism, high but differential growth rates, and bitter, emotional rivalries between insecure neighbours.

The success of states in today's world is not so much measured in terms of capacity for defending borders or creating uniquely national institutions, but in terms of ability to adapt to regional and global trends, promote exports, attract investments, and skilled labour, provide a beneficial environment for transnational companies, build attractive institutions of research and higher learning, wield political influence on the regional and global scene, and also brand the nation culturally in the international market-place.

Consequently, regional associations are fast becoming an important and effective new scene for political and economic interaction in the world. In this new environment the importance of regional community and functional groupings has been heightened. Regional, political and religious blocs of nations now provide platforms for a number of countries to exercise influence in global affairs.

Interest in greater regional economic integration, fuelled partly by the achievement of an economic union and a single currency in Europe, has grown in different parts of the world. This includes South Asia and the regional organisation known as South Asian Association for Regional Cooperation (SAARC), which has announced the goal of attaining an economic union and expressed the desire for a common currency.

SAARC is a fairly recents association, established in 1985 by the seven member states of Bangladesh, Bhutan, India, Maldives, Nepal, Paki stan, and Sri Lanka. These seven countries differ greatly in land area , GDP, and population, although they have similar levels of human and economic development. They also share the unusual feature of having a common border with one another member country.

Today world is divided into two major categories. The states whose influence goes beyond a particular region — the world powers — and those whose influence is confined to a particular region — the regional powers.

GLOBALISM

Globalism is defined as a borderless world programme that implies a tendency towards a global social system. Its historical origins reached a new stage in the post-Second World War era since the sense of geographical distance has dramatically changed; some even speak of "the end of geography". The world is now considered as one global village.

Globalisation is a new phenomenon. There is an intricate relationship between regionalisation and globalisation. Compared to regionalism with an impressive theoretical tradition behind it, globalism is a more recent concept in social sciences. Whether its consequences are seen as catastrophic or as the ultimate unification of the world, the concept of globalisation is often used in a rather loose and ideological sense.

However, there are also many definitions of regionalism. For the critics, the regionalist trend constitutes a threat to the multilateral system, on the other hand, for the enthusiasts the regionalism could form the basis for an improved multilateral system.

The effectiveness of regional governance arrangements has been recognised since the end of the Second World War. Now regionalism has emerged as one of the dominant themes of World politics in the post-Cold War era. In this world of globalisation, the nature of competition presses towards the formation of larger units, both for economic efficiency and to ensure the political power necessary to bargain effectively over the rules and institutions that govern the world economy. European Union, NAFTA, ASEAN are the examples of state-driven integration policies which are effectively responding to the challenges of international competition.

Economic integration that encompasses broad areas of socio-political, economic and cultural links with nations joining together in a forum generally belongs to one or several regions.

THE ASSOCIATION OF SOUTH EAST

Asian Nations (ASEAN), European Union (EU), North American Free Trade Area (NAFTA) are few examples of such integration. The degree of economic integration ranges from preferential trade arrangements (PTA) to free trade area (FTA), customs union (CU), common market (CM) and economic union (EU).

The study of regionalism lies in the problem of how conflict can be avoided and how cooperation and stability can be maintained.

Regionalism

Regions in international politics are described as 'a limited number of states linked by a geographical relationship and by a degree of mutual independence' and could be differentiated according to the level and scope of exchange, formal organisations, and political interdependence.

It involves formal and informal agreements marked by "explicit and implicit principles, norms, rules and decision-making procedures around which actors' expectations converge in a given area of international relations."

Regionalisation does not come about unless the states in a particular region want it. It may come about through political regime, economic policy or security but often triggers from political events that set the process in motion. The foreign policy and political events identify this change in a state as an actor in regional integration process. Region as a geographical unit is delimited by more or less through natural physical barriers and is marked by ecological characteristics that as social system imply trans-local relations between human groups. Region is organised for cooperation in the cultural, economic, and political and security fields.

Region in civil society takes shape when the organisational framework facilitates and promotes social communication and convergence of values throughout the region. Region has a distinct identity, a legitimate structure of decision-making and actor capability. Crucial areas for regional integration lead to conflict resolution within the member states and help creation of welfare, social security and regional balance. This process is similar to state formation and nation building, and the ultimate outcome is a voluntary evolution of a group of sovereign national, political units into a supranational security community, where sovereignty is pooled for the best of all.

For Deutsch, integration is a relationship among units, which makes them interdependent, and those units produce such properties within the system that they would lack in separate cases.

Cohesion of an integrated system can be measured by its capacity to withstand stress and strain, support disequilibria, and resist disruptions. Thus, strain-survival capacity of an integrated system is directly proportional to its cohesion.

Regional integration was traditionally seen as a harmonisation of trade policies leading to deeper economic integration, with political integration as a possible future result. The concept of regionalism refers to a transformation of a particular region from relative heterogeneity to increased homogeneity with regard to a number of dimensions, the most important being culture, security, economic policies and political regimes.

The convergence along these four dimensions may be a natural process or a politically steered one or, most likely, a mixture of the two. A certain level of sameness is necessary but not a sufficient condition. Furthermore, all regions are hardly equal in their potential for instituteonal formation and success. Not only do they vary in their homogeneity by the above criteria, but they also vary immensely in the resources they can bring to bear on the problems of their member states.

Changes in political regimes today typically mean democratisation and changes in economic policies nowadays normally go in the direction of economic openness. The dynamics of regionalisation thus constitute the interaction between these dimensions found at different levels in the world society.

On the global level, the changing structure of the world system provides autonomy for the regional actors, as the process of regionalisation in itself constitutes a structural change towards multipolarity and globalisation. On the level of interregional relations the behaviour of one region affects the behaviour of other regions. European regionalism is, for instance, the trigger of global regionalisation, at least in two different ways: one positive, in promoting regionalism by providing a model, the other negative, in provoking regionalism by constituting a protectionist threat. Thus regions themselves constitute arenas for sometimes competing and sometimes converging national interests for emerging as an effective regional actor.

Summits which are the highest authority in SAARC, are supposed to be held annually. South Asia's regional cooperation, international political and economic environment, poverty alleviation, advancing economic cooperation, funding mechanisms, security of small states, combating, terrorism, social, natural disasters and environmental challenge s as an agenda for third decade of SAARC.

Political cooperation and external linkages of SAARC was also discussed.

SAARC member states welcomed the request by the Islamic Republic of Afghanistan for membership and invited Afghanistan as a member, subject to the completion of formalities. SAARC member states also agreed in principle with the desire of the People's Republic of China and Japan to be associated as observers.

Meetings: 1. The Council of Ministers comprising Foreign Ministers, meets at least twice a year. Its functions include formulating policy, reviewing progress of regional cooperation, identifying new areas of cooperation and establishing additional mechanisms that may be necessary.

2. The Standing Committee comprising Foreign Secretaries, monitors and coordinates SAARC programmes of cooperation, approves projects including their financing and mobilises regional and external resources. It meets as often as necessary and reports to the Council of Ministers.

3. The Association also convenes meetings at Ministerial Level on specialised themes. The Committee on Economic Cooperation consisting of Secretaries of Commerce oversees regional cooperation in the economic field.

4. The Governors of the Central Banks of member states under the auspices of SAARCFINANCE meet regularly to consider cooperation in financial matters. For strengthening cooperation in information and media related activities of the Association, the Heads of National Television and Radio Organisations of member countries meet annually. Similarly, the SAARC Audio-Visual Exchange (SAVE) Committee disseminates information both on SAARC and its Member States through regular Radio and TV Programmes. In the field of education, the Member States cooperate through the forums of SACODiL (SAARC Consortium on Open and Distance Learning) and Heads of Universities Grants Commission/Equivalent Bodies.

Memorandum of Understanding have been signed to promote collaboration with UNCTAD (United Nations Conference on Trade and Development), UNICEF (United Nations Children's Fund), UNDP (United Nations Development Programme), UNESCAP (United Nations Economic and Social Commission for Asia and Pacific), UNDCP (United Nations Drug Control Programme), ITU (International Telecommunications Union), APT (Asia Pacific Telecommunity), WHO (World Health Organisation), UNIFEM (Untied Nations Fund for Women), CIDA (Canadian International Development Agency), EC (European Commission), PTB (German Metrology Institute), WB (World Bank), ADB (Asian Development Bank), UNAIDS (Joint United Nations Programme on HIV/AIDS) and SACEP (South Asia Cooperative Environment Programme).

Regular dialogues with other Regional Organisations such as ASEAN (Association of South-East Asian Nations), ECO (Economic Cooperation Organisation) and PIFS (Pacific Islands Forum Secretariat) are held with a view to promoting cooperation among sub-regional organisations.

The Association promotes interaction on multilateral issues of common concern to its members and has identified areas in which collective positions could be projected at international forums.

These include trade, finance, environment, agriculture, women and children, information and telecommunications.

Beyond official linkages, SAARC also encourages and facilitates cooperation in private sector through the SAARC Chamber of Commerce and Industry (SCCI), which is a SAARC Apex Body. Other such bodies are SAARCLAW and South Asian Federation of Accountants (SAFA). In addition, the status of SAARC Recognised Bodies has been accorded to professional groups in South Asia including Architects, Management Development Institutions, University Women, Town Planners, Cardiologists, Dermatologists, Teachers, Writers, Insurance Organisations, Diploma Engineers, Radiological and Surgical Care Societies. The Association of Speakers and Parliamentarians enjoy special recognition by the Heads of State or Government.

First summit

The first summit was held in Dhaka, Bangladesh on 7–8 December 1985 and was attended by the Government representative and president of Bangladesh, Maldives, Pakistan and Sri Lanka, the kings of Bhutan and Nepal, and the prime minister of India. They signed the SAARC Charter on 8 December 1985, thereby establishing the regional association, and established study groups on the problems of terrorism and drug trafficking, as well as planning a ministerial-level meeting about GATT, and a ministerial-level conference on increasing the participation of women at the regional level.[1] The summit also agreed to establish a SAARC secretariat and adopted an official SAARC emblem.[1]

Second summit

The second summit was held in November 16–17 Bangalore, India in 1986. The Heads of State or Government welcomed the signing of the Memorandum of Understanding on the establishment of the SAARC Secretariat by the Council of Ministers and their decision to locate the Secretariat in Kathmandu and appoint Ambassador Abul Ahsan of Bangladesh as the first Secretary-General of south Asian association of regional cooperation.

Third summit

The third summit was held in Nepal from 2–4 November 1987, and was attended by the presidents of Bangladesh, the Maldives and Sri Lanka, the prime ministers of India and Pakistan, and the kings of Bhutan and Nepal. The foreign ministers of the member states signed the SAARC Regional Convention on Suppression of Terrorism and an agreement to establish a South Asian Food Reserve.[2] SAARC is a summit.

Fourth summit

The fourth summit was held in Islamabad, Pakistan on 29–31 December 1988 and was attended by the presidents of Bangladesh, the Maldives and Sri Lanka, the prime ministers of India and Pakistan, and the kings of Bhutan and Nepal.[3] The summit discussed the coup attempt on 3 November 1988, declared 1989 to be the "SAARC Year Against Drug Abuse", declared 1990 to be the "SAARC Year of the Girl Child", set up a technical committee on education, and launched a regional plan called "SAARC-2000-A Basic Needs Perspective" to meet specific targets by the end of the twentieth century in areas such as food, shelter, education and environmental protection. It was also agreed to hold regular "South Asian Festivals" with the first being hosted by India.

Fifth summit

The fifth summit was held in Malé, Maldives on 21–23 November 1990 and was attended by the presidents of Bangladesh, the Maldives and Sri Lanka, the prime ministers of India, Nepal and Pakistan, and the king of Bhutan.[4] The leaders signed the SAARC Convention on Narcotic Drugs and Psychotropic Substances, launched the Special SAARC Travel Document (providing visa-exemptions for national judges, parliamentarians and academics and their immediate families), launched a Scheme for the Promotion of Organised Tourism, authorised the SAARC secretariat to share information and exchange reports, studies and publications with the European Community and the Association of South East Asian Nations, declared various SAARC years (1991-2000 AD) to be the "SAARC Decade of the Girl Child", 1991 to be the "SAARC Year of Shelter", 1992 to be the "SAARC Year of the Environment", 1993 to be the "SAARC Year of Disabled Persons", and decided to set up the SAARC.

Sixth summit

The sixth summit was held in Colombo, Sri Lanka on 21 December 1991 and was attended by the prime ministers of Bangladesh, India, Nepal and Pakistan, the presidents of the Maldives and Sri Lanka, and the king of Bhutan.

Seventh summit

The seventh summit was held in Dhaka, on 10–11 April 1993, and was attended by the presidents of the Maldives and Sri Lanka, the prime ministers of Bangladesh, India, Nepal and Pakistan, and the king of Bhutan.

Eighth summit

The eighth summit was held in New Delhi, on 2–4 May 1995, and was attended by the presidents of the Maldives, Pakistan and Sri Lanka, the prime ministers of Bangladesh, India and Nepal, and the king of Bhutan.

Ninth summit

The ninth summit was held in Male, on 12–14 May 1997, and was attended by the presidents of the Maldives and Sri Lanka, the prime ministers of Bangladesh, India, Nepal and Pakistan, and the king of Bhutan.

Tenth summit

The tenth summit was held in Colombo, on 29–31 July 1998, and was attended by the presidents of the Maldives and Sri Lanka and the prime ministers of Bangladesh, Bhutan, India, Nepal and Pakistan.

Eleventh summit

The eleventh summit was held in Kathmandu, on 4–6 January 2002, and was attended by the presidents of the Maldives, Pakistan and Sri Lanka and the prime ministers of Bangladesh, Bhutan, India and Nepal.

Twelfth summit

The twelfth summit was held in Islamabad, on 4–6 January 2004, and was attended by the presidents of the Maldives and Sri Lanka and the prime ministers of Bangladesh, Bhutan, India, Nepal and Pakistan.

Thirteenth summit

The thirteenth summit was held in Dhaka, on 12–13 November 2005, and was attended by the prime ministers of Bangladesh, Bhutan, India and Pakistan, the presidents of the Maldives and Sri Lanka, and the king of Nepal.

Fourteenth summit

The fourteenth summit of SAARC was held in New Delhi, India on 3rd-4 April 2007, and was attended by the presidents of Afghanistan, the Maldives and Sri Lanka and the prime ministers Bhutan, India, Nepal and Pakistan and the chief adviser of the government of Bangladesh.

Fifteenth summit

The fifteenth summit of SAARC was held in Colombo, Sri Lanka on 1–3 August 2008. The issues discussed were regional cooperation, partnership for growth for the peoples of South Asia, connectivity, energy, the environment, water resources, poverty alleviation, the SAARC Development Fund, transport, information and communications technology development, science and technology, tourism, culture, the South Asian Free Trade Area, the SAARC Social Charter, women and children, education, combating terrorism, and the admission of Australia and Myanamar as observers.

Food security

At the summit, one of the major points of discussion was the global food crisis. The SAARC heads of government made a statement saying "in view of the emerging global situation of reduced food availability and worldwide rise in food prices, we direct that an Extra-ordinary Meeting of the Agriculture Ministers of the SAARC Member States be convened in New Delhi, India in November 2008, to evolve and implement people-centred short to medium term regional strategy and collaborative projects." They also acknowledged the need to forge greater cooperation with the international community to ensure the food availability and nutrition security.

Sixteenth summit

The sixteenth summit was held in Thimpu, Bhutan on 28–29 April 2010. Bhutan hosted the SAARC summit for the first time. This was marked the silver jubilee celebration of SAARC that was formed in Bangladesh in December 1985. Climate change was the central issue of the summit with summit's theme "Towards a Green and Happy South Asia". Outcome of Thimpu Summit regarding climate change issue:

- SAARC leaders signed a SAARC Convention on Cooperation on Environment to tackle the problem of climate change.
- The SAARC nations also pledged to plant 10 million trees over the next 5 years.
- India proposed setting up of climate innovation centres in South Asia to develop sustainable energy technologies.
- India offered services of India's mission on sustaining the Himalayan Ecosystem to the SAARC member states saying that the initiative could serve as a nucleus for regional cooperation in this vital area.
- India announced "India endowment for climate change" in South Asia to help member states meet their urgent adaption and capacity building needs posed by the climate change.
- The seven-page 'Thimphu Silver Jubilee Declaration-Towards a Green and Happy South Asia' emphasised the importance of reducing dependence on high-carbon technologies for economic growth and hoped promotion of climate resilience will promote both development and poverty eradication in a sustainable manner.

Seventeenth summit

The Seventeenth Summit was held from 10-11 of November 2011 in Addu City, Maldives. The Meeting, which was held at the Equatorial Convention Centre, Addu City was opened by the outgoing Chair of SAARC, Prime Minister of the Royal Government of Bhutan, H.E.Lyonchhen Jigmi Yoezer Thinley.

H.E. Mohamed Nasheed was elected as the Chairperson of the 17th SAARC Summit. In his inaugural address President Nasheed highlighted three areas of cooperation in which progress should be made; trade, transport and economic integration; security issues such piracy and climate change; and good governance. President also called on the Member States to establish a commission to address issues of gender inequalities in South Asia.

The Head of States of all the SAARC Member States addressed the Meeting. The inaugural meeting was attended by Foreign/External Ministers of SAARC Member States, the Secretary General of SAARC, the Heads of Observer Delegation, Cabinet Ministers of the Maldives, Ministers in the visiting delegations and other state dignitaries.

In her address Secretary General stated that the Summit being held under the theme of"Building Bridges" provides further impetus and momentum to build the many bridges that needs to be built: from bridging the gaps created by uneven economic development and income distribution, the gaps in recognizing and respecting the equality of men and women, the closing of space between intent and implementation.

In this Meeting, the Foreign Ministers of the respective Member States signed four agreements;

SAARC Agreement on Rapid Response to Natural Disasters SAARC Agreement on Multilateral Arrangement on Recognition of Conformity Assessment SAARC Agreement on Implementation of Regional Standards SAARC Seed Bank Agreement In addition, the Addu Declaration of the Seventeenth SAARC Summit was also adopted.

Eighteenth summit

The 18th SAARC Summit was held at the Nepalese capital Kathmandu from November 26 to November 27, 2014 and was attended by the prime ministers of Bangladesh, Bhutan, India, Nepal and Pakistan, the presidents of the Afghanistan, Maldives and Sri Lanka. The motto was 'Deeper Integration for Peace and Prosperity'.

Nineteenth summit

Pakistan will host the 19th summit of South Asian Association for Regional Cooperation (SAARC) in Islamabad in 2016.

This was announced by Pakistani Prime Minister Nawaz Sharif in his address to the 18th SAARC summit being held in the Nepal's capital.

18TH SAARC SUMMIT REVIEW

The South Asian Association for Regional Cooperation (SAARC) is a multi-nation organisation that comprises eight countries located in South Asia. SAARC is an economic organisation of which Afghanistan, Bangladesh, Bhutan, India, Maldives, Nepal, Pakistan, and Sri Lanka are members. The SAARC was the talk of the town recently when Prime Minister Narendra Modi invited SAARC leaders to attend his swearing-in ceremony on May 26. The invitation was also extended to Pakistan to which its Prime Minister Nawaz Sharif readily accepted. India witnessed a historic ceremony as it was also dubbed to be a mini-SAARC Summit.

Starting on November 26, the two-day SAARC Summit will be the 18th session of the multilateral organisation. Nepal will be holding the 18th SAARC meet as the national capital Kathmandu is all set to host neighbouring South-Asian countries. The current session is abuzz with the news of India-Pakistan relations.

There are several facts and figures which one would like to know about the South Asian association. We would like to bring some facts about SAARC Summit in the light which will aptly describe the work, significance and importance of it. Look at the list below:

1. The motto of the SAARC organisation is 'Deeper Integration for Peace and Prosperity'.
2. It will surprise many but the official language of SAARC organisation is English.
3. The headquarters of the SAARC association is not in India or Pakistan, but it situated in Kathmandu, Nepal.
4. Not many know that if the Gross Domestic Product (PPP) of these eight nations is combined, it will be the third highest economy in the world, behind United States of America and China.
5. The idea to develop SAARC was first initiated in the year 1980 but it took five years to contemplate it. The first SAARC summit was held in the year 1985 on December 8 in Dhaka, Bangladesh.
6. Initially the SAARC organisation comprised of only seven countries. Afghanistan was later added as new full member of the association during the 13th SAARC Summit held in Dhaka in April 2007.
7. India has have host the SAARC Summit for three times previously viz. in the year 1986, 1995 and 2007.

Not many know that when India was at war with Pakistan in Kargil, 1999; Pakistan's Prime Minister was none other than Nawaz Sharif. The Indo-Pak relations found a fresh lease of life when Narendra Modi invited Nawaz Sharif in his oath-taking ceremony. However, Pakistan being Pakistan, the relations soon soured when Pakistani authorities held talks with separatists in Kashmir. Well, it is for sure that the 18th SAARC Summit in Kathmandu, Nepal will be shadowed with Indo-Pak relations more than anything else

OUTCOME OF THE 18TH SAARC SUMMIT IN KATHMANDU

In a word, disappointing. The theme of the summit was "Deeper Integration for peace and prosperity." But member countries failed to sign two major agreements on rail and road connectivity. The pact on energy, however, was signed, and will enable greater cooperation in the power sector.

The 36-point concluding Kathmandu Declaration, released on November 27, states that members will continue their efforts to intensify regional cooperation on connectivity, renew their commitment to a South Asian Economic Union, strengthen the Social Window of the SAARC Development Fund, and reiterate their commitment to free South Asia from poverty.

Why were the connectivity agreements not signed?

Three important agreements related to connectivity—the Agreement for the Regulation of Passenger and Cargo Vehicular Traffic, the SAARC Regional Agreement on Railways, and the SAARC Framework Agreement for Energy Cooperation (Electricity), were expected to be signed. The first two agreements were stalled because Pakistan held back, saying it still had to complete its "internal processes" regarding these pacts. The third, on energy, was signed.

Was any progress made on other key issues?

The focus of the meeting was on improving inter-regional connectivity, and alleviating and jointly combating issues of illiteracy, poverty, corruption, climate change, and terrorism.

Apart from limited progress on connectivity, discussions on the South Asia Free Trade Agreement (SAFTA) and the SAARC Agreement on Trade in Services (SATIS) also did not move forward substantively, except for a call for more effective and early operationalisation of these agreements.

NEW INITIATIVES

India promised to launch a satellite for the region by SAARC Day in 2016, set up a Special Purpose facility in India to finance infrastructure projects in the region, ease business visas by launching a SAARC business traveller card, and provide immediate medical visas for patients and attendants.

Prime Minister Narendra Modi also suggested that a SAARC regional Supra Reference laboratory can be established to fight the common diseases of tuberculosis and HIV in South Asia. In the field of education and research, he pledged to expand India's high-speed broadband National Knowledge Network, which will connect universities in India to the SAARC region, in order to help disseminate information and build regional research capabilities. In addition, Modi suggested that the South Asian University, set up in 2010 in New Delhi, can develop a partnership with at least one university in each of the member states.

FUTURE OF SAARC

First, the expansion of membership of SAARC will be up for discussion from now on. Pakistan called for a more prominent role for observers in the future—mostly China. Other member states like Nepal and Sri Lanka also support this, and China itself is actively seeking a greater role in SAARC. India responded by saying that economic cooperation between the existing members must be strengthened before expanding membership.

Second, the issue of connectivity must be resolved if SAARC is to be strengthened. For now, member states have agreed to a three-month extension for the approval of the two key agreements on rail and road connectivity that were stalled by Pakistan. The three connectivity agreements, if implemented, will enhance economic activity within South Asia and bring the goal of SAFTA closer.

Finally, if SAARC is to be an effective multilateral entity, India and Pakistan will have to work out their differences and play a more constructive role. All member countries must now move forward on the stated common goals before they meet again at the 19th SAARC Summit, scheduled to be held in Islamabad in 2016.

Sharmadha Srinivasan is a Junior researcher at Gateway House. She has earlier interned at Espirito Santo Securities in the capacity of an economist, and at the Institute of Economic Affairs in London as a researcher. This article was originally published at Gateway House: Indian Council on Global Relations, a foreign policy think tank in Mumbai, India, established to engage India's leading corporations and individuals in debate and scholarship on India's foreign policy and the nation's role in global affairs.

QUESTIONS

1. What were the new initiatives proposed by India?
2. What is the future of SAARC after this summit?
3. Examine the outcomes of 18th SAARC SUMMIT in Kathmandu?
4. Discuss the brief report of SAARC SUMMITS till date?
5. Discuss the structure and meetings of SAARC SUBMITSin detail?
6. How Globalism and Regionalism integerated with the OUTCOME of the association of SAARC?

CHAPTER 25

TERRORISM IN THE MODERN WORLD

All terrorist acts are crimes. Many would also be violations of the rules of war, if a state of war existed. All involve violence or the threat of violence, often coupled with specific demands. The targets are mainly civilians. The motives are political. The actions generally are designed to achieve maximum publicity. The perpetrators are usually members of an organised group, and unlike other criminals, they often claim credit for the act.(This is a true hallmark of terrorism.) And, finally, it is intrinsic to a terrorist act that it is usually intended to produce psychological effects far beyond the immediate physical damage. One persons terrorist is everyone's terrorist." - **Bryan Jenkins**

INTRODUCTION

The topic of terrorism is both complex and emotive. It is complex because it combines so many different aspects of human experience, including subjects such as politics, psychology, philosophy, military strategy, and history, to name a few. Terrorism is also emotive both because experiences of terrorist acts arouse tremendous feelings, and because those who see terrorists as justified often have strong feelings concerning the rightness of the use of violence. Without a doubt, terrorism evokes strong feelings whenever it is discussed. A key challenge of understanding terrorism is both acknowledging the moral outrage at terrorist acts, while at the same time trying to understand the rationale behind terrorism.

Terrorism is not a new phenomenon in human experience. Violence has been used throughout human history by those who chose to oppose states, kings, and princes. This sort of violence can be differentiated from what is termed as terrorism. Violence in opposition to a government is often targeted against soldiers and those who govern. Terrorism, however, is characterised by the use of violence against civilians, with the expressed desire of causing terror or panic in the population. Terrorism is not unique to the 20th and 21st centuries. Terrorism existed in 18th century revolutionary France during the reign of terror, as well as among the Zealots of Palestine in opposition to Roman rule some 2000 years ago. Today, terrorist activity can be found in Israel, Indonesia, United Kingdom, Sri Lanka, Colombia, and the United States, to name a few. Of particular concern here are the September 11 suicide attacks against the World Trade Center and the Pentagon and the attempted attack that resulted in the plane crash in Pennsylvania

The suicide attacks began when a passenger jetliner, hijacked en route from Boston to Los Angeles, slammed into New York's World Trade Center at 8:45 a.m. About 18 minutes after the first crash, a second plane—United Airlines flight 175, also originating in Boston and bound for Los Angeles, with 92 crew and passengers—struck the south tower. The action was so well executed that authorities concluded that the hijackers had their own pilot aboard. Plumes of smoke filled the skyline of lower Manhattan as other terror attacks were underway. American Airlines flight 77, bound for Los Angeles from Washington, D.C. with 64 people aboard, was hijacked by men wielding knives and box cutters shortly after its takeoff at 8:21 a.m.. Veering off course, the passenger plane took aim at the Pentagon just 25 miles away, crashing into the western facade at 9:45 a.m

Meanwhile, in New York, bedlam had gripped the financial district around the World Trade Center (also the target of a 1993 terrorist bomb, which exploded in the basement killing six). Thousands of people fled the buildings and surrounding area. Others who had not yet escaped the building, were helping the injured, or were simply riveted by what they saw fell victim to another tragedy. At about 10: 00 a.m., the 410-foot-tall south tower suddenly began to collapse, one floor collapsing onto the one below. Forty minutes later the second ower collapsed. In the meantime, there were reports of another hijacked airline, United Airlines flight 93, crashing in Somerset County, Pennsylvania, southeast of Pittsburgh.

For a time, panic set in, marked by incorrect reports of bombings at the U.S. Capitol, as well as the State Department. The White House was evacuated. The U.S.-Mexico border was closed, and the Federal Aviation Administration grounded all U.S. commercial airline flights. International flights bound for the United States were hastily diverted to Canada. As a consequence of those attacks, the U.S. government initiated a war against terrorism and its sponsors, targeting Osama bin Laden, a Saudi-born anti- Western, Islamic militant residing in Afghanistan, and his al Qaeda organisation.

Al Qaeda (Arabic for "the Base") is an organisation based in Afghanistan that has a history of terrorist involvement. Al Qaeda is allied to the Taliban government in Afghanistan. Using the military, law enforcement, diplomacy (including coalition formation), the treasury department, and other instruments of state, the U.S. government undertook a campaign against bin Laden and his al Qaeda group. The U.S. government has taken great pains to state that its efforts are not directed against Islam, but against the terrorism and its sponsors

Historical Perspective:-Terrorism has been around since the days of ancient Egypt. People have been killing leaders of countries to try and overthrow the government, and for the past one hundred and twenty years terrorists have had new weapons of mass destruction, such as bombs. Many political figures in the past were assassinated: King Tut in Egypt, who was poisoned and hit in the back of the head by a political rival, the members of the Roman Senate and Brutus, his best friend, killed Caesar. John Wilkes Booth, a southerner who was angry about the way the Civil War turned out assassinated Abraham Lincoln; and Lee Harvey Oswald killed John F. Kennedy.

But terrorism in revealing itself in new forms in this modern world, such as massacres, hijackings, attacks on U.S troops, and hostage taking. But there is a difference between a criminal and a terrorist. A criminal is after money or drugs, while a terrorist is after the long-term disruption of life in a country, and to attempt to overthrow its leaders. (Kingsley, 13) There are many causes of terrorism, hate, religion, politics, and power.

Defination of Terrorism

Criminal and violent acts committed by a section of the people against the Society, Humanity and the Government to get their demands accepted or work done is known as Terrorism . In other words, terrorism takes place when some section the people adopts violent means to change the democratic set up or to get their demands fulfilled. Generally, this section does not believe in negotiation or cannot achieve their aim through it.

Among many faces of the terrorism, following are the few to be named:- Sabotage, Assassinations, Derailment of trains, Hijacking of planes Kidnappings, Looting of Banks, and Exploding Bombs etc. The purpose is to create terror in the minds of the people and thereby to make their ground strong. Having no respect in the ethnic values and to the government and humanity, they resort to violence to create a panicky in the society. Satisfaction of their demands and taking revenge becomes the main aim thereby the easiest way chosen is the terrorism.

Nature of International Terrorism

In legal terms, "An act committed with any lethal weapon is classed as terrorism". Inviting support for a terrorist person, group or organisation addressing a gathering of terrorism sympathisers, or assisting in arranging a meeting where support is expressed for terrorist groups or financing of terrorist activists all come under the acts of terrorism. Terrorism has become the most un-natural, de-humanizing and politically destabilizing phenomenon of the 21st century. Terrorist movements are neither radical not revolutionary. They are destructive and usually stem from conservatism and feeling of revenge. Terrorism seems to have become endemic to modern society. It is generated by recurrent social crisis arising out of increasing marginalisation of a section by indiscriminate spread of capitalism and free market economy through vaunted process of globalisation, rising Islamic fundamentalism, availability of latest technology and know-how to the terrorist organisations, close interaction between various terrorist groups and organisations, availability of large finances through drug trafficking and lack of coordination between countries and want of common laws against terrorism.

CAUSES OF TERRORISM

The causes of terrorism appear to be varied. There does not appear to be one lone factor that leads people to engage in acts of terror. Scholars have categorised motivations for terrorism to include psychological, ideological, and strategic.

1. Psychological Perspective

Those who engage in terrorism may do so for purely personal reasons, based on their own psychological state of mind. Their motivation may be nothing more than hate or the desire for power. For example, in 1893 Auguste Vaillant bombed the French Chamber of Deputies. Prior to his conviction and subsequent execution Vaillant explained his motivation in terms of hate for the middle classes. Vaillant wanted to spoil the sense of economic and social success, by tainting it with his violence. In many respects this terrorist is interested in getting attention from others for his or her act, rather than some grand ideological or strategic goal.

2. Ideological Perspective

Ideology is defined as the beliefs, values, and/or principles by which a group identifies its particular aims and goals. Ideology may encompass religion or political philosophies and programs. Examples of terrorist groups motivated by ideology include the Irish Republican Army (IRA), in Sri Lanka the Liberation Tamil of Tamal Eelam (LTTE), and the Bader Meinhoff in Germany. The IRA is motivated by a political program to oust the United Kingdom from Ireland and unite Ireland under one flag. Similarly the LTTE seek to establish a separate state for their people, the Tamilians in Sri Lanka. Finally, the Bader Meinhoff was a terrorist group made up of middle-class adults who opposed capitalism and sought to destroy capitalist infrastructure in Germany.

3.Strategic Perspective

Terrorism is sometimes seen as a logical extension of the failure of politics. When people seek redress of their grievances through government, but fail to win government's attention to their plight, they may resort to violence. From this viewpoint, terrorism is the result of a logical analysis of the goals and objectives

of a group, and their estimate of the likelihood of gaining victory. If victory seems unlikely using more traditional means of opposition, then one might calculate that terrorism is a better option. For example, in South Africa the African National Congress only turned to the use of terrorism after political avenues were explored and failed. Of course, not just individuals may feel let down by the political process. States may use terrorists in the pursuit of their own strategic interests. States may sponsor terrorist groups, especially when the objectives of the state and the terrorist group are similar. For example, Libya used terrorists to explode a bomb aboard Pan Am 103 flying from London to New York in 1988, allegedly in response to U.S. and British bombing of Libya

Main causes of Terrorism

a. **Dissatisfaction over certain issues:**There may always be some difference of opinion or disagreement between persons, societies, regions, groups, provinces or countries, but some people could not reconcile the same and get frustrated which ultimately resorts to lawlessness, looting, killing, kidnapping and mass violence. Unemployment and poverty which arises due to regional imbalance of economic development in different parts of the world also plays vital role in promoting terrorism. Sometimes terrorism takes birth due to religious and caste conflicts also.

b. **Misuse of national and international machinery:** National and International governments often use their might where some other means could have done well, party politics, partiality and biased decisions also responsible for this severe problem. The section which are at the receiving end get depressed and frustrated and forms outfit groups who starts indulging on atrocities and disturbing the normal life trying to draw the attention of the world towards them.

c. **Technological Development:** Development in science and technology has given us several destructive and improved arms and ammunition which has somehow reached in the hand of the outfits and thereby aggravating the problems. Cross country illegal drag and ammunition trafficking also contributes havoc in this parameter.

d. **Injustice and Exploitation motive:** Tendency to exploit others is a natural phenomenon which is still very much present in almost all the corners of the world. The poor and less developed are still being exploited by the so called advanced sectors and the former thinks that the system can be set right by means of terrorism and muscle power.

e. **Assistance and encouragement from outside:** Several countries in the world are facing the aggravated terrorism problem, because of the cross border assistance provided to the anti social elements by means of pecuniary help or arms contribution or some other way and thereby making the things simply unmanageable.

Types of Terrorism

Terrorism is the use of violence (often against civilian targets) to instill fear, generate publicity, and sometimes destabilise governments. Generally speaking, small groups fighting against powerful states practice terrorism, but governments also have the ability to practice terrorism. Throughout history, terrorism has taken many forms. Just in the last two centuries, for example, terrorism has been used by Russian nihilists, nationalists in Israel, Nazi forces, environmentalists worldwide, left-wing guerrillas in Europe, discontented radicals in the United States, Latin American death squads, and Islamic fundamentalists. Terrorism is not tied to any one particular ideology or group.

Scholars generally classify terrorism into two types: terrorism practiced by governments and terrorism practiced by groups not affiliated with a government. Ideological terrorism aims to promote a particular belief system through acts of violence; it may be practiced by both governments and groups.

TYPES OF TERRORISM

Terrorism Practiced by Governments		Terrorism Practiced by Groups	
	• **State terrorism:** A government commits acts of terror against its own citizens. • **International terrorism (also known as state-sponsored terrorism):** A government supplies and trains terrorists to make attacks in other countries.		• **Antistate terrorism:** Any terrorist act not committed by a government • **Domestic terrorism:** A group with no ties to another country or government commits terrorist acts within its own country.

Some types of terrorism fit into more than one of these categories. Suicide bombings in Israel, for example, are ideological (promoting a Palestinian state and sometimes also promoting Islamic fundamentalism), state-sponsored (a number of Arab governments fund the bombers), and domestic (many are carried out by Arabs living in Israel).

Guerrillas Versus Terrorists

Although guerrillas have been known to practice terrorism, guerrillas are not terrorists. Guerrillas fight against their governments, particularly against the military, in order to provoke a regime change. Terrorists, in contrast, target civilians and members of the military in order to create a social and political crisis of international proportions. Of course, those fighting a guerrilla group might label their opponents terrorists, and some terrorists may see themselves as guerrillas.

The Purpose of Terrorism

Terrorist acts ultimately aim to undermine governments and disrupt societies. Many terrorists are young, frustrated men who feel that they have been treated unjustly. Sometimes terrorists try to destabilise a government directly, via assassinations, kidnappings, and the bombing of government buildings. Terrorists can also work to undermine governments indirectly by showing people that their leaders are too weak to prevent the attacks and that an active resistance movement exists. Sometimes, terrorists attack in order to provoke a strong response from the government, hoping that the response will alienate more people from the government and foster even more political discord.

Example: Many scholars and political analysts have argued that President George W. Bush played into al Qaeda's hands by passing the Patriot Act in 2001 and by invading Iraq in 2003. The Patriot Act gave the federal government more power to detain and question suspected terrorists—often without trial—and to monitor suspicious activity. The Iraq War, meanwhile, deeply divided Americans when it became clear that Saddam Hussein had no connection with al Qaeda and was not harboring weapons of mass destruction. The federal government's suspension of some civil liberties along with the specter of deceit has shattered much of the unity Americans felt in the wake of the September 11th terrorist attacks.

International terrorist organisations may be enumerated as-

- **Al-Qaeda**, an Islamic terrorist organisation headed by Osama Bin Laden as described above aims at the destruction of the United States, Israel and India.

- **Hizbullah,** Lebanese state terrorist group's aim is the creations of independent Islamic Lebanon by outsting any thing western. It has targeted US Embassy in Berirut, US Marine head quarter and Israeli embassy in Buenos Aires.
- **LTTE** the Liberation Tigers of Tamil Elam aims at the creation of separate Tamil Land in Srilanka. In June 1991, India's Prime Minister Rajeev Gandhi was assassinated in 1993 Srilankan President Premadasa was their victim. In 1999 an attempt was made on the life of srilankan President Chadrika Kumaratunga. Between 1987 and 2000 it has carried out 168 suicide attacks in Srilanka and India.
- **HAMAS,** The Harket-el-Mukawma-el-Islamia aims at founding Islamic state in Palestine their home land. Israel has been their target so far.
- **PIJ,** the Palestine Islamic Jehad has so far inflicted 30 suicide attacks on Israel.

EFFECTS ON INTERNATIONAL TERRORISM

The extent to which 9/11 has contributed to changing the nature of international relations .This has provided legitimacy to the American military operations in Afghanistan and the Philippines. The US attempted to use the post 9/11 international consensus about the evil of terrorism to bolster the ideological grounds for attacking Iraq. This attempt was largely unsuccessful, and resulted in a broken image of the West. While this fact is now obvious to all, there has been no real attempt by other powers to counterbalance the United States in the traditional realist sense. The massive terrorist attacks of September 11, 2001, have placed the threat of terrorism on the front burner and have exposed the failure of the U.S. government to protect its citizens. The U.S. is using the threat of terrorism to justify a series of controversial policies, including tougher immigration laws, high military and intelligence budgets, and restrictions on civil liberties. Terrorism is rooted in political problems requiring political solutions and necessitating a major reevaluation of U.S. foreign policy as a whole.

1.American Economy

It is important to know the internal economical factors which effected to U.S due to 9/11 attack, it also effected to global internal economical sectors of countries too. When the terrorist attacks occurred it was known that the U.S. economy was in a transition from an unsustainable to a sustainable rate of growth. There for after 9/11 attack I will highlight some economical aspects of U.S which effected internally.

National Productivity

Large amount of resources are and will be committed to making production, distribution, finance, and communication more secure in the United States. Resources that could have Been used to enhance the productive capacity of the country will now be used for Security. Since it will take more labor and capital to produce a largely unchanged amount of goods and services, this will result in a slower rate of growth in national productivity, a price that will be borne by every American in the form of a slower rate of growth of per capita real income.

Oil Supply and Prices

A crucial part of U.S. imports, which now amounts to about 15% of GDP, is energy, primarily in the form of oil. Sharp and prolonged increases in the price of oil, popularly termed price shocks, can have significant negative effects for GDP growth in the short run. The individuals involved in the terrorist attacks came from an area that is an important source of the world's oil production. It is possible that an oil price shock, with possible negative effects on the U.S. economy, could have followed from the attacks. In this instance it did not, except for a brief spike in prices that eased within little more than a week. Also, it is somewhat reassuring that when a major mechanism for determining current and future petroleum prices , the New York Mercantile Exchange ,was closed for a week, other commodity and futures markets filled in as did the spot market, and the oil industry was not materially affected.

2. World Economies

Because of the large size of the U.S. economy, America is an important market for some countries like Canada, Mexico, and Japan. Theses countries are important trade partners of U.S; About 40% of Canada's output is exported to the United States. Due to 9/11 attack those developed economical sectors decreases in a flow rate, which affected the global economy. Below are some sectors which effected:

International Capital Flows and the Dollar
While international trade plays an important role in the U.S. economy, it is not the only role played by international forces. Foreign capital has often sought refuge in the United States., during the bush administration; the United States is the battle ground. Even though there was no panic selling of dollar denominated assets after 9/11, it would appear that there was a short run decline in the net purchase of U.S. assets by foreigners. However, this may be due to timely action of the Federal Reserve, which restored confidence in the smooth functioning of the nation's payments system, action supporting the dollar in international financial markets by the Bank of Japan and the European Central Bank, among others, and interest rate cuts by key central banks in support of similar cuts by the Federal Reserve.

Financial Markets
While much economic analysis tends to concentrate on the determinants of output and employment, modern market economies depend to an important extent on a well-functioning financial system and financial institutions, such as insurance companies, commercial banks, pension funds, stock exchanges, etc. due to the 9/11 attack global financial market was effected.

Industry, and Geographic Effects
As the contraction of GDP in the U.S. during the first three quarters of 2001 has adversely affected some sectors and geographical areas of the economy more than others, so the costs of, the terrorist attacks have been borne disproportionately by a few industries, especially airlines, tourism, and insurance.

Airlines.
The use of commercial airplanes as assault vehicles to wreak havoc on the United States has no precedent in aviation history. At the time of 9/11, the industry was already in financial trouble due to the recession, 9/11 severely compounded the industry's financial problem. It is also believed that in the global market the customers had being decreased after 9/11 attack and some Air Lines resulted bankruptcy.

Insurance.

Insurance was one of two industries profoundly affected by 9/11. The loss of life and property gave rise to the largest property/casualty claim in history, estimated at $40 billion. While the industry as a whole has both the reserves and liquid assets to settle these claims, this will not be the case if terrorist attacks become a more frequent occurrence. The risk posed by terrorism is new and the industry has little or no prior experience upon which to base insurance rates and hold reserves. As a result, only a few insurers are offering limited, restricted, and expensive coverage for terrorism.

Agriculture and Food.

In the days following the 9/11 attack, the global agriculture sector experienced some initial economic setbacks due to the halt of commodities futures trading and losses from delayed shipments of perishable commodities by air and by sea These losses proved transitory; nonetheless, the changing geopolitical developments that have followed 9/11 have injected a significant amount of uncertainty into any predictions about world markets and their effects on the global farm sector's due new rules enforced to international transportation sectors.

Layoffs and Unemployment Benefits.

Overlaid on a labor market already weakened by recession were 462 extended mass layoffs attributable to 9/11that displaced nearly 130,000 employees. Although gave more attention for migration and immigration by enforcing new rules internally which resulted increasing global unemployment rate.

TOURISM.

Due to 9/11 and terrorism the global tourist industry had being effected. Thus people who want to travel abroad had become less because of fear, also due to global economical recession.

ENERGY SECTOR.

After 9/11 fluctuation of global oil price had increased which result, effects on the global economy.

It is believed that due to international terrorism ,international communities and societies had badly touched. They are affected in economically, politically, socially and found many disputes on international relations to Muslims societies. After 9/11 attack, in economically ,many industries had being bankrupted due to the global stock market and also with the foreign case flow devalued. Countries, foreign policy had changed to protect their country, from international terrorism. It is also to know those countries are spending huge amount of their revenue for defense, all those are propose for the protection of their nation state.

According to Social expects ,the people, had changed social view to words the Muslims communities in to negative prospects. Original religious philosophies and the culture are now decaying.

WAYS TO PREVENT TERRORISM

Terrorism. It is a word that strikes fear into many. Terrorism has been around since the beginning of time, and has caused empires to rise, fall, and allowed people to gain power. Terrorism is a growing problem in this unstable world. A simple act of terrorism can cause tensions to break between two countries, as seen with Israel and Palestine s conflicts due to religious beliefs and territory disputes. Among the various potential threats are wars with neighbouring countries, missile attacks on cites, biological and chemical terrorism, suicide bombings, and hostage taking. In an April 1999 survey the most feared terrorism was bombings on US soil. (Cole, 1) There are many ways to combat terrorism. First, would be an international team that is always on call to respond to terrorist threats, and retrieve hostages with minimal loss of life. The second is gun control, which would limit the weapons accessed by potential terrorists. The last thing is to recognise terrorist organisations before they have a chance to attack.

Ways to Combat Terrorism

1.Team fight: One way to combat terrorism is with a team that is specially designed to go into buildings, planes, or any other place hostages are taken, and rescue the hostages, and neutralise all of the terrorists. This would help not only to prevent terrorism, but save the lives of the hostages. On the morning of September 5, 1972, eight Arab commandos broke into the Olympic compound in Munich, West Germany. They shot and killed two Israelis outright, one a wrestling coach, the other a weight-lifting coach. The commandos then took nine others of the eighteen-member Israeli Olympic team hostage and settled into the compound for a siege.

Throughout the day, West German officials negotiated with the Arab commandos over their demands. These demands included the release of two hundred Arab guerrillas being held in Israel and safe passage out of West Germany for themselves and their hostages. The Tunisian Ambassador and the representative of the Arab League from Bonn tried to help the West Germans negotiate with the commandos, but to no effect. The Israeli side also did not budge from its position; Israeli Prime Minister Golda Meir repeatedly refused to release any guerrillas being held in Israel. At one point, two West German ministers of the interior even offered themselves as replacement hostages for the Israelis. The Arabs refused. {New York Times, 2)

Convinced that negotiation over the release of hostages would not work, West German officials focused on trying to get the Arabs and their hostages out of the Olympic village where West German sharpshooters could "control" the commandos. The West Germans did not intend, however, to be embarrassed for both letting the Arab commandos onto their soil and then letting them leave scot free, and they had already rejected the idea of storming the compound as potentially dangerous to the Israeli hostages and other athletes.

The West Germans negotiated until shortly after 9:00 p.m., at which point the Arab commandos agreed to leave the compound with their hostages for the Furstenfeldbruck military airport, some fifteen miles away from Munich. The Arab commandos were well trained and knew how to control their hostages; they split the hostages into two groups and tied and blindfolded them. They also knew how to avoid two potential traps the West Germans set for them. (Ibid, 3)

The West Germans then set up their sharpshooters along the path the Arab commandos had to walk their hostages from two helicopters that had flown them from Munich to a waiting jet. It was the only opportunity left them to prevent the Arabs from leaving the country. As the first group of Arabs and hostages walked to the jet, shots rang out. It is unclear whether West German sharpshooters or Arab commandos opened fire first. Whichever side opened fire first, when West German sharpshooters fired or fired back, the first group of commandos began shooting their hostages. The second commando group had barely left their helicopter. One commando fired into the helicopter, another threw a grenade into it, killing the second group of hostages.

When the shooting was over, all nine Israeli hostages had been killed, five Arab commandos had been killed, and three had been wounded. (Idid, 3)

Had there been a trained team to handle the threat, the nine hostages would not have died. It was the fault of the under-trained German police that the hostages were killed. Had there been a team specially trained to handle the situation the nine athletes would not have lost their lives.

2. Gun Control: Another way to prevent terrorism is gun control. Gun control will prevent terrorism by reducing the number of weapons accessible to terrorists. Violent crimes and urban terrorism has dropped over 33% since the introduction of the background check. (Philips, 15)

Something as simple as having a waiting period at gun shows can help reduce terrorism. It is possible for a group of people to go into the show separately, and purchase three or four weapons, and then use them to rob a bank, or take hostages. Currently at gun shows, as long as you are 18, you can buy a variety of weapons, and ammunition. Although a full ban on guns would not stop weapons from coming into this country illegally, it would limit the guns accessible to criminals and possible terrorists.

3. Detecting terrorist Organisation: Many times on TV after a terrorist-attack the news will announce that this person had terrorist connections in the past. Now if they had terrorist connections why were they allowed to live freely, where they could plan terrorist attacks? If the government had a monitoring service to keep track of people with suspected histories of terrorism, or possible connections to terrorists, the FBI could make a careful watch of a person s communications. This would help prevent terrorism from happening by not allowing correspondence between the suspect, and the organisation. Although the person would not be a prisoner, he would be on parole so to speak, so he could lead a normal, and productive life. But if he made a large purchase of any possible bomb making materials his house would be searched. This can help prevent attacks because the person would not have any opportunities to plan any attacks.

4. The use of force and violence against terrorism has been demonstrated periodically. U.S. military action against the Taliban in Afghanistan is an example of the use of force against terrorism. The Taliban, harbouring the al Qaeda organisation, was the target of U.S. military action. In another example, in 1988 three suspected members of the Irish Republican Army were shot and killed in Gibraltar by members of the British Special Air Services. Force, in this case, was used against suspected members of a terrorist organisation. The use of force is both a tit-for-tat strategy, as well as an attempt to hinder the terrorists' ability to operate.

5.Negotiation is a method for dealing with terrorism. While nations may refuse publicly to negotiate with terrorist groups, they may follow a different strategy in secret. For example, Great Britain had long refused to negotiate with the Irish Republican Army and its political wing Sinn Fein. Yet, out of the public view negotiations did proceed, ultimately leading to the Good Friday Agreements, which went far in ending terrorist attacks in Northern Ireland. Another example is the negotiation that took place between the African National

Congress (ANC) and the apartheid government of South Africa. The ANC had been proscribed as a terrorist organisation, and the government foreswore any negotiation with the ANC. Yet, behind the scenes negotiations did take place, ultimately resulting in the end of apartheid in South Africa. International agreements are another attempt at addressing terrorism.

6. Role of International Organisation: International organisations, such as the United Nations, pass resolutions and 1997 International Convention for the Suppression of Terrorist Bombings requires that parties to the convention must make it a criminal act to unlawfully and intentionally use explosives or other deadly devices in public with the objective of causing death or injuring a person. Another example of action by the international community was UN Security Council anti-terrorism resolution 1373, "Improving International Cooperation."

There are some other preventive measures that can be taken to stop bombings from occurring. One way is to put two-foot concrete pillars around federal buildings to prevent drive up bombings. But there are other ways to cause mass killings.

Biological warfare is one of the most feared forms of terrorism in the world. Capable of killing thousands within a few days, and constantly spreading, it is the most effective form of terrorism there is. (Gaines,15) All it takes is some one with a small flask of anthrax in a powdered form to get on a subway, and spread the virus, and get off. In the powdered form the dust would spread into a fine dust, and than would be breathed in by hundreds of passengers. (Snow, 15) Now some things like that can not be prevented, but a way to keep the people from getting sick is to make sure everyone born has vaccinations for any disease that can be spread, such as anthrax, and ebola. But there are not enough shots to go around. There is only one dose of anthrax vaccine per four people. The government needs to produce enough vaccine for everyone in the country.

Terrorism against the United States in other countries continues to be a serious problem. The United States has not been able to effectively deal with terrorism directed at its embassies, personnel, or military installations.

The United States has put up concrete barriers around its embassies to protect Americans from suicide bombers. In many cultures religion and politics are intertwined, it is a great honor to die for your country on a suicide mission. It happened during World War II with the Kamikaze pilots and it happened again most recently with the attack on the U.S.S. Cole. The suicide bomb is most often used in the Middle East.

The sailors on board the Cole thought the small boat coming towards them contained a couple of local fisherman. When a naval vessel arrives for a port-call there is always a lot of interest, and local people often sail out to look at the ship. The sailors on the Cole certainly did not expect a suicide bomb, but a couple of local fishermen interested in looking at the ship. The United States is going to have to work with other governments and make sure naval vessels are allowed to dock in secure locations. The crew must be vigilant against all people, which can lead to the killing of innocent civilians. Security against terrorism abroad is an area the United States must take a closer look and try new measures.

CONCLUSION

It is impossible to say for sure what causes terrorism. A person's psychological make-up certainly will play a role, but to what extent is unclear. Some may come to terrorism, not out of any love for violence, but rather to further their ideological goals. Others may be motivated to use terror simply because it appears to be a useful strategic alternative, or may further the state's objectives.Indeed, terrorism may occur for psychological, ideological, and strategic grounds all at once. An individual may decide terrorism fits his or her own view of the world—that it makes sense. A group may come to use terrorism because it furthers and is supported by their ideology. Finally, groups or persons may useterrorism because it fits with their strategic objectives and goals.

Terrorism can be reduced with prevention, detection, and action. The problem will not go away if people just sit there and not take any action against it. Society needs to create a team to counteract terrorism, have better gun control, and monitor high-risk people. With these simple steps we can reduce terrorism.

QUESTIONS

1. September 11, 2001 terrorism has shown a face like never before. In the light of above statement discuss the nature ,categories and historical perspective of International Terrorism?

2. Examine the International organisations which are indulged in spreading International Terrorism
3. The global spread of terrorism indicates that nation cannot cope up with this threat on individual basis. A time has come for the nations to pool up their resources and defines a clear cut strategy to counter this dragon. In the light of above statement discuss the different ways to combat International Terrorism
4. Discuss the different perspectives and causes on Terrorism?
5. Examine the consequences of International Terrorism on the World Economies?